THE
GRUNTLED
EMPLOYEE

THE GRUNTLED EMPLOYEE

A Holistic Approach to Creating
Success *and* Happiness at Work

Mary Vaughn

Metargy Media
Parker, Colorado

Published by Metargy Media
PO Box 4010
Parker, CO 80134

The blog posts at the beginning of each chapter have been edited for clarity and anonymity. The examples within the chapters are based on actual events. They have been modified to maintain anonymity and to demonstrate applicability in different settings.

Cover design by Dunn+Associates, www.dunn-design.com
Artwork by Kirsten Freeman
Interior design by Dorie McClelland, www.springbookdesign.com
Developmental editors: Holly Lancaster, Kathleen Goolsby
Copy editor: Tiffany McNeil
Printed in the United States of America

Library of Congress Cataloging-in-Publication Data
Vaughn, Mary
Gruntled Employee / by Mary Vaughn.
p. cm.
Includes bibliographic references and index.
ISBN 978-0-9847845-0-9

FIRST EDITION
First printing 2012

Dedicated to my father, Gilbert H. Voecks,
who was my first mentor in the business world.

Contents

Acknowledgments

I wish to express my deepest gratitude and appreciation to my editors for the 100 plus revisions of the manuscript. Holly Lancaster edited the manuscript for over three years ensuring that the concepts in the book were clearly communicated. Kathleen Goolsby helped with the initial revisions, reorganizing the material in a much more readable fashion. Both Holly and Kathleen demonstrated the book's concepts along the way by working in partnership with me to solve various problems and by providing encouragement.

I also want to acknowledge those who contributed directly to the content of this book. Lindy Vaughn, Daniel Bronstein, Jeff Blackmon, David Greenwald, and Randy Huffman all reviewed early drafts of the manuscript. Lindy Vaughn also contributed significantly to Chapter 30 Addressing Physical Causal Factors of Behavior Preferences. Also, thanks to all those who contributed stories and examples of workplace experiences: Elizabeth Finley, Kathy Menard, Jim Brandt, Jeff Blackmon, Jeanne Fontenot, Tim Otto, Gerry Voecks, Joe Furey, Randy Huffman, Lindy Vaughn, Scott Pomeroy, Kay May, Don Mueller, Steve Huffman, Pamela Thompson, David Greenwald, John Wright, Holly Lancaster, and Scott Bliss.

I also want to thank all the workgroups that I was a part of, which gave me so many examples of workplace behaviors. I'd particularly like to acknowledge the contribution that David Greenwald made over the past 6 years; he helped me apply these concepts in many different situations. I would also like to acknowledge the contributions of Randy Huffman who helped me implement interdependent business system characteristics with many of the workgroups that I managed. I'd like to thank those that provided me opportunities to apply the concepts in this book: Donna Leone, Kevin Gaulin, Joe Schechter, and Ron Schwartz. I also want to acknowledge those who helped me apply *The Gruntled Employee* concepts to their specific work situation: Narayanan Viswanathan, Ray Narragon,

Jim Edwards, Jerry Haughey, Rajesh Bhatia, Vikesh Bharat Jain, Dimple Tiwari, Prachi Wadhwa, Bindu Jayaraj, Alicia Davila, Barbara MacNiven, Claudia Taylor, and Alyce Martin.

I also want to thank those that helped me address my personal causal factors to gruntledness and success:

- Mentally – Anthony Robbins, Herrmann International, Dr. Shane Steadman from Integrated Health Systems, Susan Shor Fehmi, and Dr. Les Fehmi from the Princeton Biofeedback Center
- Emotionally – Scott Pomeroy, Jannette Wesley, the late Daniel Blecher, Marianne Williamson, Gerald Jampolsky, Diane Cirincione, Kenneth Wapnick, Beverly Hutchinson McNeff, and Karin Shola von Daler
- Physically – Dr. Gabrielle Francis, Dr. Shane Steadman, Michael Biamonte, Dr. Daniel Kalish, and Dr. Lindy Vaughn

I must also acknowledge the impact that dancing had on me; it significantly improved my mental, emotional, and physical causal factors. Thanks to my past and present dance instructors who, through dance, helped me be more gruntled and successful at work: Carter Lovisone, Jean Smith, Marion Mobley, Karen Lee Bridge, Manuel Viarrial, and Trevor and Chelsea Spika.

I'd also like to express my appreciation to Helen Schucman and William Thetford whose search for another way to work led to the book, *A Course In Miracles*. Studying *A Course in Miracles* for over 20 years helped me find a different way to be gruntled and successful in business—no matter what was going on.

Most of all, I want to thank my dad, Gilbert Voecks, who first taught me the joy of working together interdependently. Having such a great start in the working world gave me a positive attitude towards work that helped me be successful no matter what the circumstances were.

About the Author

Mary Vaughn has over 30 years of management, consulting, and technical experience in the information technology industry. Mary is currently a director at Computer Sciences Corporation (CSC).

Mary has held a number of account management, program management, and business transformation management positions. Many of the workgroups she led supported Fortune 500 clients and U.S. federal government agencies. Over the past 20 years, she has managed CSC's accounts with Sun Microsystems, AT&T, BHP Billiton (Australia), DuPont, the Internal Revenue Service, the U.S. Customs Service, the U.S. Postal Service, the U.S. Air Force, and the Nuclear Regulatory Commission. Early in her career, Mary worked for the Denver Water Department, Samsonite, and Petro-Lewis.

Through observation and experimentation, Mary developed the approach presented in this book to increase employee morale and the success rate of business strategy efforts, and to improve business operations. Over the course of three decades, she has used this approach with the various workgroups she has led. Several of these workgroups were nominated for excellence awards or were singled out at industry symposiums for outstanding strategy execution and performance.

Part 1

The Interrelated Problems of Employee Morale and Business Success

"Our almost universal tendency to fragment the world and ignore the dynamic interconnectedness of all things is responsible for many of our problems . . . we believe we can extract the valuable parts of the earth without affecting the whole . . . treat parts of our body and not be concerned with the whole . . . deal with . . . crime, poverty, and drug addiction without addressing . . . society as a whole."

Michael Talbot
The Holographic Universe

1

How Happy and Successful Are You Personally?

"The past two years, employee survey results at my company have been in the toilet. It doesn't surprise me, though, because the surveys were done at the most inopportune times. The first survey was done right smack dab in the middle of union contract negotiations. The second survey was done during the company's downsizing and many of the employees were either laid off, offered clerical jobs, or were basically told to 'Find your own job within the company or take the unemployment.' The majority of them (me included) took the minimal clerical jobs. With our holiday bonus last year we received the 'Sorry, this is your last one' letter. What's next? No more cake for your birthdays? Keep those surveys coming!"

Disgruntled Employee
Blog Post

In the movie *As Good As It Gets,* Melvin Udal, played by Jack Nicholson, asks the question "What if this is as good as it gets?" Depending on your work situation, this may be an unsettling question. What if the way things are for you right now at work is as good as it gets? Would you be okay with that, or does the thought leave you feeling depressed? Are you content in your current job or even happy with how things are at work? Or are you just holding on, hoping that things will get better?

If your job is making you unhappy, something's got to change. Do any of these complaints make you think about quitting your job?

- You're not being treated fairly
- Your contributions go unnoticed, so moving up seems impossible
- The behavior of individuals in your workgroup seems to sabotage success
- Your group leader micromanages, doesn't provide adequate direction, or even yells at you
- You must pick up the slack of deadbeat coworkers
- You're frustrated with the old-fashioned business-as-usual approach
- You're unhappy about the "no's" you continually receive from leaders
- You're stuck having to learn new technology
- You're frustrated with outsourcing, downsizing, or some other business strategy

If you're a business leader, what if your current business results are as good as they're going to get? Are your business strategies on target or missing the mark? Are your employees supporting or resisting your business initiatives? Is employee attrition high because your business strategies and organizational culture don't meld with the expectations of employees, particularly the newest generation? Do you have any of the following complaints?

- You're struggling to implement your organization's business strategies
- Your system implementation project is behind schedule and costing more money than estimated
- Your outsourcing engagement isn't going as well as expected

- You aren't getting the anticipated benefits from your mergers or acquisitions

If any of these scenarios strike a chord, or you have something else in mind that's causing job gloom, this book is for you. Over the span of 30 years I have experienced many of these work situations. When the workplace got difficult, I sought advice in the business book section, but my findings always left me feeling like I was only getting half the picture. Many business books provide advice on how to improve business performance and deliver better business results. They provide strategies for increasing revenue, reducing risks, and cutting costs. However, they don't focus on an employee's happiness or sense of fulfillment.

On the other hand, many books are directed at improving employee morale. Some discuss improving the quality of employees' lives, improving working relationships, and becoming more personally fulfilled. However, these books don't focus on improving business results.

Neither type of book uncovers the root causes that lead to workplace problems or solves problems by addressing the whole picture (that is, holistically). The reality is initiatives aimed at improving business may deliver business results, but they often have a very negative impact on employee morale, which can negatively impact the bottom line in many ways, so you're right back where you started—disgruntled and not as successful as you could be.

This book is the crossroads where business performance and success intersect with relationships that work and employee happiness. It provides a holistic approach that will improve employee morale and business results at the same time.

This book shows how you can succeed as an individual and in a workgroup. The insights, principles, and strategies in this book relate to any business situation. They are applicable to public and private sectors, nonprofit organizations, small and midsize businesses, and departments and business units within large corporations.

You'll get insight into what's really going on in the interactions between you and your boss or coworkers and how well (if at all) these interactions support business strategies. It will show you how organizations can improve employee morale and deliver business results by creating effective alignments between employee behaviors, leadership behaviors, and business systems. It will also show you what you can do about this on an individual level.

Along the way, this book will show you techniques for tapping into your personal power to improve interactions with others in your workgroup and organization. Ultimately, this book will give you the tools you need to be gruntled and successful at work—regardless of your level within the organization.

2

Gruntled Versus Disgruntled Employees

"The retail world is the worst for morale. The bottom line is profits and customer satisfaction—even if the customer is being unreasonable, trying to 'pull a fast one,' or is being generally unpleasant. Some people just always seem to have an axe to grind, and the employees have to tolerate it with a smile and a 'have a great day' attitude. If an employee happens to not be as exuberant as the company expects—even once—they will be talked to about it. That isn't good for morale. It keeps the employees on edge and makes them feel unappreciated. If retail wages were better—*much better*—maybe this would be more tolerable. However, employees are paid poorly and pushed to a point where they develop a 'who gives a hoot' attitude. It's no wonder that retail stores have a high turnover of employees. Employees simply get fed up after a time."

Disgruntled Employee
Blog Post

Gruntled is not a word that I made up. The word originated in the 1930s. The *New Oxford American Dictionary* defines it as "pleased, satisfied, and contented." A gruntled employee is one who is satisfied at work most of the time. They look forward to going to work and enjoy the work they do. They enjoy the people they work with, so they're quick to help others. They are pleased and contented during the process of meeting objectives—not just when they achieve the objectives. They support organizational goals and often go the extra mile. Gruntled employees feel a sense of calm and peace in the workplace as they do their jobs.

However, as you can see from the preceding blog, not all employees are gruntled. Many employees are just the opposite—disgruntled. Disgruntled employees are easy to spot. They manifest their feelings through complaints, bad-mouthing the organization or management, insubordination, errors, slowing down productivity, not taking care of the workplace assets, requesting transfers, frequent tardiness, and absenteeism. And to make matters worse, each disgruntled employee usually exhibits more than one of these behaviors, often at the same time.

In response to this disgruntledness, companies try to do many things to improve employee morale. Management undertakes initiatives that address organizational culture, leadership, and working environment issues. It also conducts surveys to determine if the organization is meeting employee satisfaction expectations. Human Resources (HR) works with leaders to improve communications with employees. It also sets up leadership development programs and seminars with guest speakers providing training on effective leadership. In addition, HR conducts exit interviews, trying to determine what issues may have caused employees to leave.

Management also creates employee reward and recognition programs to thank employees for meeting goals and to acknowledge positive behaviors. It sets up flexible work programs for employees such as working from home, flexible work schedules, or reduced workweeks. Furthermore, HR reviews the organization's compensation and benefit programs to ensure that they are competitive in the market and not a cause of employee disgruntledness.

Sometimes leaders try to improve employee morale with team-building exercises or community-involvement activities. They also sometimes try to inject fun into the working environment with holiday parties, picnics, or celebrating employee birthdays.

However, despite all these employee morale improvement techniques, work still needs to be done to improve employee gruntledness. Gruntledness is a critical factor in personal and professional fulfillment and is crucial to achieving success.

Employee Morale and Engagement Statistics

Research shows that employee morale problems exist in almost any organization. But very seldom do these statistics get the business exposure that they should. In many instances, organizations would rather not acknowledge what is really going on. Therefore, this section will contain many examples of what the true results really are. Consider the following statistics from *Entrepreneur Magazine's* Web site:[1]

- 46% of new hires leave their jobs within the first year
- 85% of employees' morale sharply decreases after their first 6 months on the job
- 53% of senior-level executives are dissatisfied with their current job
- 71% of workers say they have no desire to become a boss at their workplace
- 25% of workers go job hunting on their work computer even though they believe their boss monitors their Internet use
- 43% of 26- to 39-year-olds expect to leave their job within 3 years
- On average, workers in their 20s stay at each job for only 1.1 years
- 43% of employees call in sick when they aren't sick at all

These statistics are not an indication of high employee morale. In addition, the Randstad 2008 World of Work study found that only 51% of employees felt that company morale was either excellent or good.[2]

Many studies these days aim to find the level of employee *engagement*, which measures employee commitment to making the organization a success. Note that employee morale is a key factor in employee engagement. Most studies show that employees are either marginally engaged or disengaged:

- A BlessingWhite Employee Engagement Report published in 2011 found that globally only 31% of employees were engaged and 17% were disengaged[3]
- A Gallup Management Journal survey in 2008 found in average organizations 33% were engaged, 49% were not engaged, and 18% were actively disengaged[4]
- A Towers Perrin study of 90,000 employees in 18 countries in 2007–2008 found only 21% of the workers were fully engaged and 38% were either disenchanted or disengaged[5]
- A 2008–09 Employee Hold'em National Workforce Engagement Benchmark study found that 43% of the over 2300 employees surveyed were fully engaged and 32% were disengaged; the study concluded that nearly 60% of employees were reluctant to work hard but also reluctant to leave their company[6]
- A Watson Wyatt study of 14,000 employees in 10 European countries found that only 13% of employees were engaged at work with a strong commitment and good understanding of their part in making their company successful; the study also found that about 36% of employees were disengaged[7]

A quick visit to some Web sites that allow people to speak freely about their boss and organization clearly shows many employees are unhappy and dissatisfied at work. Employerscorecard.com, Glassdoor.com, Salary.com, Jobitorial.com, Vault.com, and badbossology.com are just a few of these popular sites. They are full of negative comments about managers' and coworkers' behaviors and work environments.

How Does Employee Morale and Engagement Affect Business Success?

Where would an organization be without its employees? Employees deliver the capabilities (productivity, excellent customer service, innovation) that lead to market share. An organization that recognizes that its most valuable asset is its employees has a greater chance of having more gruntled and engaged employees, which will make it more successful. The truth is, employee gruntledness has a dramatic impact on business success.

Research from numerous sources conclusively shows that employee morale is definitely a factor in an organization's success. In their book, *Contented Cows Give Better Milk,* Bill Catlette and Richard Hadden demonstrate that companies that are regarded as good places to work financially outperform companies that are less admired in their industry.[8] Sirota Consulting's research found that the share price of companies with high employee morale increased an average of 16%—compared to an industry average of 6%.[9]

The most significant finding is not the number of employees and managers who are dissatisfied and plan to look for another job but, rather, the number of disengaged employees—those who are unhappy but plan to stay with their current employer.

In addition, a Towers Perrin study of 50 global companies over a one-year period found that companies with employees that were highly engaged had a 28% earnings per share growth rate while companies with disengaged employees experienced an 11% earnings per share decrease.[10]

Gallup found that publicly traded companies with high levels of employee engagement (67% engaged, 7% disengaged) had an earning per share growth 3.9 times the rate of companies with an average level of employee engagement (33% engaged, 18% disengaged). Gallup estimated that U.S. companies lost as much as $300 billion annually in lost productivity due to disengaged employees.[11]

The 2008–09 Employee Hold'em National Workforce Engagement Benchmark study found the following as well:[12]

- 96% of fully engaged employees compared to only 56% of disengaged employees will go out of their way for customers
- 98% of fully engaged employees compared to only 34% of disengaged employees are motivated to work hard
- 97% of fully engaged employees compared to only 11% of disengaged employees will enthusiastically refer their company
- 92% of fully engaged employees compared to only 9% of disengaged employees would stay with their companies for less money
- 92% of fully engaged employees compared to only 29% of disengaged employees plan on staying with their company for the next two years

So What Do We Know So Far?

Employee morale problems persist in many organizations despite management efforts to improve them. Numerous studies show that a lot of work still needs to be done to improve employee morale and engagement levels.

Disgruntledness and disengagement negatively impact customer satisfaction and productivity, and threaten the bottom line. Disgruntled and disengaged employees create a large risk in the workplace by not meeting customers' expectations, not being motivated to work hard, not giving their organization a positive reference, and not being loyal to the organization. Gruntledness impacts the success of the organization. The next chapter explores the success rate of companies' business strategies and their relationship on employee morale and engagement.

3

How Businesses Try to Succeed

"To counter the company's dramatic losses, layoffs were implemented. But a single layoff never seemed to be enough to get the costs down. So the layoffs continued to the pace of two a year for close to 36 months. The layoffs had produced dismal employee morale, which resulted in poor job performance, which resulted in more layoffs. Then the company was convicted of laying off employees over 40. So to add more pain and misery, the company implemented a new way to do layoffs. No longer would employee past and current performance be reviewed as part of the layoff process. All layoffs were done by laying off the whole workgroup. Your tenure was then determined by the luck of the draw as to what workgroup you were in. Most employee morale hit rock bottom about that time. There was nothing that could be done performance-wise to help hold your position in the company. The best way to survive an environment like this was to just not care. And many did not."

Disgruntled Employee
Blog Post

Companies focus efforts and resources on developing unique products and services that differentiate them from their competitors. Similarly, nonprofits and government agencies focus efforts and resources on excellence in service to taxpaying citizens and other constituents. To achieve their mission and goals, companies and nonprofits or government agencies implement business strategies.

Consumers now take low prices for granted. Business customers also expect companies to provide products and services with higher quality, in shorter time frames, and for less cost. The phrase "better, cheaper, faster" is widespread in the business world. And customers of government and non-profit services now expect them to be more efficient, faster, less redundant, and delivered over the Internet.

As a result of these expectations, some business strategies focus on reducing operational costs such as increasing quality and reducing the time it takes to get products and services to customers faster. Cost-reduction initiatives include reorganizing, downsizing, outsourcing, or simplifying processes. Information technology projects reduce the cost of providing these products/services by automating and streamlining processes.

Other business strategies aim at growing revenue. Companies develop new products and services to sell to existing customers or extend their brand to enter new markets. Companies also form strategic alliances to combine complementary strengths in providing new services or developing new products. Strategic alliances are particularly helpful to companies in entering unfamiliar markets and sharing the costs and risks associated with the development of new services and products.

Many companies these days are growing revenue and market share through globalization initiatives and exporting their goods or services into new countries. Mergers and acquisitions are a much quicker way for companies to move into new markets or expand market share than developing new products or services. Mergers and acquisitions can improve an organization's competitive position in the marketplace and provide the organization with additional advantages such as different technology and experienced staff.

Business Strategies Statistics

Companies' business strategies have not had a high rate of success. An article, "Turning Great Strategy into Great Performance," in *Harvard Business Review*, stated "Most companies' strategies deliver only 63% of their promised financial value."[13] Another study in the *Harvard Business Review* found that companies' growth strategies did not deliver anticipated benefits. It found that most companies' success rate with business initiatives is only at 25%.[14] An additional *Harvard Business Review* study found that only 53% of 2000 strategic alliances returned profits greater than the partners' cost investments.[15]

Mergers and acquisitions, which are often a combination of revenue growth and cost-cutting strategies, have limited success, as pointed out in the following studies:

- A study by the global management consultancy Hay Group on mergers and acquisitions in 2007 found that more than 90% did not achieve all their objectives; only a third of those surveyed stated that they achieved significant cost efficiencies, increased shareholder value, or a significant increase in revenue or market share[16]
- A study by KPMG on acquisitions in 2006 found that only 31% created real value, and 26% actually reduced value[17]
- A study by Accenture in 2009 found that about 50% of merger and acquisition deals had either substantial or partial value erosion, and within the financial industry, banks that experienced a merger had a higher decrease in customer loyalty and trust[18]
- A study by Hewitt in 2008 found that 78% of those surveyed felt that they had not met or exceeded their merger and acquisition goals; while the majority of respondents felt that revenue synergy and increased market share objectives had been achieved, only 69% felt that increased productivity objectives had been met, and less than 48% saw a change in share price[19]

During the past four decades of companies using outsourcing as a business strategy, numerous studies on success and failure rates have been conducted. Offshore outsourcing has been popular for the past decade and has also encountered some problems. Some outsourcing relationships achieve their objectives over time, but many do not, as revealed in the following studies:

- A study by outsourcing advisory firm TPI in 2007 revealed that savings ranged from 10% to 39%—a significant variance from the market's widely touted claims of cost reductions in the range of 60%[20]
- A survey by A.T. Kearney in 2007 found that 42 large companies saved 44% by offshoring, however, 34% didn't save as much as expected, and 60% didn't hit their operational performance targets[21]
- A study by DiamondCluster in 2005 found only 62% of companies were satisfied with their offshore outsourcing, and 51% of companies had terminated their outsourcing contracts abnormally[22]
- A survey by Deloitte in 2005 found that 70% of the companies had very negative experiences with outsourcing; 44% said they didn't get the promised cost savings, particularly in the later years of the contract, and 64% of companies in the study brought the work back in-house after outsourcing[23]

Enterprise resource planning (ERP), which is a business strategy that aims to streamline processes and reduce costs, has its own issues. A study on ERP implementations found that 70% do not deliver anticipated benefits.[24] Several studies on ERP cite employees culturally rejecting the ERP system as a main cause of failure.[25,26] Management's lack of commitment to the new system is another common reason for ERP failures.

How Do Business Strategies Affect Employee Morale and Engagement?

Today's business strategies for improving business success often create problems for employees. Although technology is a key resource in an organization's pursuit of business success, studies reveal that employee resistance to technological change often impedes the success of technology initiatives. Studies find that "user involvement and participation in technology decisions are of paramount importance in the successful adoption of new technology;" without such involvement, employee reactions can "range from resistance to outright sabotage."[27]

Other business strategies such as mergers and acquisitions cause problems for employees. Kenexa Research Institute found that mergers and acquisitions and their resulting layoffs negatively impact the following drivers of employee engagement: confidence in the company's future and its senior leaders, assurance of a promising future with the company, and a guarantee that their company provides its customers with higher quality products and services than its competitors.[28]

Cost-cutting strategies such as layoffs, travel and training restrictions, reductions in size of offices and cubicles, or decreases in compensation and benefits all negatively impact employees. Many employee surveys point out the impact of cost-cutting strategies on employee morale. For example, a 2005 survey of morale among employees in the U.S. Department of Homeland Security found a high degree of disgruntledness. The problems were attributed to continued cost-cutting initiatives along with pressure to improve services at the same time.[29]

The 2004 Business Energy Survey of employee attitudes in the retail industry found that high work volume, the pace of change, the impact of cost-reduction initiatives, and management's lack of effective communication to employees about change caused employees' energy levels to drop very low.

As the above surveys show, business strategies sometimes cause more problems than they solve, and some of these problems can be far-reaching, as is evident in the following experience of a company's business strategy efforts:

Providing unique services, Company A was successful in its market for the first two years in business. But by the third year it wasn't competing well on cost or quality compared to new competitors. Potential sales in the pipeline had dwindled to almost nothing, and the company's revenue was based solely on the remaining contracts for existing customers. So it brought on board a new CEO who was tasked with achieving a turn-around, which involved several business strategies.

The CEO's actions included eliminating employees who were not add-ing to the growth of the business, training some remaining employees on new skills, firing some leaders, and hiring others to develop new capa-bilities. Some of the fired employees and leaders ended up at a competitor firm, Company C. In the turnover/reorganization efforts, Company A also developed several new competitive service offerings.

Within two years, Company A's business was so successful that it be-came the target of an unsolicited takeover bid. Company A was then ac-quired by Company B, a process that took about a year. During that year, several employees from Company A lost their jobs because of the acquisi-tion; of those who remained, many were upset about what happened to their coworkers since they'd worked so hard to help the company grow. The CEO left Company A at the time of the acquisition and was immediately brought on board at Company C, where he was tasked with another turn-around situation.

Two years after the acquisition, Company B still had ongoing perfor-mance issues with its disgruntled employees who never got over what hap-pened to them and their coworkers after Company A was acquired. And Company C had trouble with some of its employees who had heard ru-mors (from former Company A employees now at Company C) about the CEO and became wary of the real motive behind any change the CEO implemented at Company C.

So What Do We Know So Far?

The implementation of business strategies often does not deliver antici-pated business results. This is true for revenue-generating business strat-egies as well as cost-cutting strategies. Mergers and acquisitions often negatively impact the morale of employees. Cost-cutting initiatives also take their toll on employees, causing them stress as they try to do more work with fewer resources.

Employee morale is also low and management's efforts to improve it are not usually successful. The studies show that employee morale and engagement levels have a significant impact on business results.

Companies that fail in their business strategies to reduce costs quickly or transform and grow the business soon find they are not competitive in today's global economy. To make matters worse, business strategies often create unfriendly corporate cultures and working environments for employees.

There appears to be a catch-22 in the business world. Business strategies negatively impact employee morale and low employee morale negatively impacts business results. So what can be done to address the interdependencies between employee morale and business strategies? The next chapter looks at the causes of these interrelated problems.

4

How to Improve Employee Gruntledness and Business Success Simultaneously

"When our workgroup was being transitioned to a new company, we were told that we needed to change pagers to the new company's standard provider. But the new company had not bothered to check to see if the pagers would consistently work in our metropolitan area. This little fact was mentioned to our new management staff. Management did a quick test with four different models of pagers. After the test was complete, it was determined that the new brand of pagers would only receive 30% to 40% of the time. This was not particularly good since our client was a 24/7 operation. We thought that the testing would resolve the issue of pager changeover. It did not. The decision was being made 1,000 miles away at some corporate headquarters. The new company insisted that everyone needed to switch over to the new pager because of better discounts. Never mind that the people on call would miss 70% of the pages. It was difficult to care about performance when management did not understand the environment."

Disgruntled Employee
Blog Post

Trying to solve employee morale problems without addressing the influence of business strategies on morale is not really going to improve morale. Similarly, implementing a business strategy without considering the impact employee morale has on business results is not going to ensure success. These interrelated problems require a holistic solution.

Putting in place a remedy for complex and interrelated problems is easier said than done because most people tend to look at things in a segmented way rather than taking a holistic view. If you focus your attention on the problem immediately in front of you and don't look at the root cause that contributed to the problem, how can you solve problems holistically?

When organizations define strategies to improve business results but neglect to consider the impact of the strategies on employee morale, months later, management realizes that employee morale has decreased. So they implement a program to improve morale, but they don't consider the relationship between the program and business strategies.

For example, an organization may reorganize to more effectively provide the products and services it offers, but won't consider the impact to employee roles and responsibilities and how the reorganization will affect current processes. Impacts to management and information systems are also usually not considered in sufficient detail. Reorganizations, along with many other business strategies, tend to cause confusion amongst employees and workgroups, negatively impacting employee morale as Figure 4.1 illustrates.

Obviously the company where Ken was employed felt that reorganization was the solution to its problems; but as is often the case with reorganizations, the strategy caused operational issues and disgruntled employees.

Reorganizations happen all the time. Unfortunately, most reorganizations do not focus on the real cause of the business problems—people's behavior. If an organization's management team does not address the underlying patterns of behavior, it will get the same kinds of results it had before the reorganization. Management teams have a lot of influence, but they can get much better results if they approach the problem holistically, taking into account every aspect that helped to create the problem.

Figure 4.1: E-mail of disgruntled employee after reorganization

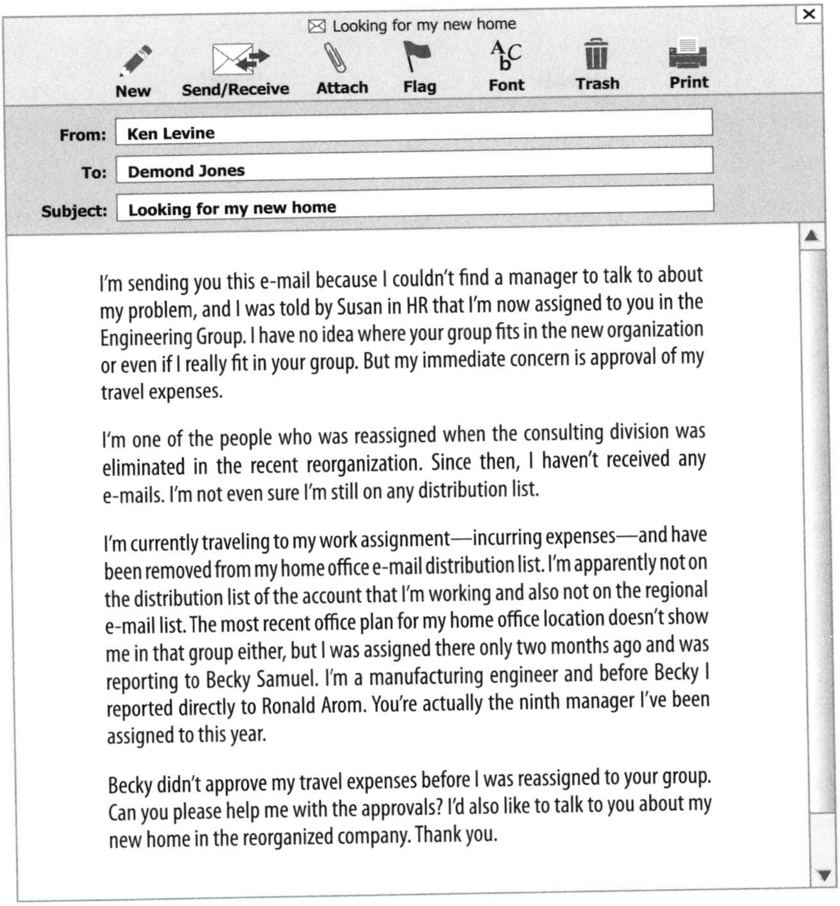
Looking for my new home

New Send/Receive Attach Flag Font Trash Print

From: Ken Levine

To: Demond Jones

Subject: Looking for my new home

I'm sending you this e-mail because I couldn't find a manager to talk to about my problem, and I was told by Susan in HR that I'm now assigned to you in the Engineering Group. I have no idea where your group fits in the new organization or even if I really fit in your group. But my immediate concern is approval of my travel expenses.

I'm one of the people who was reassigned when the consulting division was eliminated in the recent reorganization. Since then, I haven't received any e-mails. I'm not even sure I'm still on any distribution list.

I'm currently traveling to my work assignment—incurring expenses—and have been removed from my home office e-mail distribution list. I'm apparently not on the distribution list of the account that I'm working and also not on the regional e-mail list. The most recent office plan for my home office location doesn't show me in that group either, but I was assigned there only two months ago and was reporting to Becky Samuel. I'm a manufacturing engineer and before Becky I reported directly to Ronald Arom. You're actually the ninth manager I've been assigned to this year.

Becky didn't approve my travel expenses before I was reassigned to your group. Can you please help me with the approvals? I'd also like to talk to you about my new home in the reorganized company. Thank you.

Root Cause Analysis

To solve an employee morale or business results problem holistically, you must look beyond the immediate problem and find the *root cause*, that is—the reason why the problem occurred. If you look only at the immediate problem and identify the reason why it occurred, the solution is often a quick fix that may prevent the problem from occurring again but does not prevent similar problems from occurring. Finding the root cause is the only way to ensure that this and similar problems don't recur. To properly investigate root causes, you need to perform the following steps:

- Determine the causal factors that contributed to the problem at hand
- Review behavioral and systemic causal factors for the particular problem
- Determine the root cause of the problem

The investigation starts by looking for *causal factors*—the underlying reasons that contributed to the problem. When you try to find causal factors, systemic and behavioral issues surface. *Systemic issues* are problems with the business system. A *business system* comprises an organizational framework (business units, departments, and workgroups), processes (how goods and services are produced), management systems (business strategy approach), and information technology or IT (process automation and data dissemination). Michael Hammer and James Champy introduced the concept of analyzing a company's business system in their book *Reengineering the Corporation*.[30] *Behavioral issues* are problems with how employees and/or leaders interact.

When serious employee morale or business result problems occur, the underlying business system is usually a key factor. Examining the business system uncovers any issues with the organizational framework, processes, management systems, and IT that encouraged the behaviors that resulted in the problem. So the business system can be a causal factor to problematic behaviors. Addressing systemic causal factors can help encourage appropriate behaviors. But it doesn't always get to the root cause of the problem. The behaviors themselves have causal factors behind them. Here's an example of root cause analysis:

You are the owner of a restaurant. One of the customers complains that the steak he ordered is medium rare and not medium. You review with the cook how he grilled the steak, and discover that he grilled the steak for 5 minutes when he should have grilled it for 7 minutes. So your analysis leads you to determine that the cook undercooked the steak by 2 minutes.

You decide to look further into the problem and discover the cook had been undercooking medium steaks for months because he thought it was the right amount of time, which is a causal factor. In response to your discovery, you tell all the cooks they need to cook medium steaks for 7 minutes instead of 5, which irritates the cooks who already know this information. However, the announcement ensures that steaks won't be sent back for now. But you worry that it could happen again because you haven't gotten to the bottom of why your cook made this error in the first place. You wonder why your new hire orientation did not train him how to properly cook steaks.

You decide to investigate why the cook thought that 5 minutes was the right amount of time. You find out that when the cook was hired, he was given an outdated recipe book that incorrectly lists 5 minutes as the time it takes to cook medium steaks. With this information, the systemic causal factor that generated the behavior is revealed.

In order to solve the problem at the systemic level, you update the old recipe book. Doing so solves the systemic causal factors of the problem. It also points you to other outdated recipes that were causing problems—making customers and staff unhappy and costing you money every time food was sent back to the kitchen. But again, you wonder if you reached the root cause of the problem: Why is the recipe book out of date? Isn't it the head chef's responsibility to update it? He's the expert. Why doesn't he know this? Reflecting on this some more, you realize that it is your job as owner of the restaurant to inform the head chef to keep the recipe book up to date. You suddenly realize that you were the root cause of the problem.

So when you seek a solution to business strategy or employee morale problems, you need to look for the root cause. Once the root cause of the problem is identified, a holistic plan can be developed to address that cause. If the root cause isn't identified, then a holistic plan cannot be created, so the chances are greater that the problem will occur again.

As illustrated in the restaurant example, significant causal factors are often due to business system deficiencies. Changing deficiencies in the business system provides benefits beyond the problem at hand. Correcting business system deficiencies can improve overall employee morale and business results and prevent future occurrences of other types of operational errors. But the biggest impact to employee morale and business results issues comes when you address the root cause of the problem, which in the restaurant example ended up being a problem with leadership behaviors. Part 6 digs even deeper and examines root causes for employee and leadership behaviors.

Causal Factors for Employee Morale and Engagement Problems

The surveys referenced in Chapter 2 provide some insight into causal factors for employee morale problems: behavior of leaders and behavior of employees. These surveys, which were conducted for hundreds or thousands of employees across many different companies, show the causes behind employee morale and engagement problems.

The 2008 BlessingWhite survey shows that leadership behaviors make a difference between engaged and disengaged employees:[31]

- 33% of disengaged employees compared to only 3% of engaged employees do not trust their managers
- 41% of disengaged employees compared to only 3% of engaged employees do not believe that their manager encourages them to use their talents
- 52% of disengaged employees compared to only 6% of engaged employees do not trust senior leaders of the company

Other studies also show that leadership behaviors have an impact on employee morale. An independent study in Wales in 2007 revealed that more than 200,000 people (16% of respondents) claimed they were currently being bullied in the workplace. Bullying was defined as "humiliating an employee in front of other people, setting impossible tasks, or displaying aggression or violence."[32] Three-quarters of the bullying came from a manager.

Leaders that "motivate" employees using threats and negative consequences, criticize or bully employees, communicate from a position of authority, and rarely listen to employees can have a destructive effect on employee morale, which ends up de-motivating them. This type of climate does not create a high-performance atmosphere for an energized workforce.

The way that leaders behave has a lot to do with whether employees are engaged or disengaged, and gruntled or disgruntled. Solving leadership problems can decrease the number of disengaged and disgruntled employees within an organization.

Other studies show that the behavior of coworkers is another cause of low employee morale. A list of Human Resources Statistics published on Entrepreneur.com shows that managers spend an average of 7 hours or more a week sorting out personality conflicts among staff members and that 87% of employees feel that working with a low performer makes them want to change jobs.[33]

The Randstad 2008 World of Work survey shows that one of the most important reasons why employees stay is that they enjoy the relationships they have with their coworkers.[34] The survey also shows the following coworker traits to be among the most important factors for happiness on the job:

- Open to new ideas
- Friendly
- Willing to share knowledge
- Competent
- Ethical
- Willing to do extra to get the job done
- Willing to take on responsibility
- Respectful
- Able to handle a crisis

Surveys also frequently uncover lack of teamwork and cooperation as a cause for low employee morale. Improving the interactions that employees have with their coworkers can also decrease the number of disengaged or disgruntled employees within an organization.

Causal Factors for Business Success Problems

Many of the studies in Chapter 3 also point to two major factors that would improve employee performance and increase the chance of success by implementing business strategies: improved leadership and better relationships with coworkers. These studies also shed some light on typical causal factors for the failure or success rate of mergers and acquisitions:

- The study by Hewitt found that insufficient attention to people issues such as leadership selection, communications, employee retention, employee engagement, and cultural integration were major reasons why mergers and acquisitions did not meet their objectives[35]
- The study by HayGroup found intangible assets such as leadership capability, cultural compatibility, employee engagement, productivity, and skills to be as critical as tangible assets in any merger or acquisition; the survey found the following:[36]
  - 54% of leaders felt that not auditing intangible assets increased the risk of making the wrong acquisition
  - 70% of leaders did not audit intangible assets even though they recognized the importance of them
  - 63% of leaders felt a significant cultural gap after merger and acquisition integration
  - 22% of leaders reported culture shock immediately after a merger or acquisition
  - 16% described mergers and acquisitions as trench warfare
- The study by KPMG found that the difference between organizational cultures was one of the top three challenges with mergers and acquisitions, and 80% of the companies were not prepared to handle cultural issues[37]
- A 2006 study by Accenture found understanding cultural issues to be a critical factor for having successful mergers and acquisitions:
  - 22% of leaders had serious doubts that they could manage cultural differences
  - Only 44% felt confident in their ability to manage cultural differences; leadership commitment and a good communication strategy were also found to be keys to success[38]

Another notable study conducted by the Forum Corporation reveals people issues as causal factors for failed growth strategies.[39] Leadership behaviors such as communicating objectives, coaching and listening to employees, keeping employees focused on objectives, and building a climate of ownership were found to be critical to the success of all growth strategies; for mergers and acquisitions in particular, leadership's ability to bridge differences in styles and organizational culture was also important.

Studies on outsourcing success and failure rates also show causal factors.[40,41,42,43,44] Leadership behaviors such as providing little or no direction to employees, having poor or minimal decision-making skills, and demonstrating low executive commitment are often cited. The client's mismanagement of outsourcing vendors is a commonly cited reason for not getting the full value out of outsourcing engagements. This happens when client leadership provides little direction to vendor leadership on implementing their specific business objectives for outsourcing. Also, the client organization often has problems internally, such as employees not being able to accept outsourcing.

Poor performance by vendors is another causal factor for receiving limited or no value from outsourcing engagements. Employee performance problems such as inefficiently completing work, not delivering on commitments, delivering low-quality work, resolving issues with delays leading to slipping project deadlines, and not meeting agreed-upon service levels are typically cited. Other cited causal factors for outsourcing failures include conflicting communication and work styles and cultural differences.

As you can see, the relationship that employees have with their leaders and coworkers is a determining factor in the success rate of business strategies. Research shows that lack of teamwork and cooperation are a cause for business problems as well as employee morale problems. Improving the interactions that employees have with their managers and each other can increase the chance for business strategies to succeed. Of course it all comes down to people and how employees and leaders behave, because that is the root cause of all problems. Everything else is a result of what employees and leaders produce. While the list of complaints for business success problems is very different from the employee morale problems list, leadership and employee behaviors keep showing up on both lists as the reason behind those complaints.

Systemic Causal Factors for Employee Morale and Engagement Problems

Business systems also influence employee and leadership behavior patterns. These behavior patterns are related to employee morale and engagement problems.

A company's organizational framework will encourage different behaviors. For example, in a hierarchical organizational structure, managers are encouraged to take an active role and employees a more passive role. Limiting contributions of employees often leads to low employee morale and disengagement.

An organization's processes often encourage leaders and employees to behave in certain ways. For example, if a company's process is very bureaucratic, employees may be required to get management approval between each step in a task. Or if a company strictly enforces its processes even when the processes are ineffective, employees may be required to complete unnecessary steps. When employees do not see the worth in the process and are not trusted to do the job they were hired to do, motivation and engagement often decreases.

An organization's management systems are also a factor. Management plans that are generated at the upper-management level of an organization and then rolled down throughout the organization without a chance for employees to provide feedback can encourage employees to do only as their leaders direct. Employee involvement would be much different if the management system allowed each level of the organization to determine its own management plans. The more management lets employees be involved, the more engaged employees are.

Certain IT products that an organization provides to employees also show up as a factor in employee morale and engagement. IT can increase or decrease employee morale and engagement, depending on its characteristics. If a computer system is not user-friendly, it can cause a lot of disgruntledness. Also, when data is controlled by upper management, employees often have a difficult time getting the information they need to do their jobs well. This further contributes to employee morale problems.

Business systems with characteristics that encourage leaders to take an active role and employees to take a passive role often have a negative impact on employee morale. However, business systems with characteristics that encourage the opposite may negatively impact business strategies, as you will see in the next section.

Systemic Causal Factors for Business Problems

Business systems also influence business strategy and success because business systems encourage leaders and employees to behave in certain ways; these behaviors affect how business strategies are implemented, which ultimately affects business success.

Decentralized organizations tend to encourage upper management to take a more hands-off approach, which allows lower levels of management to determine how to implement business strategies on their own. If an employee has the freedom to implement a bad strategy, this too could hinder business success.

If an organization's processes are very flexible or not enforced, employees will be allowed to carry out business strategies any way they like. However, many business strategies are very complex, so companies encounter problems when processes provide too much empowerment, allowing employees to decide how to implement strategy without direction from leaders.

Management plans that are generated at each level of the organization encourage workgroups to do what they think is best. While this is empowering, it can lead to problems, particularly because most business strategies need to be coordinated across workgroups at each level. Without upper management's direction or coordination between workgroups, one workgroup's plan may be inadvertently misaligned with the organization's objectives and business strategies.

Some organizations have decentralized data, which allows each workgroup to collect and report data as they see fit. This encourages workgroups to act more autonomously than workgroups in organizations that control access to data. Decentralized data hinders implementing organization-wide business strategies because every workgroup has their own source of truth, which can undermine business strategies that are trying to get everyone on the same page.

Business systems with characteristics that encourage leaders to take an active role and employees to take a passive role often work better when implementing business strategies. However, the opposite is true for employee morale. Employees tend to be more gruntled when business systems have characteristics that encourage employees to take an active role and leaders to take a passive role.

So What Do We Know So Far?

The cause of employee morale problems and business result problems is the same—employee and leadership behaviors. Behaviors influence business success and gruntledness. Behaviors improve or degrade operational performance, determine the success of a business strategy, and impact the gruntledness of fellow employees.

Leadership behaviors have a *multiplying effect* on employees' behaviors. Certain leadership behaviors will encourage different employee behaviors and either increase or decrease employee gruntledness and the chances of business success.

The surveys referenced in this book reveal that leader and coworker behaviors are key factors in whether an employee is gruntled or disgruntled and engaged or disengaged. Certain behaviors lead to gruntledness and engagement, others to disgruntledness and disengagement. The relationships that employees have with each other, their supervisors, and their work environments make all the difference in whether the employees are gruntled or disgruntled.

Behaviors are encouraged by business systems and business systems *exponentially influence* behavior. In fact, business systems cement certain behaviors into the organization, which forces employees and leaders to behave more in line with the behaviors the business system promotes, even when those behaviors are not an individual's personal preference.

Employees tend to prefer business systems that allow a lot of freedom and encourage independent behaviors. Unfortunately these types of business systems and behaviors don't work well for implementing many of today's business strategies. Successful business strategies are often implemented by managers using more authoritarian behaviors, and many of these strategies require a business system that forces employees to behave in a certain way. However, such business systems and behaviors have a negative impact on employee morale and engagement. Fortunately, business systems can have characteristics put in place to encourage employee and leadership behaviors that will improve employee morale and business results at the same time.

So there are three causal factors for all employee morale and business problems:

• Employee behaviors
• Leadership behaviors
• Business system characteristics

Parts 2 and 3 of this book detail employee and leadership behaviors and explain how they impact employee gruntledness and business results. Part 4 describes how business systems can have various characteristics that promote different employee and leadership behaviors. Part 5 provides a holistic approach that addresses causal factors of employee morale and business result problems. It also explains how you can change behaviors and business system characteristics to improve employee morale and business results at the same time. Part 6 provides a holistic approach that explains how you can change your own behavior so that you can be more gruntled and successful personally.

Part 2

How Employee Behaviors Influence Business Results and Employee Morale

"We need each other. Staunch independence is an illusion, but heavy dependence isn't healthy, either. The only position of long-term strength is interdependence."

Greg Anderson
American author; founder of the American Wellness Project

5

Employee Behaviors Impact Gruntledness and Business Success

"This idiot I work with insists it is our responsibility to send out year-end statements to donors. When she wasn't here for 2 years, I didn't do year-end statements and only about 5–10 people called for one, which I mailed to them. But that was only 5–10 as opposed to 800. She's an absolute idiot and drives me crazy with her analness. She keeps saying she may have to quit because she doesn't like the direction the organization is going in. I keep thinking 'Here's your hat, what are you waiting for?' God, I'm such a nice person."

Disgruntled Employee
Blog Post

I n Stephen Covey's book, *The 7 Habits of Highly Effective People*, he describes three paradigms (or patterns) behind human behavior: ". . . dependence is the paradigm of you—you take care of me; you come through for me; you didn't come through; I blame you for the results. Independence is the paradigm of I—I can do it; I am responsible, I am self-reliant, I can choose. Interdependence is the paradigm of we—we can do it; we can cooperate; we can combine our talents and abilities and create something greater together."[45]

The "you," "I," and "we" paradigms shape how people behave. The people who use the "you" paradigm depend on others to get things done. Those who use the "I" paradigm want to do it all themselves. Those who use the "we" paradigm work with others to accomplish a common goal.

So why is it important to be aware of behavior patterns? Because it will help you understand your behaviors and the behaviors of the people you work with, and when you do that, you can change behaviors that negatively impact business success and employee morale.

Five Employee Activities

Employees do all sorts of activities in the workplace, and how an employee behaves while doing those activities greatly impacts employee gruntledness and business results. Some approaches to employee activities cause interpersonal and business problems, while other approaches bond a workgroup together. Most employee activities can be grouped into five activities. The five employee activities are defined and broken down into sub-activities in the following way:

1. **Decision Making.** Employees participate in decision making in several ways and regard opinions differently.
   - Participation – may defer decisions to others, make decisions for people, make decisions by themselves, or make decisions with others
   - Opinions – may disregard their own or others' opinions, consider only their own opinions, or give others' opinions some consideration
2. **Completing Tasks.** Employees accept responsibility for tasks differently and get their work done in different ways.

- Responsibility – may feel less responsible for a task than their co-workers, feel more responsible for a task than their coworkers, accept responsibility for a task on their own, or accept responsibility for a task jointly
- Work Style – may prefer to follow direction, lead, work alone, or work with others

3. **Resolving Problems.** Employees react to problems in different ways and differ in the amount of ownership they accept for resolving problems.
   - Reaction – may discount the significance of a problem, overreact to it, appreciate its significance, or see problem interdependencies
   - Ownership – may defer problems to others, solve them for others, solve only their own part of a problem, or offer support to others

4. **Conflict Resolution.** Employees approach conflicting views in different ways and have different expectations regarding who will win in the face of conflict.
   - Approach – may try to avoid conflict, use conflict to their advantage, confront conflict, or resolve conflict equitably for everyone involved
   - Expectations – may think they will not win, expect to win no matter the cost to others, expect that they have a chance at winning, or expect everyone involved will win

5. **Relating to Others.** How employees relate to others depends on their attitude towards themselves or others, their belief on who deserves respect, and their sensitivity to needs and personal boundaries. People establish *personal boundaries*, or barriers and limitations that create and maintain personal space physically, mentally, and emotionally.
   - Attitude – may have self-deprecating, arrogant, closed-minded or open-minded attitudes
   - Respect – may or may not insist on being treated with respect and may or may not treat others respectfully
   - Boundaries – may let others violate their boundaries, cross others' personal boundaries, protect their personal boundaries, or protect everyone's boundaries

Employee Behaviors and Their Patterns

As mentioned earlier, people behave differently depending on which paradigm, or pattern, they are coming from. You can attribute employee behaviors to one of these four patterns:

- Passive (dependent) behaviors (based on the paradigm of you)
- Dominant (dependent) behaviors (based on the paradigm of you)
- Independent behaviors (based on the paradigm of I)
- Interdependent behaviors (based on the paradigm of we)

Employees choose between passive, dominant, independent, and interdependent behaviors at work all the time and typically use all behavior patterns in the performance of their daily work activities. However, employees usually have a preference for a pattern of behavior. A pattern becomes a *behavior preference* when you use a particular behavior pattern during most activities and situations. Figure 5.1 illustrates how those patterns impact the five employee activities.

Figure 5.1: Relationship between patterns and employee activities

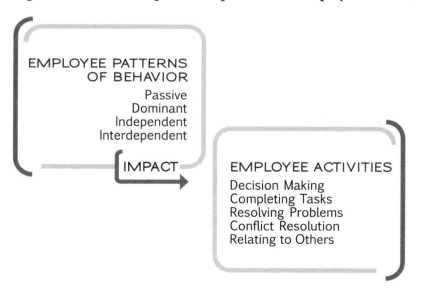

EMPLOYEE PATTERNS OF BEHAVIOR
Passive
Dominant
Independent
Interdependent

IMPACT

EMPLOYEE ACTIVITIES
Decision Making
Completing Tasks
Resolving Problems
Conflict Resolution
Relating to Others

Figure 5.2 summarizes the four behavior patterns for each of the five employee activities. Figure 5.2 is just a sample of the employee behaviors that influence business results and employee morale. Other employee behaviors can also be an influence.

Figure 5.2: Employee Behavior Matrix

EMPLOYEE ACTIVITIES	PASSIVE BEHAVIORS	DOMINANT BEHAVIORS	INDEPENDENT BEHAVIORS	INTER-DEPENDENT BEHAVIORS
Decision Making				
Participation	Defers to others	Makes decisions for others	Makes own decisions	Makes joint decisions
Opinions	Keeps opinions to self	Disregards others' opinions	Considers only own opinion	Considers own & others' opinions
Completing Tasks				
Responsibility	Less responsible	More responsible	Personally responsible	Jointly responsible
Work Style	Follows direction	Leads	Works alone	Collaborates & cooperates
Resolving Problems				
Reaction	Discounts significance	Overreacts to significance	Appreciates significance	Appreciates problem inter-dependencies
Ownership	Defers action to others	Solves problems for others	Solves own part	Supportive of others
Conflict Resolution				
Approach	Avoids conflict	Uses conflict to an advantage	Confronts conflict	Resolves conflict equitably
Expectations	Approaches conflict expecting others to win	Approaches conflict expecting to win regardless of cost to others	Approaches conflict expecting to win	Approaches conflict expecting everyone to win
Relating to Others				
Attitude	Self-deprecating	Arrogant	Closed-minded	Open-minded
Respect	Does not respect self	Does not respect others	Insists on respect	Respects self & others
Boundaries	Allows boundary violations	Crosses personal boundaries	Protects personal boundaries	Protects everyone's boundaries

Employees' behavior preferences impact operational performance and business strategy efforts; the behavior preferences also have financial impacts. Workgroups where employees demonstrate mostly interdependent behaviors usually have better business results than workgroups where employees demonstrate primarily passive, dominant, or independent behaviors. Workgroups that use primarily interdependent behaviors also tend to have higher employee morale than workgroups primarily using passive, dominant, or independent behaviors.

Appropriate and Inappropriate Behaviors

Passive, dominant, independent, and interdependent behavior patterns are completely appropriate in certain situations. However, in some situations each of these forms of behavior can be inappropriate.

People tend to develop a preference for a certain behavior pattern across most situations, although they may develop a preference for one behavior pattern in certain situations and another in other situations. For example, you may have a preference for interdependent behaviors in most situations, but when someone tries to micromanage you, you may use dominant behaviors, making it known that you're in charge.

Despite your preference for certain behaviors, you can make the choice to behave differently from that preference if the situation calls for it. Some situations appropriately necessitate leading with dominant behaviors. In other situations, it is appropriate to follow someone else's lead and use passive behaviors. Other times, it is appropriate to work alone and use independent behaviors, as well as work equally with others using interdependent behaviors. Behaving only according to your preference can lead to more inappropriate behavior choices.

The next four chapters detail passive, dominant, independent, and interdependent employee behaviors. These behaviors will be illustrated within the five employee activities.

6

How Passive Behaviors Impact Gruntledness and Business Success

"I work with a person who is a social worker but he doesn't like the actual work involved, so he documents nothing. I can only assume he is truly doing nothing. He likes to let others do his work. He especially takes advantage of using people from other organizations that work with the same clients. He'll actually send a client to them while he's got the client in his office to make an appointment for something he could have taken care of in the amount of time it took to make the call. He always has an excuse for not following through, which has been noticed but overlooked by his supervisors. He believes he is being discriminated against because he's been overlooked for promotions in spite of being with us for many years. But everyone knows he gets others to do his work for him. If you're not doing your job well in a lower tier job, you're not going to make a good manager."

Disgruntled Employee
Blog Post

People who behave passively go with the flow. Those with a preference for passive behaviors seem to get along well with others and conform easily to whatever is going on. They tend to do what is expected and not challenge those in authority. They will not rock the boat and tend to be favorably thought of. They may do this out of consideration or respect for the person taking the lead, they may not care enough to do anything differently, or they may be afraid of authority. They may use passive behaviors as their way of coping with dominant behaviors. Using passive behaviors on a regular basis to minimize stress or conflict is a passive *coping strategy*.

An alternative form of passive behavior is passive-aggressive behavior. People who behave passive-aggressively pretend to go with the flow then covertly retaliate. They care enough about the situation to take action, but are unwilling to address their concerns in open conflict. They are afraid of confronting the person directly, so they will covertly do what they think is necessary. Passive-aggressive behaviors are typically based on feeling angry about a situation but fearing to openly do something about it. Lacking respect for the person taking the lead is also a common reason for passive-aggressive behavior.

Labeling behavior as "passive" tends to have a negative connotation. However, many situations require one person to lead and others to passively follow direction. For example, suppose that you are in a car accident and taken to the emergency room. How would you feel if the nurses said that they were going to try something different than what the doctor ordered? You would probably feel more secure if the staff actually followed the doctor's direction. Many situations in business call for one person to set direction and others to follow it. Teamwork wouldn't happen if everyone were allowed to go off and do their own thing.

Passive behaviors are based on a mindset focused on *you*. Here's how these behaviors are reflected in certain work situations: If I believe that my value isn't as great as *your* value, then I might expect *you* to be better at certain activities than I am. If I believe that I'm not as responsible as *you* are on a certain task or issue, then I may expect *you* to take care of certain things for me. If I believe that I'm not entitled to something, then I may feel *you* have privileges over me.

Having one or more of these beliefs all the time or just in certain situations may lead to behaving in the following passive ways within the five employee activities:

- **Decision Making.** Defers decisions to others and keeps opinions to self.
- **Completing Tasks.** Takes on less responsibility and follows others.
- **Resolving Problems.** Discounts the significance of a problem and defers action to others.
- **Conflict Resolution.** Avoids conflict and approaches conflict expecting others to win.
- **Relating to Others.** Uses self-deprecating behavior, lacks self-respect, and allows others to cross personal boundaries.

The next sections illustrate passive behaviors across the five employee activities.

Passive Behaviors in Decision Making

Deferring decisions to others and keeping your opinion to yourself are passive ways of making decisions. Asking others what they think before voicing your opinion, not having an opinion, or just going along with others' opinions are also passive ways of making decisions. You might use these behaviors if you are less experienced or know that you don't have the best information to make a decision.

Refusing to make a decision because of a difference of opinion is a passive-aggressive approach to decision making. Such behavior may be based in the belief that the other person is a know-it-all who won't require or appreciate your help.

Decision Making—Passive Example

As a member of the procurement team, Nadine is in a meeting to decide on new copy equipment. A lively discussion is going on. Nadine thinks of something that may be important to say, but she thinks the others may have more valuable input because of how confident they all seem to be. She is worried about the group's impression of her if her concern turns out to be wrong.

Instead of speaking up and adding her concern to the discussion, Nadine continues to sit quietly, just listening to the others. Toward the end of the meeting, the team leader, Neil, notices that Nadine hasn't said anything and asks her what she would do. Even though Nadine still has her concern, she tells him that the decision sounds good.

ANALYSIS: Nadine inappropriately keeps her opinion to herself in the meeting out of fear of others' dominant behaviors toward her if she is wrong. This is an unacceptable risk to her since she isn't responsible for the team's decision. She defers the decision to other meeting participants when Neil asks her what she would do if the decision were up to her.

Passive Behaviors in Completing Tasks

Being less responsible (or uncommitted) and always following others' directions are passive ways of completing tasks. Completing your work as told without question and never challenging those providing direction are also passive behaviors. Sometimes you must be less responsible and not complete a task if there is more work than can be done in the allotted time. You may also decide that others are more knowledgeable or responsible than you in a particular task so you follow their lead or shift responsibility for your tasks to others.

Pawning a task off on others because it's not going a certain way is a passive-aggressive approach to task completion. It is also passive-aggressive to follow another's direction even though you know it's wrong just so that you can prove that fact. In addition, undermining direction while completing a task to get even with a manager is also passive-aggressive behavior.

Completing Tasks—Passive Example

Latasha is tasked with teaching her coworkers a new work process. However, she doesn't completely understand how the new process works and is very comfortable with the old way of doing things. At the next staff meeting, instead of describing the new approach that was agreed upon, Latasha tells her workgroup a slightly different approach that is basically the same as the old way with a few minor changes.

ANALYSIS: Because Latasha doesn't understand the new work process and resists change, she re-teaches the old process, which demonstrates that she is less responsible in training her coworkers in the new process and uncommitted to making needed changes. Latasha's passive task completion undermines the organization's new direction.

Passive Behaviors in Resolving Problems

Discounting the significance of a problem and deferring action to others are passive ways of resolving problems. Reacting defensively about a situation is also a passive way of resolving a problem. You might rightfully become defensive about a problem if someone unjustifiably blames you for it. You might also need to discount the significance of a problem if someone emotionally overreacts to a problem that you know isn't that important. Also, at times it is best to defer a problem to someone else if the problem is too overwhelming or advanced for you.

Not helping coworkers work through a problem because of opposition is a passive-aggressive approach to problem resolution. Refusing to solve a problem when you're responsible and capable is typically a passive-aggressive behavior that may be motivated by a past, unresolved conflict.

Resolving Problems—Passive Example

Sam has an issue with his senior editor, Susan, who keeps criticizing his work as if he doesn't understand his assignments. So he brings the issue to the attention of his manager, Nasha, the editor-in-chief.

Nasha isn't looking forward to confronting Susan who is known to overreact to criticism. Nasha is afraid that, in mentioning the issue, Susan will explode in anger and create a scene, as she has in the past. Nasha views this as a problem particularly because everyone is in cubicles and will be able to easily see and hear the commotion. So Nasha puts off bringing up the issue with Susan for a while.

Sam continues to have problems with Susan. Two weeks later, he asks Nasha what happened when she talked to Susan. Nasha blames her busy schedule for not being able to bring this up to Susan yet. She tells Sam that if it's really bothering him, he should talk to HR about it. A few weeks later, Sam and Susan seem okay to Nasha, so she assumes that it's no longer important for her to deal with.

ANALYSIS: Nasha is inappropriately non-reactive in dealing with the issue that Sam brings to her. When Sam later asks for the status on the issue, she becomes defensive and defers the problem to HR. Rather than dealing with her fear of conflict, Nasha inappropriately discounts the significance of the problem.

Passive Behaviors in Conflict Resolution

Avoiding conflict and approaching conflict expecting to lose are passive ways of resolving conflict. Accepting a losing position without really trying to win goes hand-in-hand with avoiding conflict. Not being honest about a situation to avoid conflict is also a passive approach. In addition, backing out at the first sign of conflict—even if the conflict is winnable—is passive behavior. Sometimes it is better to smooth over conflict in the interest of harmony rather than damage working relationships. It may also be appropriate to avoid a conflict if confronting the situation will have serious negative consequences.

Saying "Fine. I don't care," when you really do care and then resolving the conflict behind the scenes is a passive-aggressive approach to conflict resolution. Getting even without the other party being aware of the actions taken is also a passive-aggressive way of resolving a conflict.

Conflict Resolution—Passive Example

Gayle and Steve are working on a proposal. Gayle is a very opinionated person and decides that they should propose a part of their solution a certain way. Steve has tried that approach before and knows that it won't work. Steve tries to point out the problem with this approach, but Gayle becomes angry and demands he do it her way. Steve is intimidated by anger and backs down in response to Gayle's reaction to his points.

ANALYSIS: Steve accepts a losing position by avoiding conflict instead of confronting Gayle's approach and behaviors.

Passive Behaviors in Relating to Others

Using self-deprecating behavior, not respecting yourself, and allowing others to cross personal boundaries are passive ways of relating to others. Putting yourself down in front of others isn't usually a good idea unless you are doing it to defuse a potentially explosive situation. Any situation where you don't insist on respect is passive behavior in relating to others. Not being in touch with your own needs can allow this to happen. Allowing your manager to cross your personal boundaries, such as expecting you to answer e-mail while you're on vacation, is a passive way of relating to your manager.

Sometimes the timing of a situation necessitates using passive behaviors while relating to others. Immediately confronting a person who isn't showing respect in a public forum might cause the situation to go from bad to worse. Not saying anything, then addressing the situation later when the person is more likely to accept feedback is usually a better way of handling the situation.

Withholding feedback when a group discussion goes in the "wrong" direction and saying, "My opinion doesn't matter; it's stupid and not worth mentioning," is self-deprecating and a passive-aggressive approach to relating to others. Allowing boundary violations in order to bring them up at a later date to get even with someone is also a passive-aggressive approach.

Relating to Others—Passive Example

After a project team meeting, Bonnie tells Lakeisha about a concern she had during the meeting. Lakeisha thinks it's a valid concern and asks why Bonnie didn't bring it up. She tells Bonnie she should speak up more in future meetings. Bonnie tells Lakeisha that the others in the meeting are so much smarter than she and she really doesn't think she would add any value.

ANALYSIS: Bonnie inappropriately uses self-deprecating behavior when responding to Lakeisha.

Reasons for Moving Away from Using Passive Behaviors

Passive behaviors may be appropriate or inappropriate depending on the situation at hand. Using inappropriate passive behaviors has several problems, particularly if you develop a preference for them. Inappropriate passive behaviors negatively impact your ability to successfully achieve business goals; so they end up impacting your own success as an employee, your workgroup leader's and coworkers' success, and the overall success of the organization that hired you. If you have a leadership role, workgroup members' passive behaviors will cause problems in working together successfully.

Success Impacts from an Employee Perspective

Deferring decisions to others, being less responsible in task completion, being defensive during problem resolution, avoiding conflict, or accepting a losing position are behaviors that typically don't lead to personal success. If you use these behaviors on a regular basis, you won't stand out for a promotion. You'll be doing less than your coworkers and will be overshadowed by those using the other behavior patterns more regularly.

When you behave passively and don't bring your good ideas to the table, you miss an opportunity that could save the organization money, which could result in recognition or advancement for you. Following bad orders or undermining the direction in which your organization is heading won't win you any achievement awards either.

When you react passively to a problem by being defensive, such behavior can create customer dissatisfaction. If you're afraid of conflict, you might accept a less-than-favorable position for your organization when negotiating with another organization. Also, if you discount the significance of a problem and don't tend to it, the problem can snowball into something worse and more costly.

Gruntledness Impacts from an Employee Perspective

If you have a preference for passive behaviors, you have developed that preference for a reason. You may be intimidated by dominant behavior and may have found that passive behaviors are an effective way to cope with aggressive people in the workplace. Keeping your head down, lying low, and staying out of the limelight decrease your chances of having to deal with unpleasant dominant behaviors.

If you use this type of coping strategy to keep from experiencing certain unpleasant situations, it won't make you happy. Coping strategies are based on fear; they don't lead to gruntledness. If you have developed a fear of others in the workplace, you're not enjoying your work experience.

If you doubt your own opinion, don't voice your opinion out of fear that it's contrary to your leader's opinion, or experience others disregarding your opinion, the result will not be gruntledness. Frequently deferring decisions to others may not make you feel in control of your work situation or it may damage your self-esteem.

When you're uncommitted or feel less responsible than others when completing work, you will not experience the joy that comes from a sense of accomplishment. Others will have to finish the work for you. This may cause them to feel disgruntled and use inappropriate behaviors towards you, which will make you feel disgruntled.

Success Impacts from a Leader Perspective

Employees with a preference for passive behavior seldom are disruptive or complain. Instead, they procrastinate, make "innocent mistakes," "forget" to do something, and work inefficiently. They pretend to understand directions instead of asking for clarification. They don't share information that would favorably impact someone else's actions and don't share ideas that could enable innovation.

If you fail to address inappropriate passive behaviors within your workgroup, it will impact the group's ability to achieve goals and thus impact your own success. For example, if an employee uses inappropriate passive behaviors that lead to a problem, this will result in rework, which will increase operational costs.

Employees use passive behaviors to avoid conflict by not voicing their opinions. But numerous studies reveal that engaging in conflict resolution results in better decisions in workgroups.[46] Voicing opposing opinions actually helps to identify underlying issues, and all issues must be understood when developing new ideas or approaches.

Additionally, the extreme form of passive behavior, passive-aggressiveness, undermines business strategies. Most workgroups have at least one employee with passive-aggressive tendencies. They use the behaviors described in this chapter to intentionally undermine business strategies or not go along with the direction that you provide as the leader.

But most employees with a preference for passive behaviors are not intentionally undermining business strategies. They're just not giving 100%. The reduced effort impacts others who not only need to complete their own tasks, but depend on everyone else in the workgroup to do the same. When an employee fails to fulfill personal potential, it drags down coworkers.

As the leader, it is important to help employees move away from passive behaviors. Using more interdependent behaviors will make your workgroup—and you—more successful.

Gruntledness Impacts from a Leader Perspective

If you fail to address inappropriate passive behaviors within your workgroup, it will impact other employees' gruntledness, which will also impact your own gruntledness. If an employee slows things down or makes mistakes by behaving passively, it puts you in a position of having to demand more from other employees and force them to pick up the slack or correct mistakes, which then leads to their disgruntledness.

If an employee's passive behavior—such as delaying task completion—impacts other employees' work, the passive behavior makes coworkers look bad. Such passive behavior can also force employees to work extra hours to get things done on time, which will create a morale problem for the workgroup.

An employee behaving passively by blaming others for problems can lead to hard feelings among other employees. Passive behaviors contribute to an "us versus them" attitude. It is important for you to address passive behaviors within your workgroup to improve your workgroup morale.

Rethinking Behavior Preferences

When you develop a preference for and use mostly passive behaviors, your behaviors set the stage for disgruntledness and unsuccessful efforts at work. The result of such behavior choices necessitates learning more effective behaviors, which are presented later in Chapter 9. The next chapter covers the impact of dominant behaviors.

7

How Dominant Behaviors Impact Gruntledness and Business Success

"We formed a group of 20 people to develop a department-wide set of business templates. Within the first month, one of the members steamrolled her way into taking control of the meetings. She coordinated meeting times, assigned others to take notes for the meetings, and assigned tasks within the group. This soon became a one-person show. When one member was not able to meet his deliverables for the meeting because his workgroup had a very bad week due to production outages, the self-appointed project leader in a meeting of 20-some people asked, 'Are you just incompetent, or just too lazy to get the work done?' Of course, this lit the fuse for a major fireworks display at work. Many members of the group reported the meeting conversation to their managers in disgust. Our immediate manager had not realized just how bad the situation had become for this special project. The manager spent weeks trying to smooth this out."

Disgruntled Employee
Blog Post

People who behave dominantly determine the path to be taken. They tend to think that their way of doing things is best. Sometimes the dominant behaviors are based on the belief that their way is right for others, which makes the dominant behaviors have a degree of benevolence. They may behave dominantly out of consideration for others. They may think that they know better than others and are afraid that if someone else handles a situation, he or she will make a mistake that would be detrimental to others. People that behave dominantly in this manner have more of an attitude that they are taking care of something for another person.

An alternative form of dominant behaviors is based on a need to be in control. In this case, the use of dominant behaviors tends to be disrespectful. The dominant behavior is based on self-interest. Those who behave in controlling dominant ways also may think they know better than others but are afraid that if someone else handles the situation, they will make a mistake that would be detrimental to them personally. A person who is behaving dominantly in this manner has more of an "it's my way or the highway" attitude.

Dominant behaviors are often seen in a negative light; however, some situations call for dominant behavior. For example, suppose you have an unusual health condition. Would you prefer a doctor who is overly committed and continues to search for a solution beyond his knowledge, or would you prefer a doctor who performs only standard tests and treatment protocols? Most situations you face in the business world are not as serious as personal health care. However, many business activities, if not completed with a high level of commitment, can impact customer experience, employee livelihood, and shareholder value.

Dominant behaviors are based on a mindset focused on *you*. Here's how these behaviors are reflected in certain work situations: If I believe that my value is greater than *your* value, then I may expect *you* to not be as good at certain activities as I am. If I believe that *you* are not as responsible as I am, then I may expect that I must take care of this situation for *you*. If I believe that I'm entitled to a particular thing more than *you*, then I may feel that I am privileged over *you* in this situation.

Having one or more of these beliefs all the time or just in certain situations may lead to behaving in the following dominant ways within the five employee activities:

- **Decision Making.** Makes decisions for others and disregards others' opinions.
- **Completing Tasks.** Takes on more responsibility and leads others.
- **Resolving Problems.** Overreacts to the significance of a problem and solves problems for others.
- **Conflict Resolution.** Uses conflict to own advantage and approaches conflict expecting to win regardless of the cost to others.
- **Relating to Others.** Is arrogant, does not respect others, and crosses personal boundaries.

The next sections illustrate dominant behaviors across the five employee activities.

Dominant Behaviors in Decision Making

Making decisions for others and disregarding other people's opinions are dominant ways of making decisions. Sometimes, it is prudent to make decisions for others to make the best decision for the organization. Interrupting someone, using sarcasm, assuming that another person's opinion is not as important as your own, or stating your opinion arrogantly are ways to disregard others' opinions. Sometimes it is necessary to disregard others' opinions if their opinions aren't pertinent to a decision.

Arguing points with coworkers (or managers) until they "see the light" and give up is controlling decision making. A rationale for such behavior might be thinking that others are inferior so getting them to comply is what's best for the organization.

Decision Making—Dominant Example

Renee has just become a manager of a project team. Harold, one of the team members, doesn't agree with management's decision to make Renee the project manager.

Renee holds a meeting where the team must choose between two alternatives. As project manager, Renee has the ultimate responsibility for making the final decision and leans towards the first alternative. Harold feels strongly about the second alternative.

While Renee presents the first alternative, everyone sees Harold roll his eyes. When Renee tries to answer her team members' questions about the first alternative, Harold interrupts her and provides his own opinion. When Renee suggests that the team recommend the first alternative, Harold sarcastically says, "Yeah, as if that will ever work." Before Renee can react, Harold recommends that the team go forward with the second alternative and suggests that they bring the meeting to a close.

ANALYSIS: Harold inappropriately disregards Renee and other team members' opinions by using sarcastic comments and body language, and by interrupting Renee and team members. Also inappropriately, Harold effectively makes the decision for Renee by leading the team's discussion towards the end of the meeting.

Dominant Behaviors in Completing Tasks

Taking on more responsibility and leading are dominant ways of completing tasks. Working long hours, being persistent, and personally ensuring things are done correctly are also dominant behaviors. Sometimes, you may be required to do whatever it takes to get an important or urgent task back on track when it risks failure. Also, it is often necessary for one person to lead when a task requires more than one person to complete it. Without a leader, group tasks can take longer to complete or be completed incorrectly or inconsistently.

Taking over a task because others are handling it differently than you would is a controlling approach to task completion. Not relinquishing control when it's appropriate to do so is also controlling behavior. Stepping in to coach others without verifying whether they actually need coaching is also a controlling way to complete a task. Believing others' work is sub-par or assuming they will perform poorly without you might be ways to rationalize such behavior.

Completing Tasks—Dominant Example

Felipe is giving a presentation to a client, and Jun is in attendance to support Felipe. Even though the client is quite comfortable with Felipe and likes what he is saying, Jun doesn't feel that Felipe is delivering a strong enough message. Jun starts answering customer questions before Felipe has a chance to respond and also begins speaking up more in general. Towards the end of the meeting, Jun takes over and makes risky promises that she had not discussed with Felipe ahead of time. Unsure of how to point out that Jun's statements have major problems without "airing dirty laundry," Felipe doesn't say anything.

ANALYSIS: Jun has taken on more responsibility than what is appropriate and is overly committed to meeting outcomes with the client. She oversteps her bounds, is overly supportive, and eventually leads the meeting even though this isn't her role. By not discussing the risky promises with Felipe before proposing them to the client, Jun puts the company in an untenable position.

Dominant Behaviors in Resolving Problems

Overreacting to the significance of a problem and solving problems for others are dominant ways of resolving problems. Not recognizing your contribution to a problem and projecting blame onto others is also dominant behavior. It is appropriate to overreact to a problem to get the attention of those who have disregarded the problem for too long. It also may be necessary to use dominant behaviors if an issue has multiple contributors and no one is leading the effort to resolve the problem.

Refusing to let others who are capable and responsible solve a problem is usually a controlling way of resolving a problem. This behavior may stem from a general lack of trust because someone in the past was unreliable, so now solving everyone's problems, whether needed or not, has become a pattern. Refusing to admit that you made a mistake (when you did) and projecting the problem onto others is another form of controlling dominant behavior.

Resolving Problems—Dominant Example

Marge manages an independent quality-assurance (QA) group that tests software products. The team has several modules that must be tested for next month's product release. The first module they test was developed by Rose Mary's team. Rose Mary is one of Marge's friends. The QA team finds more bugs in this module than normal.

Marge decides to help Rose Mary find the bugs instead of reporting that the module isn't ready for QA testing. This takes longer than Marge anticipated, which causes her team to not have enough time to thoroughly test other software modules. As a result, their modules end up with more defects than they usually do after the product is released into production.

ANALYSIS: Marge inappropriately solves Rose Mary's problem by helping her find software bugs. Since they are friends, she gives the situation more attention than she normally does for other development managers.

Dominant Behaviors in Conflict Resolution

Using conflict to your advantage and approaching conflict with the intent of winning regardless of the cost to others are dominant ways of resolving conflict. Being overly confident about your position is also dominant behavior. Sometimes, situations can get out of hand if you don't use a dominant way of resolving conflict and bring the matter quickly to closure. When your viewpoint is important to resolving conflict quickly and equitably and no one appears to be listening to you, it may be necessary for you to use more forceful measures to ensure they hear you.

Unfairly resolving conflict is a controlling approach to conflict resolution. Additionally, creating conflict to get others to back down rather than calmly discussing the situation is a controlling way to resolve conflict. Forcing your opinion on others is also controlling conflict resolution.

Conflict Resolution—Dominant Example

Marcos and Sonja are in a meeting with several others discussing an idea. Sonja has voiced her opinion. Marcos has a different opinion and feels very strongly that he is correct. He tells the group his point of view in a self-righteous manner. Sonja questions the idea, trying to understand it more. Marcos raises his voice and replies to Sonja's question in an irritated tone. When Sonja states that she still doesn't understand, Marcos becomes angry and states that he doesn't have all day to explain this to her.

ANALYSIS: Marcos inappropriately creates conflict in an attempt to get his way on a topic. He wants to win the discussion and uses anger to shut down Sonja before she can say something to contradict his position.

Dominant Behaviors in Relating to Others

Acting arrogantly, not respecting others, and crossing personal boundaries are dominant ways of relating to others. Being insensitive to others' needs is also a dominant way to relate to others. Doing a coworker's job, welcomed or not, crosses a personal boundary and is dominant behavior. E-mailing, instant messaging, and texting can violate personal boundaries if employees are expected to respond during time off. Sometimes, when someone is overwhelmed, it may be necessary to help even if the individual requests to solely handle a situation. Also, it may be appropriate to overstep other employees' boundaries physically, mentally, or emotionally in emergency situations. Obviously, if a coworker is having a heart attack, it is appropriate to cross the individual's physical boundaries and administer CPR.

Saying things in an arrogant way, needing to be the center of attention, and not being respectful of other people's thoughts and feelings are controlling ways of relating to others. Critical and judgmental comments are often disrespectful to others. Not being aware of other people's needs can be behind disrespectful behavior. Shutting down others by insinuating that they are inferior in some way is also a controlling approach. In addition, sexual harassment is controlling dominant behavior that violates a person's boundaries.

Relating to Others—Dominant Example

Jonita and Jean are working together on a project with a tight deadline. Jean is behind because a lot of personal obligations are interfering with her work. So Jonita volunteers to finish Jean's project tasks.

But even after Jean's personal obligations are no longer an issue, Jonita continues to cover for Jean because she is still having difficulty completing her tasks. Jonita also gives Jean her notes for meetings and training sessions she continues to miss. When Jean doesn't read the notes and falls further behind, Jonita trains her personally and completes some of Jean's tasks.

ANALYSIS: Jonita inappropriately crosses a personal boundary by helping Jean with things that she should do herself.

Reasons for Moving Away from Using Dominant Behaviors

Dominant behaviors may be appropriate or inappropriate depending on the situation at hand. Several problems occur when you use dominant behaviors inappropriately, particularly if you develop a preference for them. Dominant behaviors can negatively impact your ability to successfully achieve business goals. This impacts your personal success, your workgroup leader's and coworkers' success, and the overall success of the organization that hired you. Inappropriate dominant behaviors can also negatively impact your gruntledness as well as the gruntledness of those you interact with.

Success Impacts from an Employee Perspective

If you have developed a preference for dominant behaviors, you may be more productive than most employees and may have found that dominant behaviors are an effective way for you to get business results. Dominant behaviors can result in getting things done: Decisions are made, tasks are completed, and problems and conflicts are resolved. With these outcomes, being overly responsible often leads to personal success in the business world today; it may even lead to a promotion.

However, problems arise when you use dominant behaviors inappropriately. If you force your opinion on your workgroup, thus disregarding others' opinions, and your opinion is incorrect, your business could lose revenue opportunities or incur costs to correct your mistake. Also, leading when you should follow can cause your workgroup to lose focus and go in the wrong direction.

Being overly committed and providing a level of quality or accuracy that negatively impacts time and cost also causes problems. Becoming overly involved in a problem may cause you to neglect another problem or assignment that is more urgent and important. If you often blow problems out of proportion, your coworkers will become accustomed to disregarding your emotional reaction to problems and may eventually ignore a problem worthy of attention. Putting your coworkers in a losing position so that you can win makes your coworkers wary of interacting with you in the future. Also, if you pressure customers or clients into accepting a losing position, they will always feel uneasy about the transaction, which may make them avoid you or your organization in the future.

Not treating others respectfully may lead them to think that you are confrontational and self-righteous, or worse, that you are personally attacking them. These people can be a key to your success in a future activity and because of the way you treated them, may not work with you in the future.

Gruntledness Impacts from an Employee Perspective

Dominant behaviors are often a coping strategy for those who need to be in control, but it's not possible to be in control all the time. Trying to control others is an exercise in futility and won't make you or your coworkers happy.

Being overly committed and more responsible may provide a sense of accomplishment, but it can eventually burn you out. It can also strain your working relationships.

If you use dominant behaviors disrespectfully, you will have a negative impact on others. How people negatively react to your behavior will most likely interfere with your own happiness. Even if you use dominant behaviors respectfully, your interactions with others will be far more enjoyable if you interact on a more equal basis instead of being dominant.

Success Impacts from a Leader Perspective

Individuals within your workgroup with a preference for dominant behaviors may regularly over-perform, but they usually won't cooperate with others. They may even compete with you and lead your workgroup in an inappropriate direction. Also, if the members of your workgroup who have dominant behavior preferences are quite vocal, they can stifle the creativity of their coworkers. In addition, when one person frequently makes decisions for others, accepts more responsibility, overreacts to problems, and controls conflict on a regular basis, it paves the way for others in your workgroup to be uncommitted and less responsible, which then impacts the productivity of your workgroup.

Two or more people within your workgroup with a preference for dominant behaviors can result in infighting, competitiveness, and back-biting. Your workgroup will probably have a hard time coming to a consensus and reaching an agreement on objectives and direction. If a task needs to be completed within a set timeframe, and your workgroup spends more time arguing and bickering than on the task itself, quality will suffer. Obviously, this affects your workgroup productivity and thus your success as a leader.

Inappropriate dominant behavior can negatively impact how people think at work, which can cause costly mistakes. A University of Florida study found that employees that were treated with dominant behaviors in the form of rudeness or verbal abuse had trouble solving problems and their creativity and productivity were undermined.[47]

Inappropriate dominant behavior can also negatively impact the bottom line. A University of South Florida study found that employees who had been treated with rude, disrespectful dominant behaviors were more likely than other employees to be rude to customers or clients and intentionally slow down work.[48]

Gruntledness Impacts from a Leader Perspective

As a workgroup leader, you need to address employees' dominant behaviors within your workgroup because they will negatively impact workgroup gruntledness. If one of your employees uses dominant behaviors disrespect-fully, the other employee(s) involved in such interactions won't feel very gruntled and may even feel the need to look for a different job.

The overall morale of your workgroup can decrease if you let dominant behaviors interfere with daily tasks. Workgroup members may use domi-nant behaviors to cross coworkers' personal boundaries by making deci-sions for others and being overly supportive. This behavior may initially come across as helpful, but the employees on the receiving end may eventu-ally tire of being told what to do.

Dominant behaviors that include politics to get ahead can also create a highly charged political environment that can cause many employees stress and angst. In such an environment, employees may spend their workday worrying about being mistreated and avoiding future interactions with people who use dominant behaviors. Some may worry about whether they should change jobs. This can result in employees being so unhappy that they quit their jobs, forcing the organization to deal with the high cost of turnover and loss of talent.

Rethinking Behavior Preferences

As with passive behaviors, dominant behaviors can be appropriate in some situations. However, inappropriate uses of and a preference for dominant behaviors fuels unwanted outcomes: disgruntledness and difficulties in implementing business strategies. More effective behaviors that produce gruntledness and business success are presented later in this book. The next chapter looks at the impact of independent behaviors.

8

How Independent Behaviors Impact Gruntledness and Business Success

"My first job out of college was working for a utility company where we were converting a batch customer information system to an online version. The two analysts that were designing the system designed the old batch system. Since they had designed the first system, they decided that they could design the online system by themselves without talking to anyone. So they locked themselves in their offices for six months and never talked to a single user of the system the whole time. Of course, the users were quite surprised with what they ended up with. I can't imagine any company today that would tolerate someone designing a system by themselves without even talking to the users of the system."

Disgruntled Employee
Blog Post

People who behave independently perform activities on their own. They have the self-esteem and sense of responsibility to deal with the situation by themselves. They trust and respect themselves. They tend to think that doing things on their own is an acceptable way to handle activities. They have the self-confidence to act independently without others. Those with a preference for independent behaviors tend to be "lone wolves." They are competent and set their own personal goals.

An alternative form of independent behavior is counter-dependent behavior. People who behave counter-dependently refuse to perform an activity with others. They may not wish to conform to the status quo. They do not trust others and do not want to perform work activities with them. They respect themselves but don't necessarily respect others. If they lack interpersonal skills, they may find it easier to solve problems and make decisions without involving others.

Independent behaviors are often appropriate. Many work activities require a person to perform them on their own. Most employees perform the majority of their work activities by themselves to an acceptable level of quality. As it should be, many work activities performed in the business world are done independently.

Independent behaviors are based on a mindset focused on *I*. Here's how these behaviors are reflected in certain work situations: If I believe in *my* value, then I will feel good about *my* participation in this situation. If I believe that *I'm* responsible, then *I* will take care of the situation. If I believe that *I'm* entitled to a particular thing, then I will ensure that *I* have certain privileges in a particular situation.

Having one or more of these beliefs all the time or just in certain situations may lead to behaving in the following independent ways within the five employee activities:

- **Decision Making.** Makes own decisions and considers only own opinion.
- **Completing Tasks.** Is responsible for self and works alone.
- **Resolving Problems.** Appreciates the significance of a problem and solves own part of a problem.

- **Conflict Resolution.** Confronts conflict and approaches conflict expecting to win.
- **Relating to Others.** Is closed-minded, insists on respect, and protects personal boundaries.

The next sections illustrate independent behaviors across the five employee activities.

Independent Behaviors in Decision Making

Making your own decisions and considering only your own opinion are independent ways of making decisions. Often, it is required and expected that you make decisions on your own. Most likely, you already have the information you need to make an accurate decision. If you need more information, you probably know how to research to make the right choice.

Refusing to seek the opinions of others in a situation that is over your head is a counter-dependent approach to decision making. Withdrawing emotionally or physically from situations that require joint decisions may also be a counter-dependent approach.

Decision Making—Independent Example

Ricardo works in a customer call center and takes a call from a client complaining about a bill she received regarding a promotional offer. Ricardo consults the frequently-asked-questions database on how to handle this type of call and finds the script somewhat unclear. He interprets the script's wording on his own and issues a full credit to the customer. Since the offer is new, Ricardo receives many calls concerning the promotion. He issues full credit to every customer who has the same complaint.

In reviewing call center statistics at the end of the week, Ricardo's supervisor notices that Ricardo issued a much higher amount of credits than the other call center representatives. After an inquiry, the supervisor lets Ricardo know that he should have issued partial credit—not full credit.

ANALYSIS: Ricardo inappropriately makes a decision on how to handle customer complaints on the new offer. He considers only his own opinion rather than asking for advice from his supervisor on how to handle the situation. His decision ends up costing the company more money.

Independent Behaviors in Completing Tasks

Being responsible for yourself and working alone are independent ways of completing tasks. Many work activities are best performed alone. Sometimes more is accomplished by accepting your responsibility and working alone rather than working with others. Most people in the workplace have the ability to successfully complete tasks on their own.

Working alone when an assignment should be completed with others is a counter-dependent approach to task completion. Focusing solely on personal commitments rather than helping a struggling teammate is also a counter-dependent approach. Insisting on doing a task "your" way rather than conforming to workgroup norms is also counter-dependent behavior. In addition, resisting help from others when you really need assistance is a counter-dependent approach. Believing that asking for help is a sign of weakness could be the reasoning behind such behavior.

Completing Tasks—Independent Example

Trevor is a programmer developing a new computer system. He gets the requirements from the project manager on what his software module is supposed to do. Trevor works by himself for the next three weeks developing the module. To save time, he doesn't attend the overall system design meeting since he understands what his module is supposed to do. When Trevor's module is system tested, it becomes apparent that Trevor didn't design or code his module to provide the correct data needed by the other modules.

ANALYSIS: Trevor inappropriately completes this task on his own. His software module is interdependent with other parts of the overall computer system. Since Trevor did not attend the overall system design meeting to understand these interdependencies, his module does not meet the requirements of other modules that interface with his.

Independent Behaviors in Resolving Problems

Appreciating the significance of a problem and solving your own part of a problem are independent ways of resolving problems. Accepting your contribution to a problem is also an independent approach to resolving problems. When you don't disregard or blow a problem out of proportion, you demonstrate that you appreciate the significance of a problem. Admitting you made a mistake rather than becoming defensive or projecting the problem onto others is accepting your contribution to a problem. Solving your own part of a problem instead of deferring to others, or becoming overly involved and solving parts of the problem that you aren't responsible for is independent problem resolution.

Insisting on resolving a problem alone that clearly needs others' involvement is a counter-dependent approach to problem resolution. Looking at only personal contributions to a problem rather than the other factors involved is a counter-dependent way of resolving problems and may prevent solving problems holistically.

Resolving Problems—Independent Example

Ram is part of a large team that ensures that errors are corrected with all sales orders before the financial close and that the company's profit centers accurately report financial results. Multiple workgroups from across the company work to resolve issues during this period so that financial results can be reported as quickly as possible.

Ram has figured out a way to resolve the issues assigned to him so that his data is available a day earlier. His approach could be helpful to others who participate in the financial close, but Ram chooses not to share his approach with them. Ram likes the accolades he receives each month for being early while his teammates struggle to get their issues resolved on time.

ANALYSIS: While Ram reacts appropriately and resolves issues for the financial close process, he inappropriately resolves issues for only his data. Ram has information that could help others, which he chooses not to share so that he can continue to be a corporate hero; but withholding that information is bad for his coworkers and his company.

Independent Behaviors in Conflict Resolution

Confronting conflict and approaching conflict expecting to win are independent ways of resolving conflict. Confronting people who are trying to gain an unfair advantage is usually a good idea. It takes a high level of self-esteem to confront conflict without being worried about the other person responding negatively. It is particularly difficult (and important) to confront people about their hostile or abusive behavior. Communicating your views on an issue expecting to win, but not forcing your opinion on others is also an independent way of resolving conflict.

Confronting conflict without hearing others out before making a decision is counter-dependent behavior. Often, both parties involved in a conflict can get what they want. Ignoring other points of view and not ensuring fair treatment in the resolution is a counter-dependent way of resolving conflict. Being "anesthetized" to the feelings of others may result in counter-dependent behaviors for resolving conflict. Frequent boundary violations in the past may be behind such unawareness of others' needs.

Conflict Resolution—Independent Example

Janice asks her vender, Pablo, to renegotiate their contract to lower her company's costs. If Pablo agrees to do so, it will lower the amount of revenue that he brings into his company. The contract in place protects Pablo from having to honor Janice's request and places her at a disadvantage in price renegotiations. She begins to plead her case, but Pablo interrupts her and tells her that he's sorry but his company wants the existing contract to be honored at the current negotiated costs.

However, Pablo doesn't know Janice's company is in bad financial shape and without some drastic changes to its financial picture, it may have to file bankruptcy. Since Pablo isn't willing to listen to her explain her immediate financial challenge, Janice decides to award the additional project work to one of Pablo's competitors.

ANALYSIS: Pablo inappropriately approaches this conflict by deciding ahead of time to win without considering the impact to his customer and the impact that it may have on him and his company in the long term. Pablo only sees his side of the conflict and doesn't consider Janice's point of view.

Independent Behaviors in Relating to Others

Being closed-minded, insisting on respect, and protecting personal boundaries are independent ways of relating to others. Being sensitive to only your own needs is also an independent approach to relating to others. When others are inappropriately criticizing you, it is appropriate to be closed-minded and not listen to what they are saying. Listening to inappropriate criticism on a regular basis can cause self-esteem issues. It is appropriate to ensure that others respect you while you interact with them and that you don't allow harassment of any kind. Hostile work environments are created when someone is allowed to be disrespectful on a regular basis. It is important to confront disrespectful behavior, whether the perpetrator happens to be your boss, peer, or subordinate, and it is appropriate to ask to discuss such behavior in private. Also, being sensitive to your own needs and insisting on respect helps ensure that you do not participate in a situation that is unfair or unpleasant to you. It also ensures that you do not allow others to cross your personal boundaries.

Refusing to listen to coworkers is closed-minded behavior that is counter-dependent. Additionally, not allowing others to cross personal boundaries, no matter how dire the situation, is also counter-dependent behavior. The frequent use of counter-dependent behavior in relating to others may stem from being emotionally abused (mistreated and/or wronged with boundary violations) in the past. A typical coping strategy to minimize the reoccurrence of such abuse may be to create emotional distance from others.

Relating to Others—Independent Example

Jane has just started working in a new workgroup and is annoyed by Ally, one of her coworkers. Ally has some personality traits that grate on Jane's nerves. Ally tells Jane how she should handle a task that was just assigned to Jane. Jane feels that Ally is overstepping her bounds by providing unsolicited advice on something that is solely Jane's responsibility. Although Ally has completed the task several times, she has no responsibility in the task and won't be held accountable if the task fails.

Jane decides to be closed-minded instead of being open to Ally's suggestions. The task fails, and the manager chooses Ally to rework the task, who successfully implements her suggestion.

ANALYSIS: Jane is inappropriately closed-minded about Ally's advice. Ally has completed the task numerous times and knows how to successfully complete it. Jane ignores Ally's advice solely because of the irritating nature of Ally's personality.

Reasons for Moving Away from Using Independent Behaviors

Several problems occur as a result of using independent behaviors inappropriately, particularly if you develop a preference for them. Independent behaviors can negatively impact your ability to successfully achieve business goals. This impacts your personal success, your workgroup leader's and coworkers' success, and the overall success of the organization that hired you. Independent behaviors can also negatively impact your gruntledness, as well as others' gruntledness.

Success Impacts from an Employee Perspective

If you have developed a preference for independent behaviors, you'll be more productive than you would with a preference for passive behaviors. Making your own decisions, being responsible for your tasks, taking action on resolving problems, and confronting conflict contributes to your personal success.

However, independent behaviors are not as effective when a business situation requires a team effort. When you behave independently, you don't get the benefit of working cooperatively and collaboratively with others.

Often, in today's complex work environment, being successful requires collaboration.

You negatively impact success in many ways when you use independent behaviors. You risk incorrectly assuming you have all the information you need to make a decision. Being closed-minded to others' opinions when making decisions can cause you to make bad decisions. Also, when you behave independently, you are really only committed to your part in a group task, and if you're falling behind and don't ask for help, you can cause your group to miss deadlines. In addition, when you independently approach resolving problems, you focus only on your part of a problem, which can cause incomplete problem resolution. You can address problems more completely when you work with others.

Gruntledness Impacts from an Employee Perspective

If you have a preference for independent behaviors, you may have found that independence is an effective way to cope with others' dominant be-haviors. Rather than being intimidated by aggressiveness at work, you may choose to work alone as much as possible to avoid dominant behaviors.

This coping strategy, as with other coping strategies, is based on fear and won't lead to your gruntledness. By minimizing the chances for negative experiences, you also minimize your opportunities to connect with others and experience the joy that comes from positive interactions.

Moving away from independent behaviors has many benefits. When you're open to collaboration, you'll likely be happy when others consider your opinions. When you hit a roadblock, working alone on a task can be frustrating. Your gruntledness level can increase significantly when you ac-cept help from others. When problems arise, if you realize that you're not alone and you can work through problems with others, you'll be happier that the burden is not yours alone.

Success Impacts from a Leader Perspective

Employees with a preference for independent behaviors create a special challenge for workgroup leaders. Such employees tend not to follow a process; they get the job done, but they do it their way. They also prefer to learn through personal trial and error, rather than risk making mistakes while learning from others.

Teamwork, rather than employees working independently, creates synergies that result in greater efficiency and effectiveness. When employees work alone, they accomplish smaller goals and have less success than they would if they had worked with other employees. Independent behaviors negatively impact cross-pollination of ideas and knowledge. In twenty-first-century businesses, knowledge sharing, teamwork, and collaboration are essential to workgroup performance and success and to your success as a leader. Allowing workgroup members to work primarily independently won't provide synergies that can optimize your workgroup's performance.

As a workgroup leader, you are responsible for ensuring employees follow labor laws/regulations and policies/procedures. Employees with a preference for independent behaviors can be challenging in today's world of Sarbanes-Oxley compliance, sexual harassment requirements, and other policies and regulations because these need to be followed. People with a preference for independent behaviors often do not like following rules.

Gruntledness Impacts from a Leader Perspective

As the leader, it's important for you to address inappropriate independent behaviors of employees in your workgroup. Allowing employees to continue with inappropriate independent behaviors can be costly. It can even lead to internal competition rather than collaboration.

Workgroups where most of the employees behave independently will not be as happy as workgroups where employees behave more interdependently. Humans are social creatures by nature and need positive interactions with others. Working mainly alone does not provide the feeling that "we are all in this together." Workgroups where employees primarily work independently miss the satisfaction that comes from collaboration.

Rethinking Behavior Preferences

As with passive and dominant behaviors, independent behaviors are, at times, appropriate. However, a preference for independent behaviors won't cause you, your workgroup, or your organization to thrive. The next chapter will look at interdependent behaviors—one of three factors that will improve employee gruntledness for you and your coworkers and also increase the success of business strategies for your workgroup and organization.

9

How Interdependent Behaviors Impact Gruntledness and Business Success

"When one can find someone who will collaborate, be supportive, etc., it's worth its weight in gold. I was placed with a [new] team of teachers. I was rather dreading the prospect of working with new people. We met as a team on a daily basis. When I would share my observations in the past, I would frequently be met with doubts and even surprise that I would 'exaggerate' the behaviors I observed. So, needless to say, I was hesitant to share observations with my new team. What I found, however, is a group of people who not only listened to my concerns or comments, but embraced the idea that my observations had some merit and then they would proceed to brainstorm possible solutions, procedures, ideas, etc. Inevitably, we'd develop a plan of action that all of us could live with. We learned to trust each other's perceptions and ideas and became a very proactive team. We were motivated to think outside the box, to keep problem solving, and to not feel despair at how difficult things were at times. We always had each other's backs during difficult parent conferences. I don't think I could have dealt with some of the problems we faced and worked through if it hadn't been for the way we were able to work together."

Gruntled Employee
Blog Post

People who behave interdependently work well with others. They have the interpersonal skills to work well with other people. They trust and respect others. Interdependent behaviors are usually exhibited peacefully. People calmly express their opinions and listen to others. They serenely go about completing work tasks and resolving problems with others. Conflict is resolved with minimal effort. Interactions with others are conducted in a respectful manner.

An alternative form of interdependent behavior is dominant/interdependent behavior. This behavior may not seem to an outsider as interdependent at all. People using this behavior still trust and respect others but express their own opinions passionately. Even though they more forcefully express their opinions, they are still open-minded and listen to others. However, they expect others to be as vocal as they are in expressing their opinion.

An incredible amount of energy is present when a person behaves dominant/interdependently. There is nothing serene in how they complete tasks and resolve problems with others. In fact they often appear to others as if they are demonstrating dominant behaviors—often leading the way, being overly involved, and stating opinions forcefully. The difference is that they are more open-minded than those using dominant behaviors, and they show respect for others. Those who prefer dominant behaviors will still see these interactions as respectful; however, those who prefer passive behaviors will not. Participation with a person using dominant/interdependent behavior will be difficult for those who have an aversion to dominant behaviors.

Interdependent behaviors are based on a mindset focused on *we*. Here's how these behaviors are reflected in certain work situations: If I believe that my value is equal to your value, then I will feel good about *our participating together* in a particular situation. If I believe that I am as responsible as you, then I will take care of the situation *with you*. If I believe that I am as entitled as you are, then I will ensure that *we* both have certain privileges in this situation.

Having one or more of these beliefs all the time or just in certain situations may lead to behaving in the following interdependent ways within the five employee activities:

- **Decision Making.** Makes decisions jointly with others and considers own and others' opinions.
- **Completing Tasks.** Takes joint responsibility and collaborates and co-operates in task completion.
- **Resolving Problems.** Appreciates problem interdependencies and is supportive of others in resolving a problem.
- **Conflict Resolution.** Resolves conflict equitably and approaches conflict expecting everyone to win.
- **Relating to Others.** Is open-minded, respects others and self, and protects everyone's personal boundaries.

The next sections illustrate interdependent behaviors across the five employee activities.

Interdependent Behaviors in Decision Making

Jointly making decisions and considering your own and others' opinions are interdependent ways of making decisions. Feeling that others can contribute to the decision at hand is an interdependent way of thinking. Realizing that listening to others' feedback will provide additional information or help you see a different perspective is an interdependent insight. To interdependently make a decision, all participants must feel comfortable expressing their opinions. Equally as important, all participants must be willing to listen to everyone else's opinions.

A passively preferred individual will probably interpret dominant/interdependent decision making as an argument. In fact, if those participating in the decision don't step up and express their opinion as vocally as others, an interdependent decision won't occur—a dominant one will. All decision participants must feel comfortable expressing their opinions as vocally as others for the matter to be decided in an interdependent way.

Decision Making—Interdependent Example

Ashok's school district is facing budget challenges, and each school within the district has been directed to cut its budget by 3%. Ashok decides to get his staff together along with several of the senior teachers to discuss ways to cut the budget. At the end of the meeting, Ashok has a list of recommendations that meet the budget-cut challenge without impacting the quality of their educational program at the high school.

ANALYSIS: Ashok appropriately pays attention to the opinions of his staff and senior teachers. The budget challenge is a complex situation that benefits from different people's perspectives. As a result, they come up with the best set of recommendations possible, considering the circumstances.

Interdependent Behaviors in Completing Tasks

Taking joint responsibility, working together collaboratively, and cooperating with others are interdependent ways of completing tasks. Many work situations require you to take joint responsibility and work collaboratively with others, ensuring that tasks are delivered on time, within budget, and with the appropriate level of quality. Often, two people working together can accomplish more than if they had worked alone. Synergy can occur when you're able to collaborate with your coworker on a task. Your coworker might be able to add further value to the task, thus completing the task in a way that couldn't have been done without the other.

A workgroup using dominant/interdependent behaviors will be jointly responsible and cooperate and collaborate on completing tasks on one hand, but will be overly committed and overly responsible on the other. This workgroup is likely to efficiently and effectively complete an impossible task in record time. However, the downside is this workgroup will leave anyone behaving passively in the dust and it will not get the benefit of their contributions. A workgroup using interdependent behaviors without a dominant flavor has a better chance of getting all team members to participate.

Task Completion—Interdependent Example

Jeanne is a social worker. One of her cases is a middle school student who is being bullied. Although Jeanne has complained to the school principal numerous times, the bullying continues. Jeanne decides to bring this subject up at the next Parent Teacher Association meeting. Jeanne volunteers to lead a team of teachers and parents to create a program to correct the situation. Many of the incidents happen in the cafeteria during the students' lunch break when they are often unsupervised. Jeanne volunteers to come to the school during the lunch break once a week to keep an eye on the students. She also calls several parents to see if they will also volunteer to supervise the lunch breaks once a week.

ANALYSIS: Jeanne appropriately works with the school principal and teachers to be jointly responsible for the bullying problem at the school. Jeanne collaborates with the teachers to create a program to reduce bullying incidents. Instead of criticizing the school for not supervising the kids at lunchtime, Jeanne provides her support and enlists the help of other parents so that the teachers can have a break during lunch.

Interdependent Behaviors in Resolving Problems

Appreciating problem interdependencies and being supportive of others when resolving and responding to a problem (regardless of who contributed to the cause of the problem) are interdependent ways of resolving problems. If someone unjustly accuses you of causing a problem, even if the claim is absurd or delivered unpleasantly, it is still appropriate to remain calm and look for the truth in the person's remarks to see if something can be worked on. Being responsible for a problem, no matter who contributed to it, allows you to focus more on problem resolution than on who is to blame. That said, it is also important to realize that you are not solely responsible for the cause of a problem. With this realization, you can look at causal factors outside your contribution. By working with others to address all the causal factors to the problem, you can arrive at a more holistic resolution.

Dominant/interdependent problem resolution is at play when most members of a workgroup are overly involved in resolving a problem. Being overachievers, the workgroup may come up with a resolution that most workgroups couldn't be successful at and wouldn't even consider as a possibility. A downside of dominant/interdependent problem solving is that those with an aversion to dominant behaviors will not be heard, and what may seem like a fair resolution to everyone else may not be to those who did not speak up. Their lack of voice could result in a missed opportunity for a better resolution or one that everyone is happy with.

Problem Resolution—Interdependent Example

Adam is an engineer working in a manufacturing plant. A piece of equipment in the assembly line fails for the third time in the past year. After Adam implements a quick solution to get the assembly line up and running again, the general manager calls Adam into his office to discuss how he handled the situation. The general manager is quite upset and blames Adam for the revenue loss and the third occurrence of the equipment failure. Adam understands the pressures that the general manager is under and reacts non-defensively, even though he accuses Adam of failures beyond his responsibility.

Adam is still intent on finding the root cause of the equipment failure and reconvenes the meeting with the manufacturing engineers once the crisis is over. They take a look at the problem from a holistic perspective and determine that a decision to change to a lower-cost supplier for equipment parts was the root cause for the equipment failure. Adam works with the purchasing department to find a new supplier.

ANALYSIS: Adam reacts interdependently despite his manager's unfair accusations. He takes on the responsibility to clear up the whole problem instead of only his part. After the crisis is over, Adam appropriately works with others in solving the root cause of the equipment failure.

Interdependent Behaviors in Conflict Resolution

Resolving conflict equitably and approaching conflict expecting everyone to win are interdependent ways of resolving conflict. It is usually appropriate to resolve conflict equitably for all involved. It is appropriate for you to communicate your position and seek to understand the other person's perspective before resolving the issue. You should demonstrate as much willingness to understand as to explain. Resolving conflict interdependently means having the self-esteem to present your position, the interpersonal skills to listen to others, and the patience to find common ground. Also, if you approach conflict resolution expecting everyone to win, you recognize that all parties are entitled to a favorable outcome, so you will work interdependently with others to make that outcome a reality.

A dominant/interdependent approach to resolving conflict is a passionate undertaking. This type of conflict resolution is often referred to as a "professional argument" because it seems like an argument when it's happening, but all parties are listening to each other's opinions.

Conflict Resolution—Interdependent Example

Jamal is working on negotiating an outsourcing contract for his company. Jamal's company needs to cut costs by outsourcing a high volume of work in a short period of time. Alexa, at the outsourcing firm, has not done this before but is confident that the approach will succeed. Jamal works with Alexa on how much risk each company should assume. They agree that both companies should share in the risk associated with aggressive cost reduction, so they draw up a contract stating that the two companies will work together to figure out how to minimize the risk.

ANALYSIS: Jamal and Alexa appropriately resolve the conflict around risk fairly and equitably for both companies. They negotiate a win-win deal for both parties.

Interdependent Behaviors in Relating to Others

Being open-minded, respecting yourself and others, and protecting your own and others' boundaries are interdependent ways of relating to others. Being sensitive to your own and others' needs is also an interdependent approach to relating to others. Being open-minded allows you to consider others' perspectives and learn new things. It is a good idea to treat others as you want to be treated. It is appropriate to not allow others to take advantage of you and for you to not take advantage of them. Respecting others in your workgroup includes accepting diversity and treating others as equals.

Some companies think that hostile work environments are only related to sexual harassment. However, these companies don't appreciate that some dominant behaviors cross personal boundaries and can create a hostile environment. Encouraging interdependent behaviors, such as treating everyone with respect, can help to address these inappropriate behaviors and ensure that everyone is treated fairly.

Dominant/interdependent behaviors look a little different. Being open-minded means being able to hear people express their opinions more vocally than others. Being respectful of others might change from interacting with each other calmly to interacting with each other passionately. One person's definition of respect might be to never yell at one another. A dominant/interdependent definition of respect might be to never leave a situation without working through the disagreement—no matter how heated it gets. Using dominant/interdependent behaviors means going to greater lengths to ensure that boundaries are protected in the workplace; standing up for those who have been mentally, emotionally, or physically abused is a dominant/interdependent approach to relating to others.

Relating to Others—Interdependent Example

Dimitri is in a meeting at work and overhears Todd yelling at Janis. Todd is quite angry about a mistake that Janis made and is verbally abusive. Dimitri waits until the incident is over and then takes Todd aside, letting him know that a better way of handling the situation would be to treat Janis with respect: Give her the benefit of the doubt and hear her side of the story before accusing her of a mistake.

ANALYSIS: Dimitri appropriately works with Todd, showing him how to address mistakes while still being respectful of the individuals involved. He explains to Todd how to address this in the future and protect others' mental and emotional boundaries.

Benefits of Using Interdependent Behaviors

Using interdependent behaviors is beneficial, particularly if you develop a preference for them. Interdependent behaviors make a positive impact on your personal success and gruntledness.

If you have a leadership role, employees' interdependent behaviors will positively impact the success and gruntledness of your group and ultimately your own success and gruntledness.

Success Impacts from an Employee Perspective

The business world is an interdependent environment. Very little of what you do at work is truly independent; most of what you do requires interacting with others. If you cooperate, support, and work well with others (in other words, use interdependent behaviors), you'll accomplish objectives more cost-effectively than employees who prefer using passive, dominant, or independent behaviors. This is because decisions will be more accurate, tasks will be completed with less rework, and problems will be solved correctly more often the first time.

If you make decisions jointly with others, you will most likely make better decisions because you will have more perspectives to choose from. The outcome in many situations can be improved if you are more open-minded, pay attention to others' perspectives, and make decisions jointly.

Often, the most productive way of completing tasks is working cooperatively with others, accepting joint responsibility for task completion, and collaborating on the best way to accomplish tasks. If you and others jointly commit to getting something done correctly, you'll have a better chance of finding ways to overcome obstacles and accomplish work more cost-effectively.

Approaching problem resolution from the interdependent mindset of "we are all in this together" and accepting that it doesn't matter who contributed to the cause of a problem will create a better result for you. The chances of achieving problem resolution are also better if you take in the whole issue and make decisions from a position of full awareness.

When you approach conflict with coworkers from a win-win perspective and work to resolve the situation equitably for all parties involved, you'll end up with a better outcome. The same is true for resolving conflict with other groups or with clients and customers. Because win-win resolutions often make companies want to do business with you in the future, your organization will end up in a better long-term financial position.

Interdependent behaviors give you more of a chance of personal success because your coworkers will support your actions. Personal success can lead to promotion; continued use of interdependent behaviors can then lead to success in your new position.

Gruntledness Impacts from an Employee Perspective

An interdependent working environment is based on connectedness, unity, and cooperation. It creates harmonious relationships, which increase employee morale.

You will probably be much happier when you make decisions jointly with others or feel your opinion has been heard and considered in the decision-making process. You will also be much happier when you work together as a team in a spirit of cooperation and collaboration. Creating something with others is enjoyable in itself and leads to a sense of team achievement.

Your gruntledness will increase when you approach problems without having to be defensive. When you can focus on the solution rather than protecting yourself, you will solve issues more harmoniously. When things go wrong, you won't be out on your own, worrying about being humiliated.

Most people feel good after a conflict is resolved fairly. If you feel you're getting a fair deal in the resolution of a conflict and that others involved are also getting a fair deal, you'll be much more gruntled. Also, with an open mind, many times conflict can result in learning. Conflict can make you aware of your weaknesses. It can also give you the opportunity to leverage the skills of others and learn from them in the process. In *The Magic of Conflict: Turning a Life of Work into a Work of Art,* author Thomas Crum describes conflict as something that is natural and neither positive nor negative—it just is.[49] It is also not a contest where one side is right and the other is wrong. He points out that conflict can be used as a motivator for change and an enabler for learning and growing.

Success Impacts from a Leader Perspective

As Lyndon B. Johnson, the 36th President of the United States, pointed out, "There are no problems we cannot solve together and very few we can solve by ourselves." This is as true in a business as it is with any other group of people.

When your workgroup primarily uses interdependent behaviors, it increases the chances of meeting business objectives. Employees put more effort into their work when they don't have to focus on people crossing their physical, mental, and emotional boundaries. And they will be more productive individually and collectively when they feel respected. Your chances of success are also greater when you aren't dependent on individual heroics to get a job done. The more you encourage your employees to use interdependent behaviors, the easier it will be for you to implement your organization's new business strategies, no matter how difficult they may be. Your workgroup members can work together to overcome most issues that come up.

The way people work together has a profound impact on a workgroup's performance, especially in adapting to change. For example, when using interdependent behaviors to deal with change, employees feel more empowered and collaborate more with coworkers. One study found that employees who use interdependent behaviors connect better to an organization's objectives and are more motivated to learn. The study also showed that interdependent behaviors enable teamwork, and holistic, cross-functional approaches to doing work.[50] Interdependent behaviors often result in employees going way beyond what is expected of them in their work responsibilities and performance levels. Interdependent behaviors in your workgroup increase the chances of business success.

Gruntledness Impacts from a Leader Perspective

As a leader, you'll benefit from having employees who behave interdependently because they'll be happier. Employees like interdependence in the workplace. In fact, one survey asked employees to identify the things that irritate them and turn the workplace into drudgery. Among the top four factors identified, respondents included "a lack of feeling part of a team/feeling we are in this together."[51]

Employees who work together using primarily interdependent behaviors are much happier because they have fewer issues when interacting, work more efficiently, and use a maximum amount of cooperation. Work disruptions and unscheduled absenteeism will be minimal. And it will be easier for you to implement change when necessary. These factors will translate to fewer problems and more gruntledness for you as the leader.

Encouraging interdependent behaviors will increase employee morale, which is a key component to engaging employees. Companies with engaged employees experience less turnover, which is an indication of higher employee morale.

Rethinking Behavior Preferences

Interdependent behaviors are one of three factors that will improve gruntledness for you and your coworkers and also increase the success of business strategies. The other two factors will be discussed in Parts 3 and 4.

10

Why Employee Behaviors Matter

"I was part of a team that made sure that we were meeting all the backup criteria for disaster recovery in two major locations. A year after a changeover reorganization had taken place, management found out that none of the East Coast offsite backup tapes were being taken offsite. The company had a one year gap in their offsite storage. Management found this out and went ballistic with good cause. It was discovered that one of the employees knew that none of the tapes were making it offsite. We all knew that if a problem had occurred, the multibillion-dollar company would have to shut the doors and file Chapter 7. No data equals no recovery. The employee was asked why he did not bring the fact to anyone's attention. His response was he was told that he only needed to make sure that the tapes made it to the back dock. The end result was that no actions were taken against the employee since he was just following his manager's directions. Unbelievable. This one individual put the entire billion-dollar organization at risk. Everyone was lucky that nothing set off an event where the offsite tapes would have been required."

Disgruntled Employee
Blog Post

D r. C. K. Prahalad is one of the world's most important and influential business thinkers; in fact, he was ranked number one in the "Thinkers 50" ranking of global business thinkers in 2007.[52] He points out that connectivity through the Internet has already changed consumer and business customer expectations of value in products and services; thus, it is also changing the competitive landscape for today's businesses.

He believes, in order to stay competitive and achieve innovation and create value in products or services, employees and entire organizations now more than ever need to work in a connected, cooperative, collaborative way with other organizations around the world and also internally at their own companies.[53] Therefore, interdependent behaviors will be a key part of the talent and capabilities that organizations will now seek in hiring, retaining, and rewarding employees.

The Impact of Employee Behaviors

Interdependent behaviors allow employees to work and interact cooperatively, which greatly improves their work efforts and creates better outcomes such as increased revenue, decreased costs, individual and business success, and ultimately, gruntledness.

Passive, dominant, and independent behavioral patterns are more common than interdependent behaviors in the business world today. Unfortunately, interdependent behaviors are not often favored by businesses. However, using interdependent behaviors should be the goal because it can eliminate unfavorable business outcomes and it enables the greatest chances of success and gruntledness.

Here's an example of what happens when a company's employees do not use interdependent behaviors in a situation where they would have been appropriate:

A pharmaceutical company put business strategies in place to double its growth. As a result, employees either met the production goals, but with lower quality, or they met the quality goals, but with lower productivity. This led to shutting down manufacturing lines, wasting raw materials, mandating overtime, delivering delayed or poor-quality shipments to customers, decreasing customer satisfaction, increasing operational expenses, and reducing employee morale.

A succession-management consultant working with the company found that the root cause of all this chaos was a lack of interdependence. The company failed to communicate to employees how their performance would help achieve business goals and failed to help them understand how to work cooperatively in an interdependent manner. So, employees behaved according to their passive, dominant, and independent behavior preferences. This resulted in inadvertently hindering each other's productivity or quality.[54]

It's important to mention that interdependent behaviors aren't always appropriate. It is inappropriate to make a decision with others when the responsibility for the decision rests with you alone or gets in the way of making the decision in a timely manner. Joint decision making can sometimes get in the way of other people's ability to focus on their own responsibilities.

Also, it is usually inappropriate to complete tasks interdependently when an activity is clearly only your responsibility. It is also inappropriate to collaborate on an activity that could just as easily be completed by one person, especially when it results in increasing the cost of doing the task.

Another point to remember is that it is not always appropriate to approach conflict with a win-win perspective without confirming first that everyone is being aboveboard. It's best to be cautious during negotiations and verify that all parties involved are being up front and honest.

That said, interdependent behaviors are appropriate in most situations. Interdependent behaviors need to become more prevalent than the passive, dominant, and independent behaviors that are the norm in the business world. But realize that it is important to use whatever behavior, whether it be passive, dominant, independent, or interdependent, that is appropriate for the situation at hand. Those that have an aversion to one of the behavior patterns will find themselves at a disadvantage because all of us encounter situations on a daily basis where passive, dominant, independent, and interdependent behaviors are appropriate.

Why There Is a Lack of Interdependent Behavior Preferences in the Workplace

In reviewing the benefits of interdependent behaviors, it's clear that they enable business success and improve employee gruntledness. So why aren't there more examples of these behaviors in the workplace?

Individuals in a workgroup have a preference for a particular employee behavior pattern for four main reasons. One reason lies in leadership. The leader may have a preference for a certain pattern of leadership behavior. Leadership behavior preferences heavily influence employee behavior preferences and create a certain organizational culture within the workgroup. Part 3 looks closely at leadership behaviors and how they influence employee behaviors.

A second reason lies in the organization's business system. The business system can have characteristics that lead to certain employee behavior patterns. Part 4 looks at these business system characteristics and how they influence behaviors, and Part 5 discusses how to improve those situations.

A third reason for a lack of interdependent behaviors in the workplace is that most people develop coping strategies based on their individual emotional, mental, and physical factors. Coping strategies serve to keep people stuck in passive, dependent, and independent behavior preferences. Part 6 will explain emotional, mental, and physical factors and will show you how to change these factors so they won't constrain your behavior.

The fourth and primary reason for the lack of more interdependent behaviors in the workplace is that the corporate world does not applaud people who prefer interdependent behaviors as much as it applauds other people. People who are frequently overly responsible and arrogant—using dominant behaviors—stand out in the business world. They get promoted more often than people who behave interdependently. However, when you use mainly interdependent behaviors, you'll eventually realize that everyone contributes to success; so you won't see the value in promoting yourself to ensure you stand out above others—especially if your manager also understands that success comes from a team of people, not just a star individual. Part 5 explains how to change this trend, using methods that enable people to move to more interdependent behaviors.

Part 3

How Leadership Behaviors Influence Business Results and Employee Morale

"People once instinctively understood and practiced the art of connectivity—to the land, to nature, and to each other. As human cultures evolved, we slowly forgot the basic partnering skills that allowed us to survive. . . . These are lessons businesses must relearn if they are to thrive in the digital age. People survive and grow by propagating connections to each other. Connectivity is critical for any business."

Stephen M. Dent
CEO, Partnership Continuum Inc.

11

Leadership Behaviors Impact Gruntledness and Business Success

"We had an ineffective principal and an assistant principal who rode my tail. I felt like [the assistant] undermined me at every turn. I was always on edge and waiting for the next ax to fall on me. He would talk to me whenever a parent would complain about some 'injustice' I had done. Rather than follow the chain of command and tell these parents to call me directly (since I was the only one besides their children who knew what occurred), he would tell them he would handle things. When I had difficulties with a couple of severe behavioral kids, he would [criticize me] rather than support or help me. I would drive home frequently in tears. My health started to fail. I was a basket of raw nerves. When a new principal came in, he exuded genuine concern and met with each of us individually. That in itself was refreshing. I found that he was not only approachable, but he was supportive. He did not assume I was doing something wrong simply because I was struggling. He would direct parents who called him to talk to me first. If they refused, he would set up a meeting to include me. I was able to calm down and not be so fearful. I knew that as long as I did what I needed to do, this principal would support me. He was like this with the whole staff. Morale went up and nerves went down. He seemed like a savior to me."

Gruntled Employee
Blog Post

I n his book, *The Founding Fathers on Leadership: Classic Teamwork in Changing Times,* Donald Phillips describes the characteristics of the men who led America through the American Revolutionary War to establish independence from Great Britain. He explains that leadership differs from modern business management: Leaders must be able to inspire and persuade others rather than command and control them.[55]

Being a leader is a difficult job because effective leading requires sensitivity to all types of employee behavior patterns. For example, a leader who has a preference for dominant behaviors may do well with employees who behave passively but may butt heads with employees who behave independently. So when you lead, you need to adjust your leadership behaviors to bring out the best in your employees. To do that, you first need to identify what your preference is and understand how it affects your leadership activities and impacts employees and business results.

Four Leadership Activities

Most leadership activities can be grouped into the following four categories: Providing Direction, Motivating, Building Team Capabilities, and Communicating. How a leader performs these activities in the workplace greatly impacts employee gruntledness and business results. Everyone within an organization acts in a leadership capacity from time to time even if they are not in a management position; thus, these activities apply to anyone in an organization. The four leadership activities are defined and broken down into sub-activities in the following way:

   1. **Providing Direction.** Leaders set direction in certain ways and to varying degrees of detail, and they vary in how they monitor implementation of direction.
      • Setting Direction – may or may not allow employees to help set direction or allow them to give feedback to refine direction
      • Implementing Direction – may be heavily involved, disengaged, or offer support when needed

2. **Motivating.** Leaders try to motivate employees by using different techniques and by recognizing different behavior.
   - Motivation Techniques – may use punishment, empowerment, or a compelling vision to achieve goals
   - Recognition – may recognize and reward different kinds of behaviors, such as following direction, or achieving goals individually or as a team
3. **Building Team Capabilities.** Leaders build capabilities by hiring and promoting employees for different reasons and by addressing employee weaknesses in different ways.
   - Hiring/Promoting – may hire and promote followers, individual performers, or team players
   - Addressing Weaknesses – may use various methods such as mentoring, coaching, or criticizing in hopes of strengthening the workgroup and addressing its weaknesses
4. **Communicating.** Leaders communicate in different ways and consciously or unconsciously set how communication flows within the workgroup.
   - Communication Style – may talk more than listen, listen without commenting, or talk and listen equally
   - Communication Flow – may not allow communication to flow, may let employees communicate freely without their involvement, or may coordinate communication

Leadership Behaviors and Their Patterns

Leaders demonstrate the four leadership activities based on the situation at hand and their preferences. Certain leaders prefer to be more involved with their workgroups so they demonstrate more *authoritarian* behaviors. Other leaders prefer to be less involved with their workgroups and demonstrate more *laissez-faire* behaviors. And some leaders prefer to interact with their workgroups on more of an equal basis and demonstrate more *connective* behaviors.

A leader will behave in a certain way, expecting that employees will behave in a corresponding manner. This expectation often influences employees' choice of behavior patterns. For example, a leader behaving in an authoritarian way often encourages employees to behave passively. The following defines the patterns of leadership behavior and the behavior the leader expects in return:

- **Authoritarian.** The leader takes on a dominant role and expects employees to take a passive role.
- **Laissez-Faire.** The leader takes a passive or independent role and expects employees to take an independent role.
- **Connective.** The leader takes on an interdependent role and expects employees to also take on an interdependent role.

Leadership behavior preference is different than "style," which is how many books on leadership categorize leadership behavior. A leadership style implies that a leader only uses one behavior preference in every situation, which is inaccurate. Although a leader may have a preference for certain leadership behaviors, all leaders—depending on the situation—use behaviors across all leadership behavior patterns. Often leaders prefer one behavior pattern over the other behavior patterns for the majority of situations.

Most likely you have experienced getting used to one leader's preferences, then the leader leaves, so you have to get used to a new leader with entirely different preferences. If the new leader's behaviors are quite different from the prior leader's, a workgroup may take a while (if ever) to accept the preferences of the new leader. Imagine the reaction a workgroup may have to a leader who micromanages when the workgroup's previous leader took a completely hands-off approach.

Figure 11.1 shows the relationship between the three leadership behavior patterns and the four leadership activities.

Figure 11.1: Relationship between patterns and leadership activities

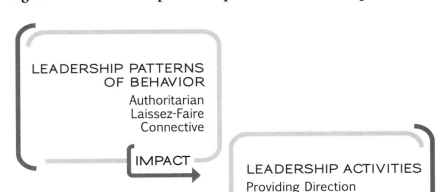

Figure 11.2 on the following page summarizes the four leadership activities for each of the three leadership behaviors as discussed in the next three chapters. Figure 11.2 is just a sample of the leadership behaviors that influence employee behaviors. Other leadership behaviors can influence employee behavior as well.

Leadership behavior preferences impact operational performance and business strategies; the behavior preferences also have financial impacts. Workgroups led by managers demonstrating mostly connective behaviors usually have better business results than workgroups that have leaders who demonstrate primarily authoritarian or laissez-faire behaviors. Leaders who use primarily connective behaviors tend to have workgroups with higher employee morale than leaders who use authoritarian or laissez-faire behaviors.

Figure 11.2: Leadership Behavior Matrix

LEADERSHIP ACTIVITIES	AUTHORITARIAN BEHAVIORS	LAISSEZ-FAIRE BEHAVIORS	CONNECTIVE BEHAVIORS
Providing Direction			
Setting Direction	Provides direction requesting minimal feedback	Provides minimal direction or allows team to set direction	Works with team to define/refine direction
Implementing Direction	Closely involved during implementation	Disengaged during implementation	Supports team during implementation
Motivating Employees			
Motivation Techniques	Motivates through negative consequences	Motivates through empowerment	Motivates through compelling vision with measurable objectives
Recognition	Recognizes those who follow direction	Recognizes individual accomplishments	Recognizes collective accomplishments
Building Team Capabilities			
Hiring/Promoting	Hires/promotes followers	Hires/promotes best individual performers	Hires/promotes team players
Addressing Weaknesses	Points out weaknesses	Expects employees to improve on their own	Coaches & mentors employees
Communicating			
Communication Style	Talks more than listens	Listens without much comment	Listens as much as talks
Communication Flow	Limits communications	Allows free-flowing communications	Coordinates communications

Appropriate and Inappropriate Behaviors

Authoritarian behaviors are completely appropriate in certain situations, as are laissez-faire and connective behaviors in other situations. However, in some situations each of these forms of behavior can be inappropriate.

Sometimes it is appropriate to use more authoritarian behaviors when leading a workgroup. The need for immediate business results during critical times may require leaders to take a more directive approach with employees. Other times, it is appropriate to use more laissez-faire behaviors with a workgroup. Employees who are delivering anticipated business results may not need much direction.

Typically, the behavior is inappropriate if it negatively impacts business results or employee gruntledness. Many times, I thought I was behaving appropriately—only to look at the situation later and realize that I was not. When I wanted to ensure my workgroup delivered business results in a difficult situation, I preferred to use authoritarian behaviors, which negatively impacted employee morale. When I wanted to improve employee morale, I preferred to use more laissez-faire behaviors. However, those behaviors didn't always deliver the business results that were being requested by management. Eventually, I discovered that connective behaviors were the best choice in delivering business results and keeping employees gruntled.

Understanding leadership behavior patterns will help you make better choices in leadership activities. Without this knowledge, your choices can negatively impact business success or employee morale. This is particularly true during times of business transformation. Many business strategies are unintentionally undermined by leaders who use inappropriate leadership behaviors while performing their daily activities.

The next three chapters detail authoritarian, laissez-faire, and connective behaviors. These behaviors will be illustrated within the four leadership activities. Chapter 15 shows how different combinations of employee behavior patterns and leadership patterns form the organizational culture for a workgroup.

12

How Authoritarian Behaviors Impact Gruntledness and Business Success

"I was laid off as an administrative assistant from a company, but was given the opportunity to go back into training to become a customer service rep again. The intense training lasted five weeks. At the end of the five weeks, all of the trainees were shown the 'Fish' motivator movie about the fish company in Seattle, WA. I left training with this upbeat positive attitude that I would not get disgruntled like so many other customer service reps and would show my smiling attitude over the phone to each customer I got. My first two days of being a phone rep were challenging, but I was thinking that I was starting to really get it. That is, until I came back from a break and had a manager (not my manager, but another team manager who had snooped at my stats) tell me that my stats sucked and that I better improve or I'd be history. I was crushed. I thought, 'Where is her fish attitude?' I needed to find a new job. In my resignation letter I talked about this incident and said it was no wonder their business was failing with managers who demean a person and don't help a person improve."

Disgruntled Employee
Blog Post

A person with a preference for dominant employee behaviors will often have a preference for authoritarian behaviors. Leading often involves some level of dominant behavior. As shown in Chapter 7, people who behave dominantly determine the path to be taken. They want their employees to do as they direct because they feel it will help the workgroup be successful. It is expected that leaders will take a more dominant/authoritarian role when giving direction. As a result, authoritarian behaviors are often the norm in the workplace.

Authoritarian behaviors range from the benevolent dictator to the feared autocrat. Those who use a benevolent dictator approach may believe that their way of leading is the best way. Even though they insist on doing it their way, their approach has a degree of kindness. Being leaders, they believe that they're better equipped to handle situations. They are afraid that if someone else provides direction, the desired results will not be achieved.

Those who use a feared autocrat approach on the other hand, are lacking any kind of benevolence in their behavior. They tend not to be respectful of others with their use of authoritarian behaviors. In fact, they are often critical and judgmental of how employees handle situations. They insist on complete obedience to their orders and often use fear as a motivator. They also have a degree of arrogance, as if their leadership role provides them with the correct insight into every situation.

Like passive and dominant employee behaviors, authoritarian behaviors are based on a mindset focused on *you*. Here's how leaders reflect these behaviors in various work situations: As a leader, if I believe that my value is greater than *your* value as an employee, then I may feel that *you* aren't as good as I am in a particular situation. If I believe that *you* as an employee are not as responsible as I am, then I may feel that I'll have to be involved in this situation to make sure *you* do things correctly. If I believe that I'm entitled to a particular thing as a leader more than *you* are as an employee, then I may feel that I have certain privileges over *you* in this situation.

If leaders have one or more of these beliefs all the time or just in certain situations, they may behave in the following authoritarian ways within the four leadership activities:

- **Providing Direction.** Provides direction by requesting minimal feedback from the team, and is closely involved during implementation of given direction.
- **Motivating Employees.** Motivates through negative consequences and recognizes employees who follow direction well.
- **Building Team Capabilities.** Hires and promotes followers and points out employee weaknesses.
- **Communicating.** Talks more than listens and limits workgroup members' communications.

The next sections illustrate authoritarian behaviors across the four leadership activities.

Authoritarian Behaviors in Providing Direction

Providing direction by requesting minimal feedback from team members, and being closely involved during implementation of direction are authoritarian ways of providing direction. Sometimes it is necessary to give detailed directions and patiently walk employees through the steps of a process. Also, it is sometimes appropriate not to let employees use their own judgment during implementation. When time is of critical importance and direction must be provided immediately, an edict may be the quickest way to accomplish implementation. Business strategies and crisis situations often need a strong leader to provide detailed direction and ensure that employees follow it. In these situations, it may also be appropriate to stay very involved with employees as they work on implementing direction—even if that means micromanaging. Providing direction in an authoritarian way may also be necessary if employees are unsuccessful in their attempts to do tasks their own way.

Trying to intimidate employees by shouting or using the authority of your position to make employees follow direction without question is a feared autocrat approach. A rationale behind using this approach while providing direction may be that a difference of opinion undermines your authority.

Providing Direction—Authoritarian Example

Quong has been a top sales performer for many years with a company that provides information services. He recently took a position with a high-tech manufacturer as its sales director, managing a group of people who have been working together for years. Quong was told that the workgroup is performing well and often exceeds their sales quotas.

Quong is determined to make his mark at the new company by increasing sales within his group. Based on his own experience, he provides detailed direction to each of his sales staff on how to close their deals. He expects his sales staff to follow his direction exactly and isn't open to feedback on why his direction may not work in this industry or for a particular client. He often accompanies his sales staff to key client meetings to ensure that they are following his sales strategy and closing deals quickly.

The members of Quong's workgroup resent the micromanagement, because they previously had so much freedom. After being cut off several times when giving feedback to Quong, several sales team members stop trying and conform to Quong's direction, feeling less responsible for results. When quarterly sales figures are next reported, the team misses its target by the largest percentage the company has ever seen.

ANALYSIS: Quong inappropriately directs his team. He doesn't give much latitude for deviation even though his team is a group of proven sales professionals who know the high-tech manufacturing industry and their clients better than Quong does. Quong's authoritarian methods cause his team to use passive behaviors, which negatively impacts business success and employee morale.

Authoritarian Behaviors in Motivating Employees

Motivating through negative consequences and recognizing followers are authoritarian ways of motivating employees. When a true disaster is looming, it may be necessary to motivate employees by communicating fearful consequences. If a situation calls for strong leadership direction, then it is also appropriate to later recognize those that followed the leader's direction.

Also, when an employee performs below acceptable levels, the kindest thing for you to do is to warn the employee of the consequences and to take appropriate action if the employee refuses to change the behavior. It is appropriate to point out undesired behavior—but also to recognize desired behavior. Doing so can bring change more quickly. Following a leader's direction is the correct thing to do in many situations.

Threatening, punishing, or humiliating employees in a public forum to instill fear is a feared autocrat approach to motivating employees. Following through on these threats to set an example for those who don't comply is also feared autocrat behavior.

Motivating Employees—Authoritarian Example

Marcie is a manager of a hotel that is undergoing renovations to the lobby, business center, and restaurants. As a result, client satisfaction scores have dropped. Marcie holds a staff meeting and tells her workgroup that there will be "hell to pay" if the client satisfaction scores don't increase by next month. Marcie's staff feels that client satisfaction scores have more to do with the renovations than their performance; but because Marcie is angry, they decide not to bring up that point.

ANALYSIS: Marcie inappropriately tries to motivate her staff through the use of negative consequences. As the survey comments point out, the client dissatisfaction has nothing to do with the service that the staff is providing. The poor survey results are mainly a consequence of the inconvenience caused by the hotel renovations. Because Marcie uses authoritarian behaviors to motivate, her staff doesn't feel empowered to voice possible solutions to improve client satisfaction during the renovation.

Authoritarian Behaviors in Building Team Capabilities

Hiring or promoting followers and pointing out weaknesses of workgroup members are authoritarian ways of building a team. You may find that the best person to hire or promote is someone who is good at following your direction and doesn't challenge your authority. Also, you may find that some situations require you to point out job-related weaknesses of employees.

Belittling employees who respectfully and correctly oppose your authority is a feared autocrat approach to team building. Unconstructive criticism is also a feared autocrat approach that induces fear to get employees "in line." Not hiring people more intelligent or competent than you because they could challenge your authority are also feared autocrat approaches to building a team.

Building Team Capabilities—Authoritarian Example

Madhur recently graduated with an MBA and has just been hired as a member of Peter's audit team. LaNell has been a member of Peter's team for years.

Madhur and LaNell work together on an audit for a key client. During the review of the audit results with Peter, Madhur brings up many points on how the audit could have been done better based on what she learned in her MBA program. LaNell notices that the more Madhur argues her points, the more Peter finds it difficult to maintain his composure. Eventually, Peter explodes: He tells her that her points are off track, he is not impressed with what she learned in her MBA program, and that she would be better off taking more of an observation role with future audits.

While LaNell agrees with Madhur's points, she is used to Peter's preference for authoritarian behaviors and remains quiet. Working for Peter over the years, LaNell has learned that the best way to get promoted is to not disagree with him.

ANALYSIS: Peter inappropriately points out Madhur's weaknesses by criticizing her suggestions. Feeling that his authority is being undermined, Peter does not listen to Madhur's correct assessment of how audits could be improved and belittles her.

Authoritarian Behaviors in Communicating

Talking more than listening and limiting communications of workgroup members are authoritarian ways of communicating. Speaking without understanding employees' perspectives on a subject is also an authoritarian approach to communicating. Authoritarian communication methods are useful when you have more information or experience than employees and need employees to pick up on your know-how. In addition, sometimes a message must be delivered as is and soliciting feedback is inappropriate. If unwanted feedback is given, it may be necessary to filter information that is irrelevant when it is important that no one contradicts or presents a different message than the one you communicate. It is often appropriate to limit communications by requesting that employees bring up issues to you before they involve others so you can try to resolve the issue first. It is sometimes necessary to communicate business information to only certain individuals. Some information is confidential and doesn't need to be made public.

Using critical, judgmental, and arrogant communication that diminishes the chance of getting feedback from employees is a feared autocrat approach to communication. Being disrespectful of employees, using overly direct, terse, and tactless communication is also a feared autocrat way to communicate.

Communicating—Authoritarian Example

Crayton holds a weekly outsourcing transition meeting and talks almost the whole time. His meetings usually run over the scheduled time slot, which doesn't allow a lot of time for interaction or questions from his transition team. Several members from his transition team find that they don't have the information they need from his weekly meetings to make decisions and complete their tasks. They end up having to go back to Crayton for clarification, which irritates him.

ANALYSIS: Crayton inappropriately conducts his staff meetings by talking most of the time and not allowing time for employees to voice concerns or ask questions. He assumes that discussions aren't required for employees to understand what he is saying. By limiting communications, Crayton's workgroup does not have the information they need to complete their tasks.

Moving Away from Using Authoritarian Behaviors

Using authoritarian behaviors creates several problems for you as a leader, particularly if you develop a preference for them. Your inappropriate use of authoritarian behaviors will negatively impact the relationship between you and the employees you lead, which will then impact your workgroup's gruntledness and success.

Moreover, if you are part of upper management and your leadership team has adopted authoritarian behaviors as part of the culture, this will negatively impact the organization's success and overall employee morale.

Gruntledness Impacts from a Leader Perspective

Even when you use authoritarian behaviors appropriately, they can sometimes be problematic. If you use respectful authoritarian behaviors, you and your employees will still miss a level of enjoyment and success that is possible only when people interact on a more equal basis. Disrespectful authoritarian behaviors are always inappropriate and problematic: Your workgroup members won't feel good about working for you.

Most employees won't be very happy if you provide direction through orders and edicts. In all industries, many employees state that micromanagement is a frequent cause for employee dissatisfaction.

Motivation through negative consequences also tends to have an adverse impact on employees' well-being. This is especially true when you use threats and punishments inappropriately.

Rarely does anyone like to hear criticism, even when it is constructive. When you use criticism inappropriately or point out employees' weaknesses more than their strengths, it will negatively affect employee morale. If employees realize that only "good soldiers" are being promoted, their level of engagement and gruntledness can be negatively impacted.

Frequent communications delivered without listening to employees' perspective can de-motivate employees. This and other authoritarian behaviors encourage employees to use passive behaviors. Employees tend not to be very happy when they adopt passive behaviors as a coping strategy.

Success Impacts from a Leader Perspective

If you have developed a preference for authoritarian behaviors across the four leadership activities, your workgroup will not be as effective as you might think. If you micromanage, motivate through negative consequences, criticize employees, and talk more than listen to your team on a regular basis, you will more than likely have workgroup members who are less responsible and uncommitted, which impacts your workgroup's productivity.

If you primarily use authoritarian behaviors to lead a workgroup, you'll end up putting more effort into work details than your workgroup members. You waste effort and talent when you inappropriately provide detailed direction and micromanage your team. This reduces the time that you could spend on strategic planning, selling new business, coaching, building your team's capabilities, and improving customer relationships.

Authoritarian behaviors limit workgroup members' thoughts and activities, which can unfavorably impact business results. For example, your behavior will likely cause employees to adopt the following attitudes: "Regardless of the organization's goals, I need to satisfy my boss," or "If I disagree with my boss, she'll think I'm challenging her authority."

Inappropriately motivating by mentioning negative consequences demotivates employees and decreases productivity. They'll perform only the minimum amount of work and will feel less engaged. Whether appropriate or not, speaking without listening may result in not obtaining valuable information from your employees that could be crucial in obtaining desired business results.

Also, when you hire or promote followers, you may not get the best talent. If you only hire employees with passive behavior preferences, and pass on employees who prefer dominant, independent, or interdependent behaviors, you may miss out on hiring someone better qualified for the job.

Since authoritarian behaviors also encourage employees to use passive behaviors, your chances for success will be further diminished. Employees who use passive behaviors don't contribute as much effort to workgroup success or to business strategy initiatives as employees who use the other behavior preferences.

Gruntledness Impacts from an Upper-Management Perspective

If most of your leaders have a preference for authoritarian behaviors, your organization is probably not going to be an employer of choice nor end up as one of the Top 100 best organizations to work for. Employee morale will probably be very low across your entire organization. Don't be shocked when your organization is labeled as a horrible place to work in a blog, on one or more disgruntled employee Web sites, or on a "Worst Places to Work" list. Also, if your organization's leaders have a preference for authoritarian behavior, it may cause high turnover rates.

A classic example of authoritarian behavior is the management theory developed by Frederick Winslow Taylor, the American management consultant known as the Father of Scientific Management. In the early 1900s, Taylor poured his efforts into improving industrial efficiency. In *Principles of Scientific Management*, he described his authoritarian system: "It is only through *enforced* standardization of methods, *enforced* adoption of the best implements and working conditions, and *enforced* cooperation that this faster work can be assured. And the duty of enforcing the adoption of standards and enforcing this cooperation rests with *management* alone."[56]

Not surprisingly, this type of management resulted in disgruntled employees. In Taylor's day, employees resented his system so much that they went on strike throughout the United States, triggering a congressional investigation.

Success Impacts from an Upper-Management Perspective

Authoritarian behaviors at your organization create a culture with an emphasis on compliance and conformity. In this kind of environment, it would be inappropriate for employees to show disagreement with the leadership team. So the authoritarian behavior stifles suggestions and information sharing, and passive employee behaviors become the norm.

Attitude impacts productivity. If your leadership team adopts authoritarian preferences, your organization's workgroups may produce the required business results; but the results will be limited, compared to what they could be if employees' hearts and minds were really into their work. A much higher degree of undermining good ideas goes on when a leader with authoritarian behavior preferences is in charge. Leaders using authoritarian behavior tell employees what to do rather than ask them for suggestions on the best approach. Thus, they cause employees to work defensively (to avoid the risk of displeasing the boss), which hinders their ability to work creatively.

If you appoint a leader with a preference for authoritarian behaviors to lead your business strategy, that leader will probably ensure that implementation activities are completed on time and within budget and will do whatever it takes to get the job done—but the leader will probably leave some "dead bodies" in the path.

In addition, although leaders with a preference for authoritarian behaviors often succeed at implementing business strategies, this type of leader is less successful at producing sustainable results. For example, a leader who micromanages operational activities and provides specific direction to employees regarding business initiatives may get desired actions or performance results from employees for a while. But such actions will be effective only as long as the leader continues to oversee operations and stay involved with the team at a detailed level. Once the leader turns attention elsewhere, the employees' performance and business results will decline.

Here's another problem: Authoritarian behaviors do not support employees' understanding about what the organization is trying to achieve. Without their leader's guidance, employees have difficulty determining whether their decisions support or hinder business objectives. Under the guidance of leaders with a preference for authoritarian behaviors, employees are not empowered to make decisions. Leaders tend not to tell employees the reasons for a given direction. They may not think employees need that information and should just do as they are told. So when employees are required occasionally to make a decision, they may hesitate because they are worried about doing the wrong thing. They often make decisions based on what will keep them out of trouble with their manager, rather than on whether the decisions are aligned with the organization's business strategy or they are best for the organization.

You sure don't want leaders to use primarily authoritarian behaviors when your company needs to implement business strategies. Outsourcing, for example, requires that employees adopt the service provider's best practices. Enterprise resource planning implementations require that employees change to new processes and application systems. Acquisitions frequently require that the acquired employees change to the new company's way of doing business. In any of these business strategies, your employees will not be equipped to make such changes quickly because they will expect and require strict guidance that may or may not be available during the transition.

Rethinking Authoritarian Behaviors

Authoritarian behaviors can be appropriate in some situations. However, inappropriate uses and, especially, a preference for authoritarian behaviors cause employee disgruntledness and can cause failed attempts in implementing business strategies. More effective leadership behaviors are presented later in this book. The next chapter will look at the impacts of laissez-faire behaviors.

13

How Laissez-Faire Behaviors Impact Gruntledness and Business Success

"When I was working at a hospital cafeteria in high school, we had a manager who would assign our jobs for the shift then sit on her butt and drink coffee at one of the tables for the rest of the day. She was lucky that she had a competent group of kids working for her, but we did take advantage of her lack of supervision—mostly because we could. We'd make giant sandwiches and eat them between [helping] customers while she wasn't paying any attention—which was most of the time. We'd 'accidentally' put a finger in a yummy dessert and say it came up that way and, 'oh too bad, I guess one of us should eat it.' This manager also had the habit of suddenly and randomly changing the schedules, but never quite erased the previous information. So since this was her habit, whenever one of us wanted a day off or needed a different time, we'd just follow her example and change it ourselves, then when she'd question us (which wasn't often), we'd simply go show her the schedule. But the clincher was the day we all decided to switch name tags and do the job of the person whose name tag we had. Our manager could never remember any of our names and we thought we'd prove it. She must have on some level known our names because she'd come up to one of us and say something to the effect of 'I thought I put you on the grill' or whatever job. We'd simply say that we were doing the job she assigned. She'd look a bit confused and comment that she thought I was so and so and I would point to 'my' name tag and 'correct her error.' I know what we did was mean, but we always got the work done."

Disgruntled Employee
Blog Post

aissez-faire is a French term for "letting people do as they choose." It originated as an eighteenth-century economic theory representing opposition to government intervention in business affairs. It is sometimes referred to as a "let it be" attitude.

People with a preference for independent employee behaviors will often have a preference for laissez-faire behaviors. As employees, they perform work activities on their own. They have the self-esteem and sense of responsibility to deal with most work situations alone. As leaders, they may assume that the members of their workgroup will behave the same way. They trust and respect their employees. They may feel that the best way for the workgroup to be successful is to empower employees to take care of problems and tasks on their own. The leader with a preference for laissez-faire behaviors believes that employees are best left on their own to achieve needed business results.

An alternative form of this behavior is passive/laissez-faire leadership. The leader with a preference for passive/laissez-faire behaviors goes along with whatever employees are doing. They may do this because they are afraid to exert their authority. Their approach also may be somewhat apathetic. They may not care enough about the situation to work with employees to do it differently. Or they may have self-confidence issues and are worried that if they provide too much direction, they will negatively impact workgroup results.

Like independent employee behaviors, laissez-faire behaviors are based on a mindset focused on *I*. Here's how leaders reflect these behaviors in certain work situations: As a leader, if I believe in the value of employees, then *I* feel good about their participation in the situation. If I believe that employees are responsible, then *I* feel they will take care of the situation on their own. If I believe that employees are entitled to certain things, then *I* will ensure they have certain privileges in this situation.

If leaders have one or more of these beliefs all the time or just in certain situations, they may behave in the following laissez-faire ways within the four leadership activities:

- **Providing Direction.** Provides minimal direction or allows team to set direction and is disengaged during the implementation of direction.
- **Motivating Employees.** Motivates through empowerment and recognizes individual accomplishments.
- **Building Team Capabilities.** Hires and promotes the best individual performers and expects employees to improve on their own.
- **Communicating.** Listens without much comment and allows free-flowing communications by workgroup members.

The next sections illustrate laissez-faire behaviors across the four leadership activities.

Laissez-Faire Behaviors in Providing Direction

Providing minimal direction or allowing the team to set direction, and disengaging during the implementation of direction are laissez-faire ways of providing direction. If your employees are very experienced in performing a task, it is appropriate to give high-level direction or to even allow workgroup members to set direction. It is often appropriate to allow a workgroup to decide how to implement direction. With any management position, it is unrealistic to know every aspect of your employees' individual duties; so a laissez-faire approach becomes a necessity in many situations. For example, it is prudent to disengage and take more of a hands-off approach when you are less familiar with a task than the employees. It may also be appropriate to allow employees to finish a task without you when you are very busy with pressing matters.

Taking a hands-off approach during a crisis situation that requires strong leadership, specific direction, and employee support is a passive/laissez-faire way to provide direction. Giving high-level direction to inexperienced employees struggling with a task is also a passive/laissez-faire approach. Additionally, not encouraging employees to perform outside their comfort zone, thus putting more importance on their aversions and insecurities and less on business results, is a passive/laissez-faire way to provide direction.

Providing Direction—Laissez-Faire Example

Denzel is head of the sales department and recently purchased a price-quoting application from an independent software vendor to improve the company's ability to give quotes to customers. Denzel has hired a very experienced consulting firm to implement the application. Because IT applications aren't his area of expertise and he has hired a firm that specializes in this, Denzel doesn't provide much direction to the implementation team.

Over the next few months, Denzel hears complaints from his staff that the application requires them to change their quoting processes to a standard process. His staff asks that the application be customized to handle the way they currently perform the process.

Denzel figures that his staff will be able to work this out with the consulting firm. The consulting firm gets approval for price increases from Denzel's staff to implement the customizations. Denzel is unpleasantly surprised when he gets the invoice from the consulting firm.

ANALYSIS: Denzel inappropriately provides very little direction to his staff or the consulting firm. Both parties need direction on whether it is more important to save money with standardized quoting processes or if it's more advantageous to spend the extra money to customize the quoting application. With lack of direction from Denzel, his team uses more independent behaviors and makes the decision to approve costly changes from the consulting company.

Laissez-Faire Behaviors in Motivating Employees

Empowering employees and recognizing individual accomplishments are laissez-faire ways of motivating employees. Empowering employees by allowing them to accomplish work activities as they see fit is often appropriate since most employees have the skills they need to do their tasks. Recognizing an employee's accomplishments, such as achieving personal objectives or quickly resolving problems is also appropriate. Recognizing employees who excel can set an example for what the organization expects regarding personal behavior in the workplace.

Recognizing employees for no reason other than to keep them happy rather than recognizing them based on business results is a passive/laissez-faire motivation technique. Conversely, not making the effort to recognize employees at all, thinking that employee empowerment is enough of a motivator in itself is also a passive/laissez-faire approach.

Motivating Employees—Laissez-Faire Example

Sue Ellen assigns Sandeep to develop an employee retention program. Sue Ellen gives him a budget to put together a team. Sandeep forms his team with people who have experience in implementing successful employee retention programs.

Sandeep is involved in several other initiatives and has very little time to work with his team. He meets with the team on a weekly basis to get a status update. The team continues to make excellent progress, so Sandeep allows them to work mostly on their own. The day before the employee retention presentation to Sue Ellen, several of the team members review their proposal with Sandeep to get him up to speed so that he is fully aware of all the strategies and can answer any of Sue Ellen's questions.

Sue Ellen is very pleased with the proposal and recognizes Sandeep at her next staff meeting for the outstanding job and presents him with a cash bonus. One of the members of Sandeep's team realizes that he took advantage of them and refuses to support Sandeep any more. She vows to make her contributions known in the future.

ANALYSIS: Sue Ellen inappropriately recognizes and rewards Sandeep for his efforts when she should have realized that the success of the employee retention program was due to a team effort; it would have been more appropriate to reward and recognize the whole team. Sue Ellen and Sandeep's behavior is a factor that causes a member of Sandeep's team to no longer be a team player and to become more competitive—making sure management recognizes her work.

Laissez-Faire Behaviors in Building Team Capabilities

Hiring or promoting the best individual performers and expecting employees to improve on their own are laissez-faire ways of building a team. Many work situations can be handled by someone working alone. In those situations, the best individual performers benefit a team because they will be able to accomplish tasks better than most. Often, it is appropriate to expect that employees will improve on their own when they understand the business consequences of their mistakes. Employees usually learn from their own and others' mistakes.

Not sharing experiences or not telling employees how to avoid making mistakes you've made in the past are passive/laissez-faire ways of team building. Additionally, under-reacting to an employee's mistake and attributing it to being part of the normal learning process when the employee is clearly unaware of the business consequences is also a passive/laissez-faire approach to team building.

Building Team Capabilities—Laissez-Faire Example

Nicholas has just promoted Zack, the best individual performer in his workgroup, to a first-line supervisory position. But since his promotion, Zack has been overwhelmed with problems.

Since this is his first time in a management position, Zack struggles with providing direction and motivating his workgroup. When his workgroup runs into trouble, Zack has a tendency to step into his old position and do the tasks for his employees. This causes friction between him and his workgroup.

Nicholas overlooks Zack's struggle, assuming that Zack will figure out how to lead the group since he was part of it so long and has all the necessary functional skills required for the position. As a result, the workgroup becomes directionless and starts to fall behind on its schedule.

ANALYSIS: It is inappropriate for Nicholas to assume that Zack can figure out his first supervisory assignment on his own. Once Nicholas recognizes that Zack is struggling, he inappropriately does not coach and mentor Zack to help him be successful in his new position. Nicholas inappropriately expects Zack to figure out on his own how to move from an individual contributor role to a leadership role.

Laissez-Faire Behaviors in Communicating

Listening to employees without saying much in response, and allowing workgroup members to communicate freely among themselves and develop their own messages are laissez-faire ways of communicating with employees. Striving to understand employees' perspectives without expressing your own opinion on a subject is also a laissez-faire approach to communicating. Hearing employees out without interruption and allowing free-flowing communications can encourage employees to take an active role in whatever they are trying to achieve. A free-flowing forum, such as blogs, where employees can voice ideas and concerns, can generate new ideas with the potential to improve business results.

Allowing vocal employees to overshadow your opinions or team members' opinions when it could lead to a bad business decision is a passive/laissez-faire way of communicating. Being overly sensitive to employee reactions, thus tiptoeing around necessary messages, often leads to watered-down communications that confuse employees. In addition, letting employees distribute information when it is imperative that the correct information gets to the right individuals is also a passive/laissez-faire way of communicating. Being overly concerned with employee issues and less concerned with business issues may also be a rationale behind choosing to use passive/laissez-faire communications.

Communicating—Laissez-Faire Example

Sharon is holding her weekly staff meeting and, as usual, they are running behind schedule. Staff members frequently comment on agenda items that they are not involved in or responsible for in any way. Even Sharon makes a recommendation on an item for which she has no role. Members often talk about issues that are not directly related to the objective that needs to be met. Sharon's staff meeting runs over its scheduled two hours by forty-five minutes. Sharon must end the meeting with two more agenda items still to discuss because she has to leave for another meeting.

ANALYSIS: Sharon inappropriately allows her staff to have too much of a voice in her staff meetings. She inappropriately allows her staff members to freely comment on topics beyond their scope of experience and responsibility. This encourages more independent behaviors with her staff. As a result, her meetings frequently take up valuable time that members of her workgroup could use more productively. Voicing too many opinions often leaves members unsure of the direction they should take.

Moving Away from Using Laissez-Faire Behaviors

Several problems can occur for you as a leader if you use laissez-faire behaviors, particularly if you develop a preference for them. Your inappropriate use of laissez-faire behaviors will negatively impact the relationship between you and the employees you lead, which will then impact your employees' gruntledness and success. Moreover, if you are part of upper management and your leadership team has adopted laissez-faire behaviors as part of the culture, this will negatively impact the organization's success and overall employee morale.

Gruntledness Impacts from a Leader Perspective

Employees will tend to be happier working for you if you use laissez-faire behaviors instead of authoritarian behaviors. However, the overall gruntledness of the workgroup still won't be as high as it could be if you and the workgroup interact collaboratively.

When you use laissez-faire behaviors, you provide minimal direction. While the employees may enjoy the freedom that results from your behavior, they'll miss the sense of connectedness with you. They'll also miss a sense of accomplishment if your high-level direction results in not meeting business objectives.

When you primarily listen and don't include your own input, you can leave a void for employees and impact their well-being. For example, leaving employees on their own to figure out how to improve their weaknesses can cause them to struggle and be unhappy.

Your laissez-faire behaviors will also encourage employees to use independent behaviors. Employees who adopt independent behaviors as a coping strategy tend to not be as happy as they could be because they are avoiding people rather than joining them.

Success Impacts from a Leader Perspective

If you have developed a preference for laissez-faire behaviors across the four leadership activities, your workgroup probably won't be as effective as it could be. Achieving productivity under laissez-faire leadership depends upon individual team members.

By using laissez-faire behaviors, you may not provide the appropriate amount of guidance that can help employees work more efficiently and eliminate confusion or mistakes. A lack of guidance can result in poorer quality work.

If you take a hands-off approach with your team, motivate by empowering employees to take action on their own, encourage employees to improve on their own, and allow employees to be primarily responsible for communications, you'll actually turn control over to your employees. Depending on your workgroup's behavior preferences, things might turn out all right; but usually business results won't be what they could be with more guidance from you.

Allowing employees to handle communications can result in employees not obtaining important information from you that will help them meet business objectives. If employees don't fully understand their part in meeting business goals because you use laissez-faire behavior, letting them make all the decisions can lead them to go against business objectives.

If you hire or promote the best individual performers, it may lower overall workgroup performance, particularly if you have business objectives that require collaboration among workgroup members. Also, recognizing individual performers de-emphasizes the importance of a team; in most cases, the team gets the lion's share of the work done.

Since laissez-faire behaviors encourage employees to use independent behaviors, your chances for success will be further diminished. Independent behaviors lack the cooperation and collaboration between employees needed to achieve optimum business results and effectively implement business strategy initiatives.

Gruntledness Impacts from an Upper-Management Perspective

Organizations sometimes become one of the Top 100 places to work when leaders use primarily laissez-faire behaviors. But these organizations probably will not retain their ranking when financial challenges come along. Layoffs and other cost-cutting initiatives tend to make employees disgruntled.

It's true that your employees will tend to be somewhat happier working with a manager who prefers laissez-faire behaviors. But this happiness is superficial because any kind of change that comes along will disrupt employee morale. With laissez-faire leadership preferences, you won't have the kind of culture where your employees and leaders feel as if they are "in this together." A laissez-faire leadership team tends to treat individual employees as though they are special; as a result, employees tend to feel entitled to special treatment. This type of happiness situation is similar to building a house on sand. The slightest deviation will cause the house to crumble. In a workgroup where leaders use primarily laissez-faire behaviors, the slightest deviation from normal treatment can cause disgruntledness.

Not everything that happens in your organization will go over well with employees. There will be good times and challenging times. Employees working with a manager who prefers laissez-faire behaviors become accustomed to the good times and don't cope well when the business climate becomes more challenging and authoritarian behaviors are used to turn things around.

Success Impacts from an Upper-Management Perspective

Business results are often negatively impacted when a business-transformation initiative, such as outsourcing, merger or acquisition, or enterprise resource planning implementation comes along that requires leadership behaviors other than laissez-faire. If your leadership team prefers laissez-faire behaviors, your organization probably won't achieve the anticipated business benefits from such initiatives. These initiatives drastically change how employees work, so employees will need more direction and leadership involvement. Leaders who prefer laissez-faire behaviors will not meet this need.

Someone with a preference for laissez-faire behaviors leading a business strategy effort doesn't have as much chance of successfully implementing the business initiatives on time or within budget. An implementation team under laissez-faire leadership tends to flounder, head in multiple directions, or complete tasks incorrectly.

Laissez-faire behaviors may cause employees to have less drive and focus. Therefore, the quality and timeliness of work products may not be as good as they could be. However, the outcome depends on individual employee behavior preferences: The business results will depend on whether individual employees decide to embrace the work.

Also, with laissez-faire behaviors, leaders offer very little encouragement and support to achieve business results, and on top of that, they provide very little follow-up to see if they are getting business results. This often results in not achieving business success. Additionally, financial stability is more difficult to sustain in organizations with laissez-faire behaviors during economically challenging times since employee decisions are not always aligned with business initiatives to reduce costs.

Although laissez-faire behaviors usually encourage independent behaviors, other employee behavior preferences can be a factor. Leaders who use laissez-faire behaviors tend to allow any kind of employee behaviors. This can be especially problematic if you accept passive behaviors. For example, employees who think it's okay to loaf on the job or withhold greater effort will be allowed to do so, which is counterproductive.

Rethinking Laissez-Faire Behaviors

Laissez-faire behaviors can be appropriate in some situations. However, inappropriate uses and, especially, a preference for laissez-faire behaviors, may cause business strategies to fail. They can also negatively impact employee morale. More effective leadership behaviors are presented in the next chapter, which covers connective behaviors.

14

How Connective Behaviors Impact Gruntledness and Business Success

"Out of the 25-plus bosses I've had, my new boss is only 1 of 4 bosses who has told me often what a good job I do, treats me with respect, and allows me to feel like my thoughts and words regarding the progress of the company means something. It's a sad example of the working world that only 4 bosses out of the 25-plus I've had over my 40 years in the business world are smart enough to recognize my talents and the talents of others they work with. These 4 bosses probably get more out of their employees in one day than most get out of an employee in a lifetime."

Gruntled Employee
Blog Post

As illustrated in the past two chapters, authoritarian and laissez-faire behaviors leave a lot to be desired. Authoritarian behaviors may be slightly better than laissez-faire behaviors in delivering business results, but they often cause employee morale problems. Laissez-faire behaviors may be somewhat better than authoritarian behaviors in improving employee morale, but they often don't deliver the needed business results, particularly when business strategies are being implemented. Connective behaviors are the answer to the problem of how to improve employee morale and improve business results at the same time. Unfortunately, authoritarian and laissez-faire behaviors are more prevalent with today's leaders. Connective behaviors are appropriate in far more situations than most leaders think.

A person with a preference for interdependent employee behaviors will often have a preference for connective behaviors. As employees, they enjoy working collaboratively with others. As leaders, they appreciate the contribution of their employees. They may feel that the best way for the workgroup to be successful is to cooperate and collaborate with their employees. Leaders who behave connectively work well with their workgroup members. They have the interpersonal skills to deal with employees.

Connective behaviors are usually exhibited peacefully. Leaders calmly express their opinions and listen to employees. They serenely go about providing direction, motivating employees, building team capabilities, and communicating to employees. They interact with employees in a respectful manner. Gandhi is an example of a leader who had a preference for connective behaviors. He united the people of India and led them through many changes in a calm and peaceful way through non-violent civil disobedience to British rule.

However, an alternative form for connective behaviors is dominant/connective. Leaders using the dominant form of connective behaviors still trust and respect their employees, but they provide direction passionately. No one would dare accuse these leaders of being apathetic. Even though they tend to be more forceful in communication and motivation, they are still open-minded and listen to employees. However, they expect employees to be as outspoken as they are when expressing opinions. They do not serenely perform their leadership activities; they are high-energy and vivacious. A person with an aversion to dominant or authoritarian behaviors will probably find it difficult to participate with a leader who uses such behaviors.

Like interdependent employee behaviors, connective behaviors are based on a mindset focused on *we*. Here's how leaders reflect these behaviors in certain work situations: As a leader, if I believe that each employees' value is equal to my value, then *we* will feel good about participating together in a situation. If I believe that employees are as responsible as I am, then *we* will take care of the situation together. If I believe that employees are as entitled to things as I am, then *we* will ensure that we both have certain privileges in this situation.

If leaders have one or more of these beliefs all the time or just in certain situations, they may behave in the following connective ways within the four leadership activities:

- **Providing Direction.** Works with team to define or refine direction and supports the team during implementation of direction.
- **Motivating Employees.** Motivates with a compelling vision with measurable objectives, and recognizes collective accomplishments.
- **Building Team Capabilities.** Hires and promotes team players and coaches/mentors employees.
- **Communicating.** Listens as much as talks and coordinates communications within and between workgroups.

The next sections illustrate connective behaviors across the four leadership activities.

Connective Behaviors in Providing Direction

Working with your team to define or refine direction and supporting the team during implementation of direction (without micromanaging) are connective ways of providing direction. Connective methods of direction can be very useful when faced with a new and complex problem because employees can benefit from your input and you, theirs. Listening to someone who thinks differently from you can help you discern if something is missing from your direction; diversity leads to a more complete solution. Staying involved with your team and supporting implementation of direction will ensure that your team is on track and aligned with objectives. Also, letting your team complete its work with appropriate checkpoints ensures that no misunderstanding occurs. In addition, business-transformation efforts such as mergers and acquisitions, outsourcing arrangements, and enterprise resource planning implementations usually benefit from upper management forming direction collaboratively and refining it from team members' feedback. The vision has a much greater chance of success when team members can help set strategies and refine direction.

Providing detailed direction through orders coupled with listening to feedback from team members is a dominant/connective way of providing direction. Sometimes direction must be somewhere between an edict and collaboration to prevent a crisis from happening or prevent matters from getting worse. When faced with a crisis situation or a tough circumstance, a dominant/connective approach to providing direction may be more effective than a connective approach. Another dominant/connective way of providing direction is following up with the team during implementation; the leader is supportive but also leaning towards micromanaging. This approach may be necessary when implementing a new strategy.

Providing Direction—Connective Example

Shante's company has just signed a deal to acquire another company. As head of the IT department, Shante's workgroup will need to do a lot of work to integrate the acquired company. Over the years, Shante's company has grown significantly by acquisition and has an integration process in place.

Shante meets with her direct reports to start planning the integration. She tells her staff about the unique challenges that they will face with the acquisition. They brainstorm ways to meet challenges, and base their decisions on lessons learned from past acquisitions. Together, they develop a detailed implementation plan that identifies and adopts the best practices from the acquired company.

The IT department meets with people from the acquired company to give them a chance to provide feedback to refine the plan. The members from both companies' IT groups make joint decisions and feel responsible, which leads to completing the integration on time and with few issues.

ANALYSIS: Shante appropriately collaborates with her team while setting direction and also refines that direction with feedback from the new team members from the acquired company. As a result of her connective methods, she encouraged all parties to voice their opinions and be part of the decision-making process to create a better outcome for all involved.

Connective Behaviors in Motivating Employees

Providing a compelling vision with measurable objectives and recognizing team accomplishments for meeting objectives are connective ways of motivating employees. The best business results are usually achieved when leaders motivate employees with a compelling vision and set measurable objectives for the workgroup so it can monitor its progress. Also, giving individual employees their own measurable objectives lets them see if they are contributing to the overall success of the workgroup. Recognizing team accomplishments also motivates employees to work together, especially if a "hero" culture has developed as a result of leaders inappropriately recognizing individual accomplishments.

Using dominant/connective motivation techniques means inspiring through a compelling vision but also ensuring that employees realize the negative consequences if measurable objectives aren't achieved. In today's environment, true disasters loom. Businesses will fail if they don't figure out how to be competitive in a global economy, and it may be necessary to inform employees of these fearful consequences.

Recognizing team accomplishments, but warning the team of the consequences if it performs below acceptable levels, and taking appropriate action if the team refuses to change the behavior are also dominant/connective ways of motivating employees. Sometimes it is necessary to disband a team if it is working together to undermine a leader's direction. It is appropriate to point out undesired team behavior—but also to recognize desired team behavior. Doing so can bring about change more quickly.

Motivating Employees—Connective Example

Amiya runs the product development group within her company. The executives have just decided that in order to cut product development costs, a majority of the work must be performed with offshore resources in India.

With the help of a third-party advisor, Amiya puts together a presentation that shows the benefits to the company and the individuals who will be a part of the new global organization. She provides a compelling vision of why this change is needed and how the company will lose market share if it doesn't become more cost competitive. She also defines measurable objectives for each of her twelve teams, which measure the success of the offshore outsourcing initiative in terms of increased quality, greater productivity, reduced product-launch time frames, and reduced costs.

During implementation, some of the teams struggle with meeting the objectives, but all have the ability to self-monitor and make necessary changes to meet their goals. Amiya continues to motivate the teams by publicly recognizing and rewarding early-adopters, giving the other teams a clear picture of the benefits of their efforts. As a result, the company completes offshoring product development work two months ahead of schedule without negatively impacting the next product ship date.

ANALYSIS: Amiya appropriately motivates her team with a compelling vision of the future. She provides measurable objectives so that each team can track its own progress and fine-tune direction as needed. She also appropriately recognizes and rewards team accomplishments to increase motivation within the workgroup. Amiya's connective methods for motivating employees enable the company to smoothly transition into becoming a global organization without impacting the product schedule.

Connective Behaviors in Building Team Capabilities

Hiring or promoting team players, and coaching or mentoring employees are connective ways of building a team. The best business results are often obtained by staffing a workgroup with employees who demonstrate cooperation, collaboration, and open-mindedness. It's best to react to employees' mistakes like they are errors in judgment that can be corrected instead of "sins" that need to be punished. If someone is performing below par, you can give the employee the benefit of the doubt until the cause of the issue is determined. Employees can also learn from leaders' mistakes. Sharing experiences and previous mistakes with employees is an effective connective team-building method to help employees grow.

Dominant/connective team building might be appropriate when an employee has been coached in the past and continues to make the same or similar mistake. It may be necessary to privately point out an employee's weakness and to provide more focused coaching to identify the problem and suggest ways to improve.

Some workgroups that are given near-impossible objectives may benefit from having lots of employees with dominant preferences. Using a dominant/connective team-building approach such as hiring or promoting dominantly preferred employees may be the best way to meet such objectives. However, this approach is only recommended if you have strong interpersonal skills; you'll most likely have to deal with a higher number of conflicts between employees.

Building Team Capabilities—Connective Example

Samir works for a book publisher and needs to hire a new synopsis writer. Samir decides that in addition to seeking someone who has good writing skills, he wants to hire someone who works well with others. Samir believes that the candidate should possess good interpersonal skills, be a team player, and be open to coaching.

Samir hires Holly after she demonstrates these skills. He mentors her and gives her tips on effective writing shortcuts. Within a month of joining the team, Holly meets the quota of five synopses per week and her coworkers appreciate her contributions and suggestions.

ANALYSIS: Samir appropriately hires a person who establishes that she could be a team player. Samir appropriately spends time with Holly, ensuring that she has what she needs to quickly become a productive member of the workgroup. As a result of Samir's connective team-building approach, Holly is quickly up to speed, performs at a high level, and contributes to the team's success.

Connective Behaviors in Communicating

Listening equally to workgroup members' views while presenting your own views and coordinating communications within and between workgroups are connective ways of communicating. During most business initiative efforts, it is important to hear employee feedback and help employees understand the topic by including both the business and employee perspective in the communication. Also, it is appropriate to use connective communication techniques, such as coordinating communications to ensure that information is disseminated in a meaningful way to all stakeholders.

Using dominant/connective communications means communicating from a position of authority but still listening to employee perspectives. In a crisis situation, dominant leadership is needed, but it is also important that employees understand what needs to be done and that they are on board. Also, it is entirely possible that your information is incorrect. Listening to employee feedback will give you the opportunity to correct the problem.

Communicating—Connective Example

Brian's company has conducted a study on whether it should do business process outsourcing (BPO) of its finance department. Rumors are starting to run rampant that many people's jobs will be outsourced. Brian convinces upper management that it is time to let employees know what is going on even though the company hasn't quite made the final decision.

Brian volunteers to create a communication presentation with a team to let employees know where things stand. He ensures that the presentation to the finance employees will cover employee concerns as well as management's perspective. Brian also ensures that the meeting allows enough time for employees to ask questions. In addition, his communication team makes packets for finance employees and employees in other departments who are supported by the finance group so that all stakeholders hear consistent and coordinated communications.

As a result of Brian's efforts, the staff members feel like they are a part of the process rather than objects of a business decision. They are informed and able to participate in some of the detailed BPO decisions. Even with the uncertainty surrounding some people's jobs, attrition does not increase during this period.

ANALYSIS: Brian appropriately makes sure that the communication presentation covers both management and employee perspectives. He also structures the agenda so that those presenting have enough time to adequately explain what is going on with the BPO initiative and that employees also have enough time to express their comments and concerns. Also, the team coordinates communications appropriately to all BPO initiative stakeholders. Brian's connective communication methods enable staff members to be informed about and prepared for the BPO decision.

Benefits of Using Connective Behaviors

Using connective behaviors has numerous benefits, particularly if you develop a preference for them. Connective behaviors positively impact your workgroup's gruntledness and success. In addition, if you are in upper management and have adopted connective behaviors as part of the organizational culture, you will positively impact your organization's success and overall employee morale.

Gruntledness Impacts from a Leader Perspective

Workgroup members are much more content and satisfied working for a leader with a preference for connective behaviors than they are working for a leader with a preference for authoritarian or laissez-faire behaviors. Your workgroup is more gruntled when your employees can work collaboratively with you in setting and implementing direction.

Your employees can also become energized when you give them a compelling vision of the future. Setting measurable objectives to show employees how they fit into the vision can also improve employee morale. Measurable objectives provide employees with positive feedback on how they are progressing towards the vision or non-judgmental negative feedback that allows them to refocus and improve their activities by themselves. Coaching employees and respectfully working with them to improve in areas help your employees' self-worth and improves their gruntledness.

Also, better communication often leads to increased employee morale. Well-coordinated communications take into consideration your perspective and your employees' perspective, ensuring that employees are heard.

Most importantly, connective behaviors encourage employees to use interdependent behaviors. Employees tend to be much happier when they have a chance to use more interdependent behaviors.

Success Impacts from a Leader Perspective

The best business results come from workgroups led by leaders with a preference for connective behaviors. These workgroups accomplish more and have fewer problems than other workgroups.

Both employees and the organization benefit when you define direction collaboratively with your workgroup. Any strategies that you allow employees to refine will be more on target to deliver business results and easier for employees to accept than strategies you didn't involve them in at all. The success rate of business strategies improves when you provide a compelling reason for accomplishing something, provide measurable goals and objectives to track progress, celebrate successes, and recognize/reward teamwork.

You will greatly enhance workgroup performance when you mentor employees on how to perform work more effectively and coach them through changes necessary to implement business strategies. Most work situations are improved when the workgroup members are free to work together with you and as a team.

When your employees are as empowered as you to communicate their thoughts and feelings, they can bring differing perspectives forward, which can benefit problem solving and decision making. When communications are coordinated throughout the entire organization, everyone hears needed information, which reduces mistakes.

Since connective behaviors also encourage employees to use interdependent behaviors, your chances for success will be further increased. Interdependent behaviors help a workgroup be more successful and are particularly important during the implementation of business strategy initiatives.

Gruntledness Impacts from an Upper-Management Perspective

If your leaders primarily prefer connective behaviors, your employees will perceive your organization as an employer of choice, so you'll be in a better position to recruit the best talent and to retain your best employees. Your turnover rates will be much lower, thus decreasing costs for temporary staffing, recruitment, training, and retention.

While challenging times for a business might impact employee morale somewhat, it won't take a nosedive. Connective behaviors create a feeling of "we are in this together," which leads to deeper employee commitment. The gruntledness that comes with connective behaviors enlists the hearts and minds of employees under many different circumstances and isn't as fragile as the gruntledness associated with laissez-faire behaviors.

Success Impacts from an Upper-Management Perspective

When your leadership team adopts connective behavior preferences, your workgroups have a better chance of supporting business initiatives and producing the required business results. Since leaders with connective behaviors provide direction collaboratively with their team, motivate with a compelling vision of the future, provide measurable objectives, and communicate from a management and employee perspective, employees are more engaged in their work. Business strategies under a leader with connective behavior preferences usually complete implementation activities on time and within budget. These leaders know how to enlist the help of the employees who will do whatever it takes to get the job done.

Leaders using connective behaviors are more prone to succeed at achieving business strategy results because they're more likely to get employees to change behaviors to support business objectives. The leader is there to provide the support that employees need to make these changes.

Connective behaviors facilitate your employees' understanding of what your organization is trying to achieve. Employees can then determine whether their decisions support or hinder business objectives without guidance. Employees will make the right decision most of the time because they understand how things fit together.

Connective behaviors also create an environment that is conducive to obtaining greater knowledge. Employees and workgroups are encouraged to share knowledge so their knowledge increases, which leads to business success.

In addition, many employees naturally fear the unknown, even if they think it might lead to success. They feel it's easier to stay safe in their comfort zones and live with disappointment rather than risk the unknown. Connective behaviors can help employees address fears that hinder them from taking risks necessary for creativity and innovation.

Rethinking Behavior Preferences

Connective behaviors are one of three factors that will improve gruntledness for you and your coworkers and also increase the success of business strategies. The first two factors, employee behaviors and leadership behaviors, form the organizational culture for your organization. The next chapter will discuss organizational culture in more detail. Part 4 will examine the third factor, business systems.

15

Different Forms of Organizational Culture

"I worked for a small start-up company that prided itself in being 'cool.' We would have 'Beer Friday' in the office in the afternoon, paid lunches for company-wide meetings, and unofficial happy hours at the local bar. Our manager trusted us to do our jobs—and rightfully so—we worked hard, put out great products, and met our deadlines. Then we got a major contract and all hell broke loose. Management started to micromanage us. We got yelled at every other day for not meeting new, impossible deadlines and for having bad attitudes. Most of us stopped participating in 'Beer Friday' because we no longer had time for it. Management stopped the company-wide luncheons for the same reason: too busy. Happy hours turned into gripe sessions, and if management dared show up, they were given the cold shoulder. But was there any wonder? The culture went from 'easy going' to 'police state' overnight."

Disgruntled Employee
Blog Post

A cause-and-effect of behaviors exists between leaders and their employees. For example, if a leader has a preference for authoritarian behaviors, then employees may develop a preference for passive behaviors. If the leader prefers laissez-faire behaviors, then employees may develop a preference for independent behaviors. If the leader prefers connective behaviors, then employees may develop a preference for interdependent behaviors. The converse is also true. If employees have a preference for passive behaviors, then the leader may develop a preference for authoritarian behaviors, and so on.

These employee and leadership behaviors encourage certain dynamics that, over time, become the *organizational culture* at a workgroup level (*micro level*). When similar dynamics occur between leaders and their employees for multiple workgroups, it forms a certain organizational culture at an organizational level (*macro level*). Often, top management sets the pace for macro-level organizational cultures. It's possible for an organization to have multiple cultures, depending on how large the organization is and on how much autonomy each workgroup has. The following lists three common organizational cultures:

- Passive behaviors and authoritarian behaviors
- Independent behaviors and laissez-faire behaviors
- Interdependent behaviors and connective behaviors

Your organizational culture probably has not been described in this manner before. Yet, these are the bases of human interaction. People either interact dominantly or passively with each other, do not interact much at all, or interact more as equals. When these types of interactions happen on a regular basis between leaders and their workgroup members, then a *passive/authoritarian, independent/laissez-faire,* or *interdependent/connective* organizational culture will form.

Complementary and Noncomplementary Cultures

There are three *complementary organizational cultures:* passive/authoritarian, independent/laissez-faire, and interdependent/connective. With these three types of organizational cultures, there is less conflict between leadership behaviors and employee behaviors; each is behaving in a way that the other expects. However, other variations can occur. Any combination of employee behavior patterns can be combined with any combination of leadership behavior patterns. Complementary organizational cultures work better than *noncomplementary organizational cultures* such as independent/authoritarian or passive/laissez-faire. Noncomplementary organizational cultures cause more frustration for the employees and leaders since their behavior preferences are incompatible with each other.

Interactions Between Employees and Leaders

Employee and leaders interact at work in many ways. They hold meetings either in person, by teleconferences, or on the Internet. They interact through phone calls, e-mail, instant messaging, and text messaging. However, no matter the method, how a leader interacts with employees has a huge impact on how employees behave.

Macro-level organizational cultures tend to form based on the top leader's behavior preference. For example, top leaders with a preference for authoritarian behaviors often hire others with a preference for dominant or authoritarian behaviors. Even leaders without a preference for authoritarian behaviors will tend to use authoritarian behaviors more if that's how their manager interacts with them. Leaders at all levels of the organization tend to imitate how top leaders interact with employees. If their immediate manager has a certain behavior preference, they often will follow suit whether it be with authoritarian, laissez-faire, or connective behaviors.

Conversely, how employees interact with their leaders impacts how leaders behave. If employees don't challenge inappropriate leadership behaviors, then leaders will continue to behave according to their preferences. If employees challenge leadership behaviors, then leaders have a choice to make. They can continue to behave inappropriately according to their behavior preference or they can change their behavior. Over time, these challenges can change the employee/leader dynamic. Sometimes leaders learn from these challenges, particularly if multiple employees confront inappropriate leadership behaviors. As a result, the leader may start to prefer different leadership behaviors, which in turn, can change the culture of the workgroup. However, if leaders come down hard on employees who challenge them, then most likely, other employees will chose passive behaviors to avoid their leaders' wrath, which then lessens the chance of a change in leadership behavior.

The symbol for the Chinese concept of yin and yang succinctly illustrates such interactions—intertwined with and complementary to each other. Figure 15.1 graphically represents common interactions and organizational cultures.

Figure 15.1: Interrelatedness of employee and leadership behavior patterns

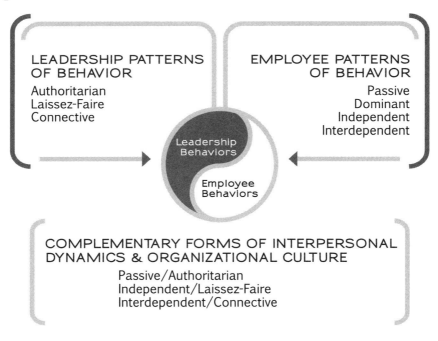

Passive and Authoritarian Organizational Culture

Authoritarian behaviors can encourage passive behaviors. Leaders with a preference for authoritarian behaviors provide direction requesting minimal feedback from the team, motivate employees through negative consequences, point out employees' weaknesses, and limit communications from employees. As a result, employees tend to defer decisions to the leader, only do as the leader says, avoid conflict with the leader, and become defensive when problems arise. Conversely, when employees develop a preference for passive behaviors, leaders may use authoritarian behaviors even it's not their preference.

Organizational Culture—Passive/Authoritarian Example

Jim just replaced a manager who gave employees a lot of freedom to decide how to accomplish their work. Jim thinks that this new assignment will be a good fit for him since he also likes to give employees a lot of freedom. When Jim finds out that the workgroup's client feels that the quality of their work could be a lot higher, Jim talks to the workgroup. He discovers that most of the employees are fairly passive in completing work, doing the bare minimum to get by. The workgroup tells Jim that the client complains a lot and feels that the complaints aren't really justified.

Jim realizes that his normal approach will not work with his new workgroup if he is to meet client expectations. He therefore becomes more authoritative in giving directions and following up with employees. He also finds it effective to point out negative consequences to several employees for not doing what he has directed since they tend to ignore his direction. He finds himself communicating more from a position of authority than what he is comfortable with since it appears to be more effective in getting his workgroup members to produce higher quality work products.

ANALYSIS: Jim prefers to use laissez-faire behaviors with employees. But when he realizes the collective behavior preference of his new workgroup is passive, he switches from using his preferred laissez-faire behaviors to using more authoritarian behaviors.

The members of Jim's workgroup don't believe that they need to be responsible for meeting the client's expectations. They believe that it's okay to discount the client's complaints about the quality of their work.

Jim does not share in these beliefs. He believes that the client's complaints are founded and that his workgroup members should be responsible for producing higher quality products. He believes that the collective behaviors of his workgroup members are inappropriate and works to change them using authoritarian behaviors. This has created a passive/authoritarian culture, which is more effective than a passive/laissez-faire culture in Jim's workgroup.

Independent and Laissez-Faire Organizational Culture

Laissez-faire behaviors can encourage independent behaviors. A leader with a preference for laissez-faire behaviors provides minimal direction, motivates employees through empowerment, allows employees to improve on their own, and allows free-flowing communications within the team. Workgroup members usually respond by making their own decisions, completing tasks, resolving problems as they see fit, and feeling empowered to confront conflict on their own. Conversely, when employees develop a preference for independent behaviors, leaders may feel comfortable or obligated to use laissez-faire behaviors.

Organizational Culture—Independent/Laissez-Faire Example

Samuel's manager tells him that while the quality of the invoices that his workgroup produces has been acceptable in the past, the new company-wide quality program requires his workgroup to do even better. During his next staff meeting, Samuel explains the situation to his workgroup members and lets them know that each needs to reduce the amount of errors in the invoices that they produce. Samuel tells them that he doesn't care how they go about reducing errors, as long as they figure it out soon. The workgroup members figure out on their own the best way to improve the quality on the invoices that they produce.

ANALYSIS: Samuel uses laissez-faire behavior by providing his workgroup members with minimal direction and expecting them to respond with an independent behavior: to complete the task on their own with little information. The workgroup responds as Samuel expects with independent behavior. Samuel's leadership behavior is often based on his belief that employees provide value on their own. This belief is based on Samuel's own preference for independent employee behaviors and the fact that most of his workgroup members do what is necessary to get the job done.

Most of the employees within Samuel's workgroup believe that they provide value on their own, which is complementary to Samuel's belief. Most of them also prefer to work alone. The complementary beliefs and work styles between Samuel and most of his workgroup members have led to an independent/laissez-faire culture for the workgroup.

Interdependent and Connective Organizational Culture

Connective behaviors can encourage interdependent behaviors. Leaders with a preference for connective behaviors provide direction collaboratively with the team, recognize team accomplishments, coach and mentor employees, and talk and listen equally to the team. As a result, employees tend to make joint decisions with leaders, be jointly responsible for completing tasks, and work cooperatively with leaders. Conversely, when employees develop a preference for interdependent behaviors, their leaders feel free to use connective behaviors.

Organizational Culture—Interdependent/Connective Example

Donna just reviewed a report from a new sales application that shows the revenue figures for most of her sales team to be much lower than normal. Donna calls her sales team together and presents the problem to them. During the discussion, Donna finds out that most of her sales staff thinks the new sales application is cumbersome so they avoid adding in all of their sales transactions. Donna asks her team what they recommend should be done about the situation. One workgroup member says that he found some shortcuts in the system to make entering sales data easier and that he would be glad to show them to the others. Another workgroup member proposes that they submit some suggested improvements to the IT department to further streamline the process of adding sales data. The group then spends a half hour brainstorming suggested improvements for the IT department.

ANALYSIS: Donna initiates an interaction with her workgroup in a connective manner by asking her workgroup members what is behind the problem and how they would suggest solving it. Her workgroup members respond with interdependent behavior by collaborating with Donna on how to solve the problem.

Donna feels that she provides equal value to her workgroup members. Donna also believes that she is jointly responsible with her workgroup for meeting business objectives. She also feels both she and those who work with her are entitled to be treated with respect during all interactions. Due to these beliefs, most of the interactions that Donna has with her workgroup are initiated with a connective behavior.

The members of Donna's workgroup also believe that they provide as much value as Donna. Most of them recognize their own particular contribution to the workgroup's success. Due to these beliefs, Donna's workgroup members usually respond interdependently. This has created an interdependent/connective culture within Donna's workgroup.

Rethinking Organizational Culture Dynamics

All complementary combinations of organizational culture are appropriate in certain situations. For example, a crisis situation may call for a passive/authoritarian culture for a period of time until the crisis passes. However, usually passive/authoritarian and independent/laissez-faire organizational cultures negatively impact organizational success and employee morale, or both. At the very least, business success and employee morale will not be as high as they could be with these two organizational cultures.

Interdependent/connective organizational cultures tend to have a positive impact on success and employee morale in most situations. For example, many organizations think a passive/authoritarian culture is best for cost-cutting initiatives because they think cost-cutting decisions should be made by leaders. But this backfires because employees in a passive/authoritarian culture will not be privy to the big picture, so they may unintentionally make a decision that goes against management's intention for cutting costs. Furthermore, when employees do not understand the reason behind cost-cuts, this can negatively impact employee morale. An interdependent/connective culture is a better choice for cost-cutting initiatives because it helps to ensure that everyone understands what needs to be done and why, which will prevent daily decisions from unintentionally undermining cost-cutting objectives and won't negatively impact morale.

Interdependent/connective cultures also support revenue and profit growth initiatives since teamwork creates synergy. Workgroups that work together collaboratively typically have higher employee morale. Working with upper management, employees can focus their attention on revenue growth opportunities and ensure they are implemented profitably. In independent/laissez-faire cultures however, the organization is usually not as successful in growing the business profitably because employees do not receive the guidance from upper management that they need to capture new business.

To improve business performance and employee morale in an organizational culture, you must begin with the dynamics at the micro level—between the leader and workgroup members. Overall organizational success and being recognized as a great place to work start at the workgroup level. Improving the organizational culture within each workgroup positively impacts business success and employee gruntledness for the whole organization. Additionally, business systems characteristics can play a role with organizational culture dynamics, particularly at the macro level. Part 4 will examine in more detail how certain business system characteristics impact organizational culture.

16

Why Leadership Behaviors Matter

"I transferred into a department that 'needed help' on several projects. After about the first week, it became apparent why they needed help. The Director of the group was a young woman that wanted to become the next CEO in the worst way. She would do anything to make herself look good, including taking credit for work produced by her team. She would always volunteer her group to take on additional work and then scream at us in a team meeting that 'heads would roll' and we'd be fired if we didn't complete the task/project on time. When five out of the seven team members went to HR complaining of intimidation and harassment, HR just pooh-poohed the issue and did nothing. After about seven months, productivity and morale sank pretty low, she was transferred to another department. Three weeks later four of the seven of us were let go from the company. I had 29 years and 8 months with the company and that year was the only year I received a 'not meeting standards' review in my whole career."

Disgruntled Employee
Blog Post

The authors of *The Cynical Americans: Living and Working in an Age of Discontent and Disillusion* state that 43% of American workers are cynics—that is, they don't trust management and believe their companies will take advantage of them.[57] Whether you're a workgroup leader or in upper management, how far do you think you can go in trying to achieve your organization's business strategies with cynical employees?

According to the book, employees become cynical after leaders treat them unfairly. However, the book explains that employees don't want to be cynical. They would rather help their companies succeed; they want to make a difference and want to support what they help create. The way to defeat cynicism is to enlist the employees' hearts and minds in the business. Using connective behaviors more frequently will support that outcome.

The Impact of Leadership Behaviors

In twenty-first-century businesses, leaders do more than just set the agenda of objectives to achieve. Leaders' behaviors are instrumental in motivating employees and even more importantly, instrumental in creating an environment that has a capacity for ongoing change that leads to success. Whether leaders demonstrate the four leadership activities appropriately or inappropriately impacts the success of a business and the happiness of employees. A Fast Company article "The CEO's New Clothes" reported that "Boards are increasingly looking for CEOs who can demonstrate superb people skills in dealing with employees" and that "farsighted, tolerant, humane and practical CEOs" returned "758% over 10 years, versus 128% for the S&P 500."[58]

Inappropriate leadership behaviors have a greater impact on company revenues and profitability than an individual employee's behavior. The higher up a leader is in the organization, the greater number of employees the leader influences. A first-level leader only influences the behavior of the employees who directly report to the leader. At the top of the ladder, the CEO's leadership behavior can influence the behaviors of every employee within the organization.

Leadership behaviors are critical to employee morale. The relationship between an employee and a leader often makes the difference between a gruntled employee and a disgruntled employee. This relationship also has the power to either enhance employees' passive, dominant, and independent behaviors or encourage employees' interdependent behaviors. It is the organizational culture, this leader-employee interaction, that determines business success.

Connective behaviors can improve an organization's business results and increase employee gruntledness more often than the other two forms of leadership behaviors. Using connective behaviors will increase your own gruntledness and productivity, positively impact the morale of your workgroup, and positively impact your organization's success.

Why There Is a Lack of Connective Behavior Preferences in the Workplace

I first learned about connective leadership ten years ago when I read an article about it.[59] Since then, I still haven't seen much that integrates this type of leadership behavior into the business world. Surprisingly, connective behaviors have not yet become common knowledge in the business world. Most management and leadership discussions still promote authoritarian and laissez-faire behaviors or variations on them.

The reason business-improvement efforts don't work as well in the business world as they could is directly related to the lack of connective behaviors. Leaders could implement business strategies much more successfully with connective behaviors. Looking at the benefits of such behaviors, it is clear that they enable business success and improve employee gruntledness. So why don't we have more examples of connective behaviors in the workplace?

One reason lies in leadership's tendency to stick to a certain behavior pattern, typically the one that's already in place and used by the top leader. So if the top leader prefers an authoritarian or laissez-faire pattern of behavior (which is often the case), the other leaders may imitate how the top leader interacts with employees.

Also, it could be that the majority of employees demonstrate a particular employee behavioral pattern. In response to the pattern, the leadership team may resort to a complementary leadership behavior pattern to get the job done. For example, if employees prefer passive behaviors, leaders may resort to authoritarian behaviors to get business results even though they do not have a preference for authoritarian behaviors.

Another explanation may be that the business system in place promotes a particular leadership behavior pattern. For example, certain business systems will encourage employees to use independent behaviors and leaders to use laissez-faire behaviors. Part 4 will discuss how business system characteristics influence employee and leadership behavior patterns.

Also, sometimes promotions up in the management ranks are based more on individual performance than the performance of a leader's workgroup. Leaders with a preference for connective behaviors don't stand out as individuals. Those with a preference for dominant behaviors do, so they tend to get promoted more often.

Businesses seem to be content with bi-modal leadership behaviors. In other words, when upper management wants business results, they bring in a leader with authoritarian preferences who will get the job done at all costs, even if it means upsetting employees in the process. When employee morale gets too bad, they bring in HR to smooth things over, or in drastic situations, replace the leader with someone with laissez-faire preferences who will bring stability back to the workgroup. Unfortunately, most businesses just don't realize that there is a third choice—connective behavior. Part 5 will discuss methods for moving towards a more interdependent/connective organizational culture.

Part 4

How Business System Characteristics Influence Business Results and Employee Morale

"A system is a network of interdependent components that work together to try to accomplish the aim of the system. A system must have an aim. Without the aim, there is no system."

W. Edwards Deming (1900–1993)
American statistician, professor, author, and consultant

17

Business Systems Impact Gruntledness and Business Success

"When I worked in my first retirement job, I thought I had it made. I was in an environment (or so I thought) where I would not only be comfortable, but I would have fun. What I soon discovered was there seemed to be no system in place. It became apparent that the owners knew how they wanted things to flow and could do it without any kind of formalized system. My problem was that since I didn't know what was in their minds, it didn't make sense to me. When service tickets came in, there was no real system in place to track the progress and ultimate completion. If something went awry, I would be asked what happened, and didn't have any explanation for them because I honestly didn't know what had happened. I decided to create a system of my own (with final approval of the service manager and the owners, of course), but that didn't entirely alleviate the problems because the service manager didn't always follow through with my 'system' and the owners didn't seem to hold him accountable for his part."

Disgruntled Employee
Blog Post

ike employee and leadership behaviors, a business system influences gruntledness and business success. A business system is composed of four components: organizational framework (used to organize employees into workgroups), process (used to produce goods and services), management system (used to meet business objectives), and information technology or IT (used to automate processes and disseminate information). A business system ensures that employees and leaders follow the organization's business rules and industry regulations, and it heavily influences employees to behave in certain ways with each other, customers, vendors, and other external entities.

Organizations of all sizes typically describe the business system as "the way we do things here." It is put in place to achieve the organization's purpose. Business systems attempt to reduce risk to an organization and ensure a proper return on business investments. Upper management sets up business systems so they can run their organization as effectively and efficiently as possible. Despite upper management's efforts to make a successful organization, they tend to overlook the impact their decisions regarding business system components have on employee and leadership behaviors and culture. But upper management can design business systems to support an organizational culture that promotes employee gruntledness and business success simultaneously.

Interconnectivity Between Employee Behaviors, Leadership Behaviors, and Business Systems

The three gruntledness and success factors—employee behaviors, leadership behaviors, and the business system—interconnect with and rely on one another in the following ways:

- Employee behaviors influence leadership behaviors, and leadership behaviors influence employee behaviors; the dynamic between employees and leaders form the organizational culture
- The business system influences organizational culture; the organizational culture can influence how upper management defines the business system

Many companies suffer because they fail to look at all the causal factors for business and employee morale problems. Employee behaviors, leadership behaviors, and the business system are all possible causal factors, each needing consideration. Employees and leaders must be able to work together to accomplish the organization's aims within a business system that efficiently and effectively supports their efforts. So achieving business goals requires understanding the interdependencies between employee behaviors, leadership behaviors, and the business system, and ensuring these three causal factors are aligned.

Some business strategies address only a part of a business system and ignore the behaviors that make up the organizational culture. For example, reorganizations often focus only on the organizational framework. Moving managers around within the organization and reassembling employees into different workgroups have limited effectiveness and often do not bring about needed behavior changes. If passive employee behaviors and laissez-faire behaviors (that is, a passive/laissez-faire culture) are causal factors for business problems, then reorganizing the same people into different workgroups and management positions won't address the root cause of the problem. Implementing a business initiative that changes management systems, processes, and information technology in addition to the organizational framework has a greater chance of meeting desired business objectives; however, the business system components also need to be aligned to an appropriate organizational culture.

Behaviors are typically the most ignored factor and yet the most important because they have great impact on business results and employee gruntledness. Ignoring behavioral impact does not provide the most effective business system for the organization and can cause operational performance problems and disgruntledness.

Figure 17.1 shows the relationship between employee and leadership behaviors and the four business system components.

Figure 17.1: Interconnectivity between behaviors and the business system components

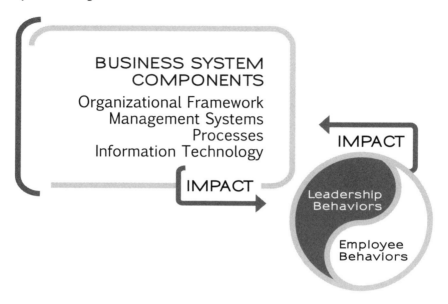

Behavior and Characteristics of Business System Components

Business systems are designed to influence how employees and leaders behave. Organizational frameworks define the roles and responsibilities of employees, leaders, and workgroups, and have a major effect on how employees behave. Management systems attempt to get employees to behave in a certain way to meet business goals and objectives. Processes specify how employees and leaders should behave to accomplish work tasks. IT provides tools for employees to accomplish their work, typically forcing employees to accomplish work in one particular way, which encourages employees and leaders to behave in a certain way.

The four business system components are defined and broken down into subcomponents:

1. **Organizational Framework.** Arranges employees into workgroups and organizes the workgroups within an organization.
   - Roles and Responsibilities – define duties for employees by job function
   - Organizational Structure – organizes multiple workgroups to work together

2. **Management Systems.** Provide the means for accomplishing an organization's business objectives.
   - Management Plans – define an approach to meet goals and objectives
   - Management Reviews – compare business results to business objectives and refines management plans accordingly

3. **Processes.** Define the way that an organization will conduct its business in producing goods and services.
   - Workflow – moves work between those involved in process activities
   - Enforcement – enforces the organization's processes and procedures

4. **Information Technology.** Automates many processes and provides data throughout the organization.
   - Data Architecture – gives employees the information needed to perform their duties
   - Technology – provides employees with the tools needed to perform their duties

Each business system component and subcomponent can have dependent, independent, or interdependent characteristics. For example, if an organization limits employees' access to technology, this is a dependent characteristic for the Information Technology component. While it is recognized that business systems are an attempt to get employees to behave in certain ways, it is not widely recognized that certain business system characteristics encourage different types of employee and leadership behaviors, which lead to different kinds of organizational cultures. For example, certain types of business system characteristics such as limited roles and responsibilities can encourage a passive/authoritarian organizational culture while other charac-teristics such as unclear roles and responsibilities can encourage an indepen-dent/laissez-faire organizational culture.

The Three Types of Business System Characteristics

As Peter Senge wrote, if people from different backgrounds behave simi-larly, the reason must lie in how the system is set up.[60] When you apply Senge's principle to an organization, a relationship between certain types of business system characteristics and organizational culture is evident, as shown in the following list:

- **Dependent Business System Characteristics.** These characteristics promote passive behaviors in employees and encourage leaders to use authoritarian behaviors, resulting in a passive/authoritarian organiza-tional culture.
- **Independent Business System Characteristics.** These characteristics tend to encourage employees to act independently from their leader and encourage the leader to use laissez-faire behaviors, resulting in an independent/laissez-faire organizational culture.
- **Interdependent Business System Characteristics.** These character-istics encourage employees to work interdependently with each other and their leaders and encourage leaders to use more connective behav-iors, resulting in an interdependent/connective organizational culture.

Figure 17.2 shows the interconnectedness between business system characteristics and organizational culture.

Figure 17.2: Interconnectedness between business system characteristics and organizational culture

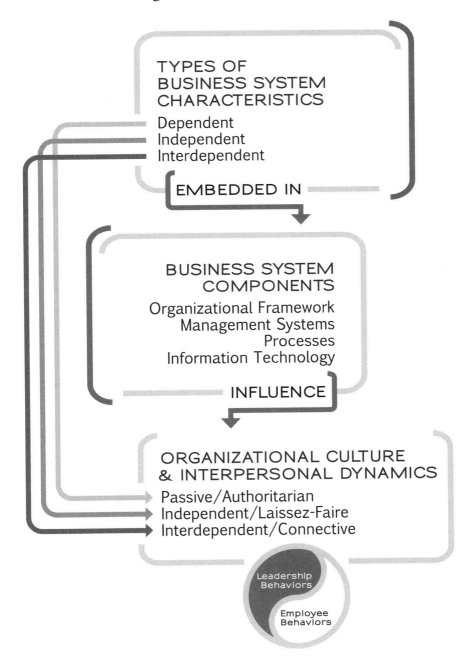

To put this all together, Figure 17.3 compares the dependent, independent, and interdependent characteristics for each business system component.

Figure 17.3: Business System Characteristics Matrix

BUSINESS SYSTEM COMPONENTS	DEPENDENT CHARACTERISTICS	INDEPENDENT CHARACTERISTICS	INTERDEPENDENT CHARACTERISTICS
Organizational Framework			
Roles & Responsibilities	Limited	Unclear	Helpful
Organizational Structure	Cumbersome	Not clearly defined	Supportive
Management Systems			
Management Plans	Top-down	Decentralized	Aligned
Management Reviews	Upper management only	Decentralized	Aligned
Processes			
Workflow	Bureaucratic	Flexible	Supportive
Enforcement	Strictly enforced	Unenforced	Institutionalized
Information Technology			
Data Architecture	Controlled data	Decentralized data	Shared data
Technology	Limited access	Uncontrolled access	Planned access

Each characteristic alone (listed in the second, third, and fourth columns) will not necessarily encourage a certain organizational culture. But the more characteristics a business system has from either the dependent, independent, or interdependent column, the more likely that set of characteristics will encourage the corresponding organizational culture. Each characteristic will be defined in the next three chapters.

Figure 17.3 is just a sample of the business system characteristics that influence organizational culture. Other characteristics can influence culture as well. Also note that some business systems suffer from schizophrenia; they have no common thread and contain multiple dependent, independent, and interdependent business system characteristics.

How Business System Characteristics Influence Organizational Culture

Dependent business system characteristics encourage employees to be more dependent on their leaders for direction. This leads to employees using more passive behaviors. Dependent business system characteristics also encourage leaders to use more authoritarian behaviors. Dependent business system characteristics encourage a passive/authoritarian organizational culture.

Independent business system characteristics encourage employees to act more independently and to rely less on their leaders. This leads to employees using more independent behaviors. Independent business system characteristics also encourage leaders to use more laissez-faire behaviors. Independent business system characteristics encourage an independent/laissez-faire organizational culture.

Interdependent business system characteristics encourage employees to work more collaboratively with their leaders and each other. This leads to employees using more interdependent behaviors. Interdependent business system characteristics also encourage leaders to use more connective behaviors. Interdependent business system characteristics encourage an interdependent/connective organizational culture.

Understanding the effect that certain business system characteristics have on organizational culture can help organizations design an effective business system. The three forms of business system characteristics have an exponential effect on an organization's culture. In fact, they cement certain behaviors into the organization, thereby forcing employees and leaders to behave more in line with the behaviors promoted by the business system characteristics, even when those behaviors are not the individuals' personal behavior preference.

How Organizational Culture Influences Business System Characteristics

In certain situations, business system characteristics can depend on organizational culture. A specific organizational culture (passive/authoritarian, independent/laissez-faire, or interdependent/connective) can influence whether the business system has more dependent, independent, or interdependent characteristics. For example, when an established workgroup gets moved to a new company (as happens in acquisitions or outsourcing) the culture of that particular workgroup can change business system characteristics of the company. So in this scenario, if the infused workgroup had an independent/laissez-faire organizational culture at their old company, they may ignore bureaucratic workflow and continue to use the more flexible processes that they used before acquisition or outsourcing. Because of the infused workgroups' decision, the business system for this workgroup now contains an independent process characteristic even though it was an informal decision.

Employees' behavior preferences from a former organizational culture can also inspire leaders to change business system characteristics. Here's what may happen in an acquisition situation:

- If new employees prefer passive behaviors and do not meet business objectives because leadership prefers laissez-faire behaviors, upper management will probably add more dependent characteristics into the business system to help out the employees
- If new employees prefer independent behaviors and meet business objectives with little direction from leadership, upper management may add more independent characteristics into the business system to give the employees more freedom to do their jobs
- If new employees prefer interdependent behaviors and exceed business objectives through collaborating with their leaders, upper management may add interdependent characteristics into the business system to encourage more of the same behaviors

The next three chapters describe dependent, independent, and interdependent business system characteristics. Each characteristic encourages a certain organizational culture, which is either appropriate or inappropriate for the organization. Each chapter describes how business system characteristics promote an organizational culture and impact business success and employee gruntledness.

18

How Dependent Business Systems Impact Gruntledness and Business Success

"[Just after] 9-11, I received a forwarded e-mail from one of the senior vice presidents. The VP was looking for qualified people to assist in the recovery of a major New York bank. According to the e-mail, the president of the company had given his personal assurances that his company would fully assist in the recovery of the bank. The VP then went on to say that this was to be a high-priority ramp-up to get the technical people involved ASAP. Unfortunately, there were seven levels of management forwarding this letter to their direct reports. Each stop took a few days before being forwarded on. I finally received the e-mail during the second week of October. Banks need to be recovered in hours, not weeks."

Disgruntled Employee
Blog Post

The collective behavior preferences of employees can encourage upper management to add new characteristics or change the existing characteristics of their business system. A workgroup may regularly exhibit inappropriate passive behaviors, negatively impacting business results. To turn things around, upper management may establish some dependent business system characteristics to limit the risk associated with employees' decisions and actions.

That said, upper management's behavior preferences trump the collective behavior of employees most of the time. One leader with a strong preference for authoritarian behaviors will do more to define the workgroup's culture than employee behavior. It's only when the collective employee behavior preferences are the same and very strong that they influence the workgroup culture more than the leader.

Upper management's behavior preferences of dominant and authoritarian behaviors can also lead to implementing dependent characteristics into business systems. If upper management believes that leaders provide more value than employees, employees are not as responsible as leaders, and leaders are more entitled than employees, the business system will probably contain dependent characteristics.

An organization may also implement dependent characteristics into their business system without realizing that it encourages a passive/authoritarian organizational culture. Dependent business system characteristics include the following:

- **Organizational Framework.** Limited employee roles and responsibilities and cumbersome organizational structures.
- **Management Systems.** Top-down management plans and upper management-only reviews.
- **Processes.** Bureaucratic workflow and strictly enforced processes.
- **Information Technology.** Controlled data and limited employee access to technology.

The next sections illustrate the impact of each of these dependent business system characteristics and their impact on organizational culture.

Dependent Organizational Framework Characteristics

Two characteristics of an organizational framework promote a passive/authoritarian organizational culture: limited employee roles and responsibilities and cumbersome organizational structures.

Most employees have a job description that defines the responsibilities for the role that they need to fulfill within their workgroup. Some organizations limit the responsibilities their workgroup members have in order to ensure that management's authority isn't undermined. More responsibility is given to the manager for decision making, problem resolution, and approval of work products. Limited employee roles and responsibilities require employees to check in with their manager before making decisions and doing certain tasks; employees are not encouraged to do these activities on their own.

Some organizations, particularly large corporations have cumbersome organizational structures (such as hierarchal or complex matrix structures), which means they are difficult to work with. Getting anything done in cumbersome organizations is a challenge. Often such organizations require employees to obtain approvals, which can drag tasks out for incredibly long periods of time. The expectation of a hierarchical organization is that employees get direction and approval from upper levels of the organization. The lowest level of a hierarchical organization is seen as subservient to all the management levels above it. In a complex matrix organization, an employee may be grouped in with others with similar skills under the guidance of an administrative manager and then assigned to work on different projects under the guidance of another manager. Complex matrix organizations can be cumbersome if employees need to get approval from two managers before completing a task.

Limited employee roles and responsibilities encourage a passive/authoritarian culture by providing more responsibility to managers than employees. As a result, employees take a passive role with many activities, and managers take an authoritarian role in an attempt to ensure that decisions, problems, and tasks are done correctly.

Cumbersome organizations encourage a passive/authoritarian culture because employees are encouraged to get management approvals rather than take the initiative to decide how to proceed on their own. They may even take less responsibility in getting things done correctly and more responsibility in doing what it takes to get approvals.

Organizational Framework—Dependent Example

Richard works in the IT department for a financial services company. He hears at his boss's weekly staff meeting that the chief information officer (CIO) is going to standardize a particular kind of server. While Richard is an authority on servers, purchasing servers is not included in his job description. Richard has conducted tests on numerous servers from multiple vendors and knows that, while this particular server is cost-efficient, it has performance issues with high transaction volumes.

Richard knows from past experience that if he wants to raise an issue to the CIO, he must go through a chain of command to reach him. He must first convince his boss that this is the wrong decision. His boss then has to discuss it with the director who, in turn, must talk to the vice president. If the vice president is convinced that the server decision is incorrect, he then will bring it to the CIO's attention. Richard decides that this is a futile effort, and due to past failings, not worth trying to convince everyone in the management chain between him and the CIO that the decision should be reversed.

ANALYSIS: This cumbersome, hierarchical organization encourages Richard to use passive behaviors. Since he feels it would be a waste of his time to convince his manager he decides not to act. Richard, as the lowest-level employee in the hierarchy, has the least amount of authority and decision rights and is encouraged to defer decisions to those at higher levels even though he is an authority on servers and his decision would be a better choice for the company.

Dependent Management Systems Characteristics

Two characteristics of an organization's management systems promote a passive/authoritarian organizational culture: top-down management plans and upper management-only reviews.

In an organization using top-down management plans, upper management defines business strategies and objectives at the highest level of the organization and rolls them down throughout the organization. Top-down management plans try to ensure that every workgroup within the organization is working on the goals and objectives that higher-level management wants them to work on.

Some organizations conduct reviews of business results only at higher levels of the organization. Upper management reviews a summary of the overall results and compares them against planned objectives. However, when overall results look bad, upper management cannot see which workgroups are contributing to the problem because individual workgroup results are not available. Since only upper management has access to the business results, only they can determine improvement actions.

Top-down management plans encourage a passive/authoritarian culture because when upper management alone defines business strategies and objectives without feedback, employees are likely to feel less responsible and less committed to getting work done. Being less responsible, employees may do only what is necessary to meet the objective and nothing more. Also, if employees have any questions about the management plan, they must defer it to their manager who may need to escalate it to his/her manager until they get an answer, which is a passive way of completing tasks. This type of management system attempts to ensure that the day-to-day decisions that employees make, the tasks that they work on, and the way they resolve problems are in accordance with upper management thinking and the overall management plan for the organization.

Only conducting upper management reviews of business results encourages a passive/authoritarian culture. Individual workgroups are dependent on upper management to analyze and determine the actions necessary to improve results. Since upper management alone has access to business results, they can use more authoritarian behaviors in determining improvement actions. Since lower-level workgroups and employees do not have access to their own business results, they have no choice but to act passively regarding improvement decisions, completing improvement tasks, and resolving problems identified by upper management's analysis.

Management Systems—Dependent Example

Rodney is the superintendent of a school district that has had relatively low scores on a statewide standardization test for the past two years. After Rodney analyzes the latest test results, he spends his summer defining standard teaching plans for each grade level. Rodney presents these plans to the elementary school principles a week before school starts. The principals then inform their teachers of this new approach. One of the principals asks if Rodney could meet with his teachers to discuss the approach in more detail.

Even though several of the teachers voice concerns over the standard teaching plans, Rodney says that they are required because they are in line with the No Child Left Behind Act. Rodney also points out that his standard teaching plans will bring much-needed improvement to the standardized testing scores. The special education teachers in particular will have a difficult time implementing Rodney's standardized teaching plan since they often have multiple teaching techniques depending on the special needs of their students.

ANALYSIS: Rodney defines standard teaching plans for his whole school district, and rolls them down to all the teachers without regard to their particular situation. Making these plans a requirement encourages passive behaviors; the teachers do as they are told even though they do not agree with Rodney. Also, Rodney conducts the management review of standardized testing results for his school district and each elementary school by himself. Reviewing only at the upper-management level leads Rodney to use more authoritarian behaviors when defining improvement actions with the principals, which in turn, causes teachers to use more passive behaviors when following Rodney's direction.

Dependent Processes Characteristics

Two characteristics of an organization's processes promote a passive/authoritarian organizational culture: bureaucratic workflow and strictly enforced processes.

Organizations define processes to provide guidance on how work should flow through the organization. *Bureaucratic workflow* occurs when an organization's processes include unnecessary process steps. Needless process steps prevent timely decision making and required actions from taking place. An unhelpful level of detail makes it difficult for employees to perform their tasks efficiently and effectively. In government circles, bureaucratic workflow is often referred to as "red tape."

Some workgroups and organizations strictly enforce their processes. Employees' actions are monitored to ensure that they are in compliance with the processes. A separate quality organization may do compliance audits to see whether or not the various workgroups are following processes. Noncompliance issues are reported to higher-level management. Process compliance is expected whether or not the processes add value and the workgroups benefit from using them.

Bureaucratic workflow encourages a passive/authoritarian culture because employees passively follow the process as specified even if some of the steps are unnecessary. Employees follow very detailed procedures rather than use their own judgment on how to get a task done. If the process doesn't address an issue that arises, it forces employees to defer the issue to management for a decision. This encourages management to use more authoritarian behaviors and assume more responsibility for completing tasks.

Strictly enforced processes encourage a passive/authoritarian culture because workgroup leaders encourage employees to follow processes regardless of whether it is appropriate or not. Employees find it easier to do what the processes state rather than appear on a noncompliance report. Consequently, employees may avoid conflict with managers by following processes even when it doesn't make sense. Upper management uses strictly enforced processes in an effort to ensure employees perform them exactly as defined.

Processes—Dependent Example

Gladys works for a tax consulting firm and frequently travels to client sites. Gladys's firm has just issued a policy that prohibits employees from booking travel arrangements outside their firm's specified travel service. The CFO wants employees to use the travel service so that the firm can get a discount at the end of the year. If an employee feels an exception to this policy is warranted, then a waiver process must be followed that requires written justification for not using the company's travel service and approval by a company vice president. The process also requires management approvals by all lower levels before the vice presidential approval. Any noncompliance to this policy is reported by the CFO to the employee's manager.

Gladys has been assigned to the same client for a year. Because Gladys's firm charges clients for travel, her client has requested that she use their travel service when their rate is cheaper. For her next trip, Gladys makes her reservations using her firm's travel service even though the rate is better through the client's travel service. Although Gladys can file a waiver, she decides not to because she knows from past experience that getting all the required approvals will take two weeks and the airfare will increase by the time she's ready to book the flight. The client becomes quite upset when he sees the higher rate on the invoice from Gladys's firm and he threatens to do business elsewhere.

ANALYSIS: Since processes are strictly enforced in her company, Gladys is concerned that not following the new travel service policy will get her in trouble with management. Additionally, the waiver process is overly bureaucratic and not efficient in getting approvals on a timely basis. As a result, Gladys passively follows the required procedure even though it doesn't make sense in this situation. The strictly enforced process by the CFO encourages authoritarian behaviors by Gladys's manager since any noncompliance is reported to him to address.

Dependent Information Technology Characteristics

Two characteristics of an organization's information technology promote a passive/authoritarian organizational culture: controlled data and limited employee access to technology.

Controlled data occurs when information is collected and shared only at higher levels in an organization and is not made available to lower levels. In some organizations, data may be made available to lower-level workgroups but only to the workgroup leader.

Sometimes an organization limits employees' access to technology, such as the Internet, handheld devices, cell phones, or certain applications or tools that automate work functions. This could be for financial reasons or because upper management does not see the value in having certain employees use some technologies. Upper levels of management may have access to technology that lower levels of the organization do not.

Controlled data encourages a passive/authoritarian culture because upper management has all the information it needs, but lower-level workgroup managers and employees do not, so they are unable to make informed decisions by themselves. When problems arise, employees may take less responsibility and defer to leaders to make decisions, complete tasks, and resolve problems. Additionally, if the manager of a workgroup is the only one that has access to data, this enables dependence between a manager and his/her workgroup members.

Limiting employees' access to technology encourages a passive/authoritarian culture because those that do not have needed technology are dependent on those that do. Employees may be dependent on managers to perform a task that requires certain technology. Likewise, a workgroup may be dependent on another workgroup with the necessary technology to perform a task.

Information Technology—Dependent Example

Lindy's Retail is opening a new branch store and is looking to hire 250 employees. The corporate office sends in a staffing team to fill all openings for the new store. Ten days before the store opening, the staffing team reports back to corporate that all openings are filled. One week before the store opens, Catrina, the store manager, realizes she can't completely fill in the schedule because only 185 people are available. Catrina isn't sure why she is short people to fill her schedule but reports the problem to corporate. Corporate, assuming that Catrina made a mistake, sends in a team to investigate the problem. The team finds out that the staffing team made job offers to the selected candidates, but did not build in time for other actions that needed to occur before the new hires could show up to work, such as drug testing, giving two weeks notice to their current employer, and training. If Catrina had had access to the corporate-held staffing application, she would have seen the staffing team's timeline omission and could have let them know that they needed to add this information.

ANALYSIS: Since corporate is the only one with access to all the information, it assumes a more authoritarian role when solving this particular problem. Catrina is forced to behave passively, deferring her responsibilities to corporate because she does not have access to the staffing application.

Moving Away from Dependent Business System Characteristics

Dependent business system characteristics can negatively impact your workgroup and organization's gruntledness and success. Such business systems encourage a passive/authoritarian organizational culture. This often leads to disgruntled employees and negatively impacts workgroup success. These problems are compounded if many of these dependent business system characteristics are organization-wide.

Gruntledness Impacts from an Upper-Management Perspective

Dependent business system characteristics negatively impact employees. This is because employees are not as happy when they are working in a business system that limits their contribution. This type of environment says to employees, "You can't be trusted." It also may give employees the feeling that business results are more important than employee morale.

Cumbersome organizational structures such as highly hierarchical organizations keep employees separated from upper management, which can lead to upper management being out of touch with employees' perspectives. Employees tend to be happier when they feel that their opinions are heard and understood by management.

Top-down management plans and upper management-only reviews limit employees' creative input for meeting business objectives. Limiting employee creativity can lead to disgruntledness.

In addition, bureaucratic workflow limits employees' ability to meet customers' needs. Strictly enforcing processes when they aren't applicable for a unique situation also limits employees. This frustrates employees and customers.

Controlled data does not provide the needed information for employees to make informed decisions. This can lead to employees feeling helpless in certain situations. Finally, limiting access to technology can frustrate employees if doing so makes it difficult to perform their responsibilities.

Success Impacts from an Upper-Management Perspective

A business system with a lot of control built into it can limit revenue growth. Dependent business system characteristics tend not to go over well with entrepreneurial types of people—the people necessary for growing your business. Dependent business system characteristics usually don't support business strategies well either since they don't provide the flexibility necessary for successful implementation.

A cumbersome organizational structure can become more internally focused than externally focused. It will be detrimental to your company and your customers if this internal focus leads your company to be out of touch with industry trends and its competition.

Management plans that upper management define and roll out throughout the organizational hierarchy miss the benefit of lower-level employee feedback. Such plans also tend not to be understood as well by employees, nor do the plans enlist employee support. Also, upper management-only reviews do not provide employees the information they need to fine-tune their activities to meet business objectives.

Bureaucratic processes often limit employees, making it difficult for them to get their jobs done. Such processes require employees to get frequent approval from their leaders. This in turn can slow down the task that they are trying to complete, which can impact the timeliness of delivery. Additionally, strictly enforced processes do not allow employees to work together effectively to meet unique circumstances that require a different approach or solution. Having processes that inhibit customer satisfaction is counterintuitive to business success.

Controlled data inhibits employees at lower levels of the organization from making decisions, completing their tasks, and resolving problems. Information is not readily available, which is necessary for performing job duties correctly. Also, limited access to technology can undermine business initiatives if employees need certain technologies to meet the needs of the organization.

Rethinking Dependent Business System Characteristics

Dependent business system characteristics can be appropriate for some organizations that require a lot of structure (for example, organizations that manufacture pharmaceuticals). However, dependent business system characteristics often contribute to employee disgruntledness and can limit the success of implementing business strategies. More effective business system characteristics are presented later in this book. The next chapter will look at the impacts of independent business system characteristics and how they encourage an independent/laissez-faire organizational culture.

19

How Independent Business Systems Impact Gruntledness and Business Success

"[There was] a problem with the lack of a formal organization. I would be told by one of the owners to do something in a particular manner, then told to do it a different way from another owner. Either way, I was chastised for not doing an appropriate job. It was discouraging, frustrating, and seemed disjointed in my mind. I never felt like I completely had a handle on things or that I understood the whole operation. That is not a recipe for competence. It's a sure way to prove inadequate performance. I never want to experience that kind of work environment ever again. I think there's a decent portion of working people (like me) who need to 'know the rules' in order to perform their jobs in a competent manner. There is a place for those of us who need an organized work environment."

Disgruntled Employee
Blog Post

A workgroup may, on a regular basis, exhibit independent behaviors that produce favorable business results. Management may add independent characteristics to the business system over time to continue to support the workgroup's behavior. If a workgroup's independent behavior preference is strong, the behavior preference can influence the workgroup culture more than the leader's behaviors. But one leader with a strong preference for laissez-faire behaviors will usually define the workgroup's culture more than the workgroup's behavior.

If upper management has a preference for independent and laissez-faire behaviors, they may also embed more independent characteristics into the business system, allowing employees more freedom to do their own thing. If upper management believes that employees provide value on their own, are responsible, and are as entitled as managers, the business system will probably have more independent characteristics.

It is also possible for leaders to implement independent characteristics into their business system without realizing that they encourage an independent/laissez-faire organizational culture. Independent business system characteristics include the following:

- **Organizational Framework.** Unclear roles and responsibilities and not clearly defined organizational structures.
- **Management Systems.** Decentralized management plans and decentralized management reviews.
- **Processes.** Flexible workflow and unenforced processes.
- **Information Technology.** Decentralized data and uncontrolled access to technology.

The next sections illustrate these independent business system characteristics and their impact on organizational culture.

Independent Organizational Framework Characteristics

Two characteristics of an organizational framework promote an independent/laissez-faire organizational culture: unclear roles and responsibilities and not clearly defined organizational structures.

Some organizations have job descriptions that do not clearly define employee responsibilities. The job descriptions (if they exist at all) are often missing critical details like what tasks employees are responsible for, who has the needed information to start a task, who the subject matter experts are on the task in case employees have questions, and who approves work.

Some organizations don't clearly define their organizational structure. Some organizations are very decentralized, meaning they are organized according to autonomous business units that are loosely tied together. Without a good description of the overall organization, customers, vendors, and employees often have difficulty navigating the organization for support.

Unclear roles and responsibilities encourage an independent/laissez-faire culture because employees will make decisions, complete tasks, and resolve problems whether they are responsible for them or not. Employees may do the right thing, but then again, they may not. Since they haven't been provided guidance, they have no option other than to guess what they should work on.

An organizational structure that isn't clearly defined encourages an independent/laissez-faire culture because employees are unsure of where to go to for help, so they make more decisions on their own, complete tasks more autonomously, and resolve problems on their own. These activities could be more prone to error since they are completed without needed support.

Organizational Framework—Independent Example

Jasmine is in orientation training for a major retail chain. She sits through a training video and reads a training manual. The training materials explain that the register will cue her on what needs to be done, but they don't spell out her responsibilities. They also don't tell her who to go to in case she has questions.

During her first day at the register, Jasmine is unclear on whether she has the authority to handle several types of transactions. Since her manager is busy, Jasmine completes all transactions on her own. The register allows her to complete all the transactions, so Jasmine assumes she has the authority to do so.

However, the front office, in reviewing transactions, realizes that Jasmine has made some mistakes. Her manager explains to Jasmine that refunds of any kind require management approval. Jasmine responds with a "deer in the headlights" look and asks who she should get approval from when managers are preoccupied with other customers. Jasmine's manager apologizes and states that Jasmine can always call the front office if she has a customer requesting a refund.

ANALYSIS: Because the training video and training manual are unclear about Jasmine's responsibilities and who to go to for support, Jasmine is forced to use more independent behaviors in figuring out what she is responsible for. Unclear responsibilities and organizational structure lead to Jasmine approving refunds that require management approval. Had Jasmine's responsibilities been clearer in the training materials, Jasmine would not have made this mistake.

Independent Management Systems Characteristics

Two characteristics of an organization's management systems promote an independent/laissez-faire organizational culture: decentralized management plans and decentralized management reviews.

Some organizations allow each lower-level workgroup to define their own objectives and strategies, which results in decentralized management plans. Each level of the organization defines their own set of objectives and strategies without regard to the higher-level objectives and strategies. In addition, individual employees may define their own personal objectives, which may or may not support their workgroup's or organization's objectives.

An organization with decentralized management reviews allows each individual workgroup to review their business results on their own. Business results are collected, analyzed, and reported by each workgroup throughout the organization. Individual workgroups review their own business results but have no visibility on how they contributed to overall organizational objectives. Each workgroup determines their own actions to improve business results for their workgroup.

Decentralized management plans encourage an independent/laissez-faire culture because upper management lets lower-level workgroups make their own decisions regarding strategies and objectives. When management plans are decentralized, often they are not aligned with organization-wide objectives or they are in conflict with other workgroups' management plans. This may lead to conflict between workgroups if they have competing objectives and overlapping responsibilities.

Decentralized management reviews encourage an independent/laissez-faire culture because each workgroup looks at their own set of business results and determines their own improvement actions, regardless of the organization's objectives. This may lead to several workgroups working on similar improvements without the knowledge of what each other is doing, costing the organization more to implement improvements than necessary. Improvement actions of the workgroups might even be contradictory to each other.

Management Systems—Independent Example

Twyla switched jobs 6 months ago, taking on her first management position at a biotechnology company in the San Francisco Bay area. Her company allows each workgroup to define their own management plans and review their own performance. Twyla, a Six Sigma black belt, decides that it would be best to review defect trends for her workgroup during their weekly staff meetings. She sets an objective for the workgroup of reducing defects by 12%. Her team reviews defect results during the meetings and comes up with improvement actions.

Six months later, Twyla has the charts to show that measuring defects was worthwhile; quality defects have trended downward by 15% since she started. Unfortunately, her boss has a report that shows she has been overrunning her budget for the past few months.

Twyla is dumbfounded. She thought for sure that reducing quality defects would also reduce costs. However, the report shows that for the past few months, several members have been working overtime to meet her new quality assurance objectives.

ANALYSIS: The independent management plans and reviews that Twyla conducted with her workgroup did an outstanding job of reducing defects. However, the management plans did not consider overall company objectives to reduce costs and increase productivity. If management reviews had been aligned between workgroups, Twyla would have known much sooner that her quality performance measures were in conflict with the company's cost-reduction measures.

Independent Processes Characteristics

Two characteristics of an organization's processes promote an independent/laissez-faire organizational culture: flexible workflow and unenforced processes.

Some organizations allow employees to determine their own process workflow without a lot of management involvement. The workflow process might also be defined only at a broad level, which allows employees a lot of flexibility in deciding how to accomplish the details of a task. Such workflow also allows workgroups or employees to determine how to tweak the process to meet unique business needs. Some organizations do not even define their processes, which gives employees the most amount of flexibility on how to complete their work.

Some organizations do not enforce usage of their processes. The processes themselves might be flexible or bureaucratic in nature, but no one monitors employees' actions to ensure that they are conducting work according to the organization's processes. These processes are often not utilized as a result. Employees may ignore the processes because there is no system in place that encourages their use.

Flexible workflow encourages an independent/laissez-faire culture because employees can define how to complete work without management involvement. Flexible workflow doesn't encourage employees to check with management for advice or needed support. Also, since process steps are less detailed, employees must figure out the finer aspects of tasks on their own. Consequently, workgroup results depend more on the individuals involved. If employees use good judgment, then everything will be fine; if they don't, then problems can occur.

Unenforced processes encourage an independent/laissez-faire culture because the decision on whether or not employees should follow processes is in the hands of employees rather than management. When processes are unenforced, management inadvertently allows employees to do whatever they feel like doing. As a result, employees may change processes, define them on the fly, or do whatever is required to complete tasks. While this gives employees a great deal of flexibility to address situations as they see fit, it also undermines the intent of defining a process in the first place. When processes are not enforced within a workgroup, employees do not get the benefit of company best practices and lessons learned by others within the organization.

Processes—Independent Example

A company that makes custom and pre-configured cabinets for residential and commercial clients hires Philip, a consultant, to look for ways to improve its quoting process. One of the company's clients has recently complained that the differences in quotes received over the past few months for a particular type of cabinet don't make sense.

Phillip checks the company's process manual and sees that the quoting process is defined very broadly. The manual also provides suggestions for the sales representatives, but it doesn't require them to follow any specific steps. It mentions that if the sales representatives have questions, they can use the most current labor rate table and that they can check supplier catalogs for quotes on more expensive materials. Phillip also finds that no one in the company checks to see if employees follow the process.

Phillip interviews the company's three sales representatives to get to the bottom of why the client is getting different quotes. The first sales representative provides quotes without validating current supplier material prices. The second sales representative provides quotes by reusing her last price quote without checking to see if the labor rate table has been updated. The third sales representative provides quotes by checking the labor rate table and vendor catalogs for every piece of material in the cabinet, which often takes a much longer time to provide the quote than necessary. None of the three sales representatives are providing quotes as suggested in the quoting process.

ANALYSIS: Since the quoting process is broadly defined and makes suggestions rather than require employees to complete quotes in a certain way, the sales representatives make their own decisions on how to produce a quote. The resulting independent/laissez-faire culture gives them a lot of leeway in whether or not to use the vendor's catalogs and labor rate tables. As a result, three different quotes on the same cabinet cause conflict with a client.

Independent Information Technology Characteristics

Two characteristics of an organization's information technology promote an independent/laissez-faire organizational culture: decentralized data and uncontrolled access to technology.

When an organization has *decentralized data*, everyone in the organization is allowed to create, access, and use whatever data they need. Individuals are allowed to create their own data with spreadsheets on their laptops.

Allowing workgroups and employees uncontrolled access to technology provides them with the capability to perform their jobs as they see fit. Each workgroup can purchase its own application packages to perform certain tasks. Additionally, distributed servers and computers enable workgroups and employees to develop their own applications. They can also download applications to their computer or handheld device. Employees may also make their own technology decisions, such as buying a Mac, PC, or iPad. They can choose between conventional cell phones or smart phones (such as iPhone or Blackberry) with a multitude of technology features, such as Bluetooth, cameras, GPS navigation, text messaging, and media players.

Decentralized data encourages an independent/laissez-faire culture because each workgroup (or employee) can act autonomously from upper management and other workgroups, since they have their own data. When employees maintain their own data on their laptops, this further encourages them to make their own decisions, complete tasks on their own, and resolve problems based on their own information. Decentralized data can lead to data redundancies and inconsistencies.

Uncontrolled access to technology encourages an independent/laissez-faire culture because it allows employees to work self-sufficiently and to solve problems on their own. However, allowing everyone to make their own technology decisions usually increases support costs and makes sharing data across different technologies more difficult.

Information Technology—Independent Example

Brett is a programmer within his company's IT department. The finance department had one of their programmers develop a new financial application, but the users of the application are complaining that the programmer is not available to support the application after business hours and on weekends. Brett's manager asks him to take over the support of the new financial application.

Since Brett started supporting the application a month ago, 11 application outages have occurred. Because the programmer in the finance department used non-standard technology, when an outage occurs, it takes Brett several hours to bring the application back online. Brett has also been preparing for an internal security audit of the financial systems he supports. Because the finance department created their own financial system, Brett is unsure whether the system complies with the company's security standards and if it will pass the audit.

ANALYSIS: The finance department has uncontrolled access to technology and can make their own decisions regarding their financial application. The resulting independent/laissez-faire culture encourages the finance department to acquire these technologies without guidance from the IT department and not follow the security standards. As a result, the systems are much less stable, more difficult to support, and at risk of failing an audit.

Moving Away from Independent Business System Characteristics

Independent business system characteristics can negatively impact your workgroup and organization's gruntledness and success. Such business systems encourage an independent/laissez-faire organizational culture. Although employees tend to be happier with this type of culture than with a passive/authoritarian culture, the independent nature of the culture may make it difficult for employees to meet business objectives and leverage the teamwork that is so often required to successfully implement today's business strategies.

Independent business system characteristics provide employees the freedom to complete work and resolve problems as they see fit. Therefore, success is more dependent on what employees do in lieu of any kind of guidance provided by leaders. The workgroup may succeed, but then again, it may not. An independent business system is often missing the checks and balances that are necessary to ensure a workgroup is on track.

Gruntledness Impacts from an Upper-Management Perspective

Some employees prefer independent business system characteristics over other types of characteristics. But some will miss the sense of team or connectedness when working in an independent/laissez-faire culture.

Employees have more freedom and possibly enjoy their work more with unclear roles, responsibilities, and organizational structures. However, isolated employees miss the opportunity to learn from and partner with their peers. Unless they develop their own network, they are left to resolve problems on their own. They may miss the camaraderie and connectedness that comes from working with others in the organization.

Decentralized management plans provide workgroup leaders with the creativity to meet their own business objectives. However, such plans can cause conflict between workgroups if they have competing objectives and overlapping responsibilities. This conflict negatively impacts employee gruntledness. Also, employees are much happier when they can see how their particular objectives are aligned with and support overall business objectives.

Employees who work with flexible processes tend to be happier than those who work with bureaucratic processes. But their happiness can be increased if the processes provide the support they need from their leader and coworkers to get the job done correctly and with ease. When processes aren't enforced, it may provide employees a sense of freedom; however, employees aren't as happy when mistakes occur that could have been prevented by following company processes.

Decentralized data provides the information employees need to make decisions and gives employees a sense of empowerment and freedom. However, their happiness can be increased when they have access to information that is correct and shared across the organization.

Success Impacts from an Upper-Management Perspective

Independent business system characteristics are often helpful when an organization is in growth mode. Start-up organizations require a more entrepreneurial spirit, which is better supported by decentralized management plans, flexible processes, and decentralized data. Although some independent business system characteristics support growth, they are not as effective in supporting cost-cutting initiatives. For example, business units with unclear roles, responsibilities, and organizational structures have a tendency to do things their own way, which is often contrary to reducing costs.

Decentralized management plans may not align with the management plans of supporting workgroups. As a result, the company may not get synergistic benefits, such as leveraging common capabilities or sharing customer information that could increase sales. Sometimes decentralized management plans lead to conflict between business units if they have competing objectives and overlapping responsibilities.

Unenforced processes do not provide employees the opportunity to leverage best practices and lessons learned from others within the organization. Organizations often include steps in their processes to prevent previous costly mistakes from being repeated. Without process enforcement, the same costly mistakes can be made over and over again.

Although decentralized data allows employees to create and maintain needed information, data in one application may be inconsistent with other workgroups' data or employees' personal data. When inconsistent data exists, then decisions are often based on bad data. If someone makes a decision based on incorrect data, the mistake can be costly to correct and can undermine business strategies. Uncontrolled access to technology can lead to ignoring various government regulations (such as Sarbanes-Oxley) and IT standards. Uncontrolled technology can also be more costly to enhance or replace down the road.

Rethinking Independent Business System Characteristics

Independent business system characteristics can be appropriate for some organizations that would be stifled with more structure. The success of a start-up company, for example, often depends on the entrepreneurial spirit of its employees and their willingness to do whatever it takes to get the company off the ground. This entrepreneurial spirit is often best supported by independent business system characteristics. While independent business system characteristics are often popular with employees, they usually are a hindrance to successfully implementing business strategies. The next chapter will look at the impact of interdependent business system characteristics, and illustrate how they encourage an interdependent/connective organizational culture, which improves employee morale and increases business success simultaneously.

20

How Interdependent Business Systems Impact Gruntledness and Business Success

"I worked for a large pharmaceutical company that was interdependent with high independence. Upper management communicated very well throughout the company. At the lower levels of the company there was quite a bit of independence of how we completed tasks. We were allowed to make the majority of the decisions on how to resolve problems. As a general rule, management gave details of what we were responsible for, and said 'Let me know if you have any problems that I may need to help with.' That was about it. Much of the success of this environment was the management structure. There were only two people between myself and the VP on the org chart. And even then, the VP was very accessible. If we needed information from the VP, a couple of us would get our manager and walk over to his office for a five-minute discussion. That was about all it took to keep projects moving. Very seldom were we waiting for an e-mail to be returned with our answer. The projects progressed exceptionally fast as compared to the 'silo style' of management that many organizations still have today."

Gruntled Employee
Blog Post

I f a workgroup exhibits primarily interdependent behaviors that produce outstanding business results, leaders may add interdependent characteristics to the business system to cultivate the behaviors that led to the results. Workgroup members with a strong preference for interdependent behaviors can influence the workgroup culture more than the leader's authoritarian or laissez-faire behaviors. However, one leader with a strong preference for connective behaviors can define the workgroup's culture regardless of employee behavior.

Upper management's behavior preferences usually are behind implementing interdependent characteristics into business systems. If upper management believes that leaders and employees provide equal value, employees and leaders are equally responsible, or leaders and employees are equally entitled, then the business system will probably have more interdependent characteristics. Interdependent business system characteristics include the following:

- **Organizational Framework.** Helpful roles and responsibilities and supportive organizational structures.
- **Management Systems.** Aligned management plans and aligned management reviews.
- **Processes.** Supportive workflow and institutionalized processes.
- **Information Technology.** Shared data and planned access to technology.

The next sections illustrate these interdependent business system characteristics and their impact on organizational culture.

Interdependent Organizational Framework Characteristics

Two characteristics of an organizational framework promote an interdependent/connective organizational culture: helpful roles and responsibilities and a supportive organizational structure.

Job descriptions that clearly specify roles and responsibilities to meet business objectives help workgroup members know where they fit in when performing tasks, making decisions, or solving problems related to business objectives. Most job descriptions only specify functional roles and responsibilities and neglect to mention how this particular role contributes to meeting business objectives. Some companies use a responsibility matrix to clearly define what each role is responsible for. A responsibility matrix can be defined using a Responsibility, Accountability, Consult, Inform (RACI) chart to specify what role is responsible for the task, what role is accountable for the task and must approve resulting work products, what role needs to be consulted if there are questions regarding the task, and what role needs to be informed after a decision is made regarding a task.[61]

A supportive organizational structure is clearly defined, so anyone within the organization knows where to go for support. Networks can also be set up as additional supportive organizational structures. Networks encourage cooperation and collaboration between workgroups. Networked workgroups share information, cooperatively make decisions, and collaborate to accomplish goals and objectives.

Ensuring that role and responsibility definitions are helpful encourages an interdependent/connective culture because doing so specifies how the various roles work together to accomplish a task, make a decision, or solve a problem. A RACI chart further encourages an interdependent/connective culture by providing another level of detail on how roles can work together to accomplish a task.

Supportive organizational structures encourage an interdependent/connective culture because they ensure that every employee understands the organizational structure, which makes it easy for employees to reach out to the appropriate person or workgroup for support. With a supportive organizational structure, employees get the support they need to make better decisions, complete tasks more efficiently or effectively, and resolve problems more completely. Networks encourage an interdependent/connective culture by helping workgroups cooperate with each other.

Organizational Framework—Interdependent Example

Benjamin has just become the CIO of an automotive company that has numerous problems with the IT department. The company perceives the IT department as being unresponsive to its needs, particularly when it comes to making enhancements to the application systems that support processes. Also, numerous outages with critical applications have negatively impacted the business. While researching the problem, Benjamin discovers that the IT roles and responsibilities are very unclear about how to interact with the business. He also discovers that the business users are unsure of who to contact within the IT department when they have an issue.

Benjamin meets with business executives to collaboratively define the roles and responsibilities for the IT department. They decide to define responsibilities to clarify the interactions that IT has with the business, and to better align IT with business goals and objectives. He sets up a team between IT and the business to see how his department impacts processes, which will give him a clearer perspective on how application outages affect business transactions. He also defines points of contact within his IT department for common issues or questions that business users have. The resulting new partnership between IT and the business better aligns IT services with business requirements.

ANALYSIS: Benjamin works with others in the business to define IT's responsibilities, which better aligns IT services with their internal clients. With more helpful roles and responsibilities and a more supportive IT organizational structure, Benjamin encourages an interdependent/connective culture. Consequently, the IT department is in a better position to collaborate with the business to figure out ways to meet business requirements.

Interdependent Management Systems Characteristics

Two characteristics of an organization's management systems promote an interdependent/connective organizational culture: aligned management plans and aligned management reviews.

Senior management may align an entire company to its overall business strategy by allowing each workgroup and employee to translate organizational objectives into workgroup and personal objectives. Further alignment is achieved when upper-management plans are refined after reviews of lower-level plans. Hoshin Planning, a technique developed by Professor Kaoru Ishikawa of Japan in the 1950s, is very useful in aligning management plans throughout the organization and tapping into the power of collective employee thinking.[62]

Aligned management reviews are conducted at various levels of the organization so that each workgroup can see the business results applicable to their workgroup and how those results contributed to overall business results. Upper management reviews a summary of the overall business results. Then each lower-level workgroup can look at a subset of the business results applicable to their workgroup. Organizations can use data warehouse and business intelligence tools to facilitate viewing business results by specific workgroup and at various summary levels from the same source of information. When overall business results look bad, management can see who is contributing to the problem. Since everyone is looking at the same source of business results, they can determine improvement plans at whatever level is appropriate within the organization.

Aligned management plans encourage an interdependent/connective culture because employees must work together to define workgroup objectives that will support organizational objectives. When goals and objectives are further broken down to the individual employee level, it allows employees to work more collaboratively and cooperatively with each other and their manager. Additionally, employees at all levels of the organization understand how to meet their workgroup's objectives and how their workgroup supports organizational objectives. This ensures that the day-to-day decisions employees make, the tasks they work on, and the way they resolve problems is aligned with organizational objectives. Aligned management plans ensure that every workgroup within the organization is working towards the same organizational goals and objectives.

Aligned management reviews encourage an interdependent/connective culture because they measure progress against objectives at each level, which helps workgroups and employees see how they are either supporting or hindering overall business results. This encourages employees to work more collaboratively and effectively inside and outside their workgroup.

Data warehouse and business intelligence tools provide multiple views into business results so that the various workgroups can work on their part of the problem but still be in support of each other.

Management Systems—Interdependent Example

Chantal, the CEO of a carpet manufacturing company, launches some business initiatives that will focus the company on growth. The company needs to expand to maintain its current market position. However, not every workgroup understands their part in meeting the new growth goal. HR has set an objective of 65 days to get a person on board. The facilities workgroup has set an objective to open up a new facility within 6 months. It becomes apparent to Chantal that the HR and facilities objectives will not help her meet her growth targets within her time frame.

She hires Jason to facilitate management planning across her company. Jason holds a workshop for Chantal's leadership team to define workgroup objectives and strategies to meet the company's growth goals. Jason then meets with each workgroup to define how they will support the corporate objectives.

HR is given a new target of having new employees hired within 30 days—particularly for the additional sales staff that Chantal wants to hire so that they can expand their sales territories. The HR management team defines a strategy to meet these new objectives by prescreening all applications as they are received so that a pool of qualified candidates is available before anyone requests a new hire.

The facilities workgroup is also given challenging targets that will encourage them to find space quicker for additional employees. The facilities management team conducts a brainstorming workshop to figure out how to meet their new objectives. They come up with a strategy to allow employees to work at home some of the time. They also suggest to share offices, because 15% of the staff is usually out on business travel, vacation, or sick time. This would allow the existing facility space to be used more effectively to support new hires and Chantal's growth objectives.

Over the next few months, HR and the facilities workgroup conduct their own management reviews and monitor progress against their new objectives. All the department managers, including HR and facilities, report their results during Chantal's monthly review meetings. Corrective actions are coordinated between all workgroups and other workgroups are supportive of additional actions required to meet Chantal's growth objectives.

ANALYSIS: Chantal and Jason's approach to aligning management plans increases workgroup interdependence by encouraging members to find ways to support overall company objectives and corrective actions. Each workgroup defines workgroup objectives and actions that align with company goals and objectives. This results in the workgroups having joint responsibility and commitment in implementing the overall business strategy.

Interdependent Processes Characteristics

Two characteristics of an organization's processes promote an interdependent/connective organizational culture: supportive workflow and institutionalized processes.

Supportive workflow occurs when an organization's processes provide a necessary amount of detail on how various roles work together for task completion. One way to have supportive workflow is to define processes from an end-to-end perspective, that is, define how a transaction is processed from initiation to final completion across organizational boundaries. A *SIPOC* (acronym for supplier, input, process, output, and customer) is a Six Sigma tool that helps define processes from end-to-end.[63] Using a SIPOC helps employees understand how workgroups must work together to process a transaction from beginning to end.

When an organization's processes become adopted, or *institutionalized*, this means employees willingly utilize the processes to accomplish work activities. Processes usually become institutionalized with management encouragement and employee buy-in. When employees see a process as a useful way to get their job done, they will readily use it. Supportive workflow can also aid in institutionalizing processes. Unlike unenforced processes, which encourage employees to focus on defining their own processes, institutionalized processes allow employees to focus on improving process-es for everyone's benefit.

Supportive workflow encourages an interdependent/connective culture because it encourages employees and workgroups to be jointly accountable for problem resolution or task completion since they can see the overall process flow. Also, employees can work more interdependently with other contributors to the process if they know who to go to at a particular stage in the process.

Institutionalized processes encourage an interdependent/connective cul-ture because employees and workgroups can work together in the same way across the organization instead of each doing their own thing, which may conflict with what others are doing. Additionally, employees can submit process improvements so that everyone can complete work more efficiently and effectively.

Processes—Interdependent Example

Terrence runs a large landscaping company. One workgroup designs the landscapes and gives estimates to his clients. Another workgroup imple-ments the landscape designs, and a third workgroup maintains the land-scapes. He consistently works with one nursery that supplies all the flowers, shrubs, and trees for his landscaping jobs.

Terrence has just won a major contract with a home builder to do the landscaping for their new housing development. This contract will almost double the size of his workforce. Since Terrence will be hiring new work-ers to meet this increased demand for his services, he decides to document the process that he uses for landscaping from end-to-end. Terrence creates a workflow chart showing the roles and process steps for his landscaping design team, the landscaping implementation team, and the landscaping maintenance team. He also documents the process steps that are required to get plants from the nursery.

As new employees are hired, Terrence requires them to read the process-es from beginning to end. When the landscape technicians bring an issue to Terrence that is covered in the process, Terrance tells them to consult the end-to-end workflow chart to see who they should work with to resolve the issue. Requiring new hires to read the documented process and revisit it each time they have a process question helps to institutionalize the process.

ANALYSIS: Providing an end-to-end workflow process allows Terrence's landscape technicians to be jointly responsible and committed to completing the landscaping for the customer. When an issue arises with a client, the workflow chart tells them specifically how to resolve the issue either by collaboratively working with Terrence, another workgroup, or the nursery. Requiring new hires to read the process encourages an interdependent/connective culture because it ensures that everyone understands what Terrence expects of them and shows them how they need to work with each other.

Interdependent Information Technology Characteristics

Two characteristics of an organization's information technology promote an interdependent/connective organizational culture: shared data and planned access to technology.

Shared data allows everyone in the organization access to needed information from the same source. Some organizations use an *enterprise data architecture* to provide a model of the data needed by workgroups. An enterprise data architecture identifies the sources of the data, how the data is to be maintained, who uses the data, and who needs access to it. Organizations can also use data flow diagrams to show how data flows through an organization and how each workgroup processes and uses that data.

Some organizations have planned access to technology, which means they create a technology plan that identifies and distributes the technology needed by workgroups to meet business objectives. Implementing the technology plan also ensures that everyone has access to the technology they need to perform their jobs efficiently and effectively. The technology that employees may need includes laptops, desktop computers, printers, or handheld devices such as smart phones. It also includes application software such as enterprise resource planning packages, e-mail, knowledge management systems, and Web services.

Shared data encourages an interdependent/connective culture because when everyone has access to the same accurate data, they are able to make decisions based on common information, which facilitates collaboration within a workgroup or between workgroups. Also, when organizations use data flow diagrams it makes it clear where the data came from (all the upstream organizations that have modified the data so far) and where the data is going (all the downstream organizations that will use the data afterwards). This allows those that touch the data to collaborate when using the data.

Planned access to technology encourages an interdependent/connective culture because employees and workgroups have the tools they need to collaborate with coworkers, vendors, and customers. Enterprise resource planning packages allow employees to work interdependently with each other in their daily activities by automating end-to-end processes and providing access to shared data. Web services enable collaboration between organizations. Knowledge management systems permit the sharing of knowledge between all those who have access to the knowledge base. The Internet allows employees to find information that others want to share with the world.

Information Technology—Interdependent Example

MacKenzie is the CIO for his state's Department of Revenue, which includes the Division of Motor Vehicles (DMV). Lately, MacKenzie has been receiving numerous complaints about server outages that are impacting the DMV's processes for obtaining or renewing a driver's license. MacKenzie knows that the rise in outages is due to aging equipment, but he was not aware of the outages' impact on the DMV.

After researching on the Web, MacKenzie decides to implement some of the concepts that he finds on an IT Service Management (ITSM) Web site. MacKenzie sets up a team to create a system that documents which applications are supported by each of the servers and network components. The team is also tasked with documenting which applications support each of the DMV's processes.

After implementation of the new system, MacKenzie and the rest of the executives have the data to see which servers have the highest amount of downtime. He also can see which DMV application systems have been impacted by this downtime and what the impact has been to the associated DMV processes. With this information, MacKenzie develops a technology plan to replace the aging hardware that supports the most critical processes for the DMV.

ANALYSIS: Using data shared on the Internet and data gathered by his new system, MacKenzie develops a technology plan to best support internal customers within the DMV. The data that MacKenzie collects and shares with his team allows his IT department to be more supportive of their users. This creates a more interdependent/connective culture, encouraging his IT staff to pay attention to the customer's experience and make joint decisions with the business since they better understand how their responsibilities impact their customers.

Moving Towards Interdependent Business System Characteristics

Interdependent business system characteristics have numerous benefits. Such characteristics positively impact your workgroup and organization's gruntledness and success. Employees are much happier in work environments supported by an interdependent business system. They have the ability to connect with others and are supported by upper management to get the job done as efficiently and effectively as possible. Interdependent business system characteristics allow leaders to help employees adapt to change more quickly and more effectively. This is particularly important with complex business strategies such as outsourcing, mergers and acquisitions, and technology implementations.

Gruntledness Impacts from an Upper-Management Perspective

Many people report that their happiest times at work are when they are working as part of a team. Employees feel trusted and supported. Helpful roles and responsibilities and supportive organizational structures provide opportunities for employees to interact and collaborate with their coworkers. Networks provide opportunities for camaraderie and connectivity across workgroups.

Aligned management plans and reviews promote employee success, which helps with their gruntledness level. Employees are happier when they see how their efforts contributed to workgroup and overall organizational objectives.

Supportive workflow ensures that employees get what they need from their managers and each other to be successful. They also support employees in working with other workgroups, reducing potential friction between them.

Planned access to data and technology provide employees with the information they need to accomplish their tasks easily. Employees are less frustrated when they have access to correct and shared information.

An interdependent business system increases gruntledness because it encourages employees to contribute value and inspires leaders to recognize employees' input. At the same time, this model facilitates feedback, which allows workgroups to monitor their own performance and change their behavior as necessary. Employees get the support they need from the organization and are less frustrated with their jobs. Anything that supports employees and workgroups working together cooperatively and collaboratively usually makes employees happier.

Success Impacts from an Upper-Management Perspective

Interdependent business system characteristics often provide the best solution in today's business world where cost-cutting and revenue-growth initiatives co-exist. They also increase the chance of success for any business strategy implementation and can improve operational results. Interdependent business system characteristics provide employees the freedom and support to complete work and solve problems in a timely and accurate manner. Their chances of success are far greater under interdependent business system characteristics.

Helpful roles and responsibilities and supportive organizational structures provide the opportunity for workgroups to work together to see how each workgroup impacts the other. These structures also make apparent any synergies between workgroups that can be leveraged.

Aligned management plans help employees understand how their objectives support other workgroups and the organization's objectives. When employees translate organizational objectives into personal and workgroup objectives, this reduces the chance of a workgroup heading off in the wrong direction or even unintentionally making decisions, completing tasks, or resolving problems that undermine business objectives.

Institutionalized processes ensure that all workgroups are using a common approach to complete tasks. This helps them work together effectively and efficiently. When employees are actually using the processes, it allows employees and workgroups to work together and improve processes to meet business objectives. Additionally, supportive workflow allows employees and managers to work together collaboratively, each contributing as appropriate to work activities.

Interdependent IT characteristics enable organizations or workgroups to share information with each other. An enterprise data architecture improves the flow of information enterprise-wide, so employees will all be "on the same page" with access to the same information to support whatever services they provide. Planned access to technology provides a plan for IT departments to implement so that various workgroups can collaborate with each other using the right tools to meet business objectives.

Considering Interdependent Business System Characteristics

Interdependent business system characteristics are appropriate for most organizations and situations. They can improve employee morale and business results simultaneously and are often the most efficient and effective way to implement business strategies. The next chapter describes the important role that business system characteristics play in employee gruntledness and business success.

21

Why Business Systems Matter

"One of my first employers after graduating college was a small company. This was a unique company because of the way they ran the software development business. They created a high-caliber environment, which presented a unique work environment. This was an interdependent workgroup to the max. All of the development staff had a very good idea of what the other groups and individuals were working on. Problems and possible delays were public information so that they could be resolved ASAP.

This interdependent attitude was outside the software development workgroup as well. Sales and Marketing were well aware of what products were in release stage, and what products were still in development stage. That is to be expected. But the Sales and Marketing people were also well aware of the details of the products. It was common to see a salesperson sitting at the computer learning just what the product could and could not do. And on the other side, many of the technical staff worked close with Sales to make sure that all customer questions could be answered to the highest degree. This open communication and work together attitude made a very enjoyable work environment with high satisfaction."

Gruntled Employee
Blog Post

As mentioned in Chapter 10, Dr. C. K. Prahalad's book, *The New Age of Innovation*, states that to remain competitive, companies must change the process of creating value in products and services.[64] Based on innovation and consumers' expectations, customers define value by being able to co-create the products or services that they purchase. Delivering value in this way depends on a supporting global ecosystem of small and large companies working together to deliver the customer's designation of "value." An interdependent business system within and between these companies would increase their chances of success in creating value through innovation and co-creation.

Without a doubt, the new business model he describes will be disruptive because of the amount of change required. Competitive advantage heavily depends on leveraging employee talent, technology, and processes. This requires collaboration and connectivity, which is difficult to consistently achieve without transforming the business system to have interdependent characteristics.

For example, outsourcing agreements are perfect opportunities for a partnership, but often the relationship takes on a more dominant/passive nature. If the organizations involved in the outsourcing agreement have a customer and vendor mindset, then the two organizations (customer and outsourcer) may have a business system with dependent characteristics. The outsourcer may become just another layer in the customer's organizational structure. Or the outsourcing contract may be used in a way to implement management system goals and objectives in a top-down fashion from customer to outsourcer. The outsourcing contract may also be used to ensure that the customer's existing processes are strictly enforced.

These dependent business system characteristics encourage the outsourcing employees to behave more passively, following the lead of the customer. These characteristics also encourage the customer to take a more dominant and authoritarian role in the relationship when providing direction to the outsourcer. Outsourcing relationships achieve greater mutual value outcomes when both parties take a more cooperative, collaborative, partnering approach and share responsibility for achieving their mutually beneficial goals.

Additionally, when employee behaviors, leadership behaviors, or business system characteristics are in conflict with each other, the organization doesn't operate as effectively as it could, and employee morale isn't as high as it could be. For example, a workgroup with an independent/laissez-faire organizational culture and dependent business system characteristics won't produce the best business results. Neither will it produce very high levels of gruntledness when the group has employees who prefer doing their own thing but are working under a business system that limits their responsibilities and authority. When employee and leadership behaviors and business system characteristics are in harmony and are appropriate for the organization, the organization will produce better business results and more gruntled employees.

Other problems can arise when an organization changes an existing business system to implement a new business strategy and ignores how organizational culture will factor in. If a current culture doesn't readily accept a business system-changing business strategy (such as outsourcing, mergers and acquisitions, and enterprise resource planning or other technology implementations), this can cause problems during implementation, such as missed dates and a far-exceeded budget.

On the other hand, sometimes the business strategy can change the business system in a way that encourages a different culture—one that may not be favorable to the business or employees. So the business strategy fails after implementation (for example, profitability is impacted or business results are not delivered).

How Moving to an Interdependent Business System Impacts Gruntledness and Success

A business composed of interdependent employee behaviors, connective behaviors, and interdependent business system characteristics will usually provide the best business results and improve employee gruntledness. Dependent business system characteristics tend to be effective in meeting an objective but not efficient: They will get the job done but at more cost and more time than is necessary. Independent business system characteristics tend to be efficient but not effective. These characteristics allow for things to proceed quickly but often do not meet intended objectives. For the most part, only interdependent business systems are both efficient and effective in helping the organization meet business objectives.

However, there are times when dependent or independent forms of business system characteristics might be more appropriate. The appropriateness of business system characteristics can vary by workgroup and industry. For example, the IT workgroup of a technology manufacturing company may need different business system characteristics than an IT workgroup for NASA. Information systems supporting manned spacecraft need more rigor than software supporting hot technology products with short life spans. It is important to ensure that business system characteristics are appropriate to your organization and workgroup and support the desired organizational culture. Certain interdependent business system characteristics may not be appropriate for the industry.

Regulated industries may require more dependent business system characteristics. For example, a pharmaceutical company that produces drugs according to US Food and Drug Administration (FDA) requirements may require certain dependent business system characteristics. This type of environment requires bureaucratic workflow and highly structured and strictly enforced processes that encourage employees to do as they're told and follow processes. In this case, improving processes and initiating change would be the responsibility of the research and development departments, whose staff would study the impacts of such changes before trying them in production.

Certain forms of business system characteristics are not appropriate for all workgroups within an organization. For instance, sales organizations often need the freedom that independent business system characteristics provide. Research-and-development environments also often benefit from more independent business system characteristics. Finance in any industry needs some of the rigor and bureaucracy that certain dependent business system characteristics provide. Most IT departments would be more respected in their companies if they had more interdependent business system characteristics in place to encourage collaboration and partnership with the workgroups they support. Understanding characteristics and the impact they have on organizational culture and business results will help in implementing business system changes.

The best chance for success often is employees working together interdependently under the guidance of connective leaders in an environment with interdependent business system characteristics. This is particularly true for business transformation strategies such as outsourcing, mergers and acquisitions, and enterprise resource planning implementations, where people need to find ways to work together differently. Most change efforts are doomed when leadership doesn't understand how the current business system characteristics affect and change organizational culture.

Why There Is a Lack of Interdependent Business System Characteristics in the Workplace

In reviewing the benefits of interdependent business systems, it is clear that interdependent business system characteristics often enable business success and improve employee gruntledness. If business strategies aren't working, the business system is often a key factor. Many business strategies could be greatly improved with the use of more interdependent business system characteristics.

So why don't we have more examples of interdependent business system characteristics in organizations? Because organizations are just not aware of its impact on business success and employee gruntledness. Without this awareness, leaders tend to define a business system based on their preferences for certain behavior patterns (for example, a leader with a preference for authoritarian behaviors may design a dependent business system).

The goal with interdependence is to create a fair and pleasant working environment and improve an organization's chance of success. Hopefully, increasing awareness of the benefits of an interdependent business system will inspire leaders to adopt more interdependent and connective behavior preferences and instill interdependent business system characteristics into their business. Part 5 will discuss how to adopt more interdependent characteristics into a business system and change the organizational culture.

Part 5

Addressing Causal Factors of Business Success and Employee Morale Problems

"You cannot continuously improve interdependent systems and processes until you progressively perfect interdependent, interpersonal relationships."

Stephen R. Covey
Author and Vice Chairman of Franklin Covey

22

A Holistic Approach to Improving Gruntledness and Business Success Simultaneously

"The morale of one company I worked for was low from what many in the company would describe as problems with the owner/managers. Complaints usually went like this: 'The owners are scared out of their minds and are breathing down our necks,' or 'The owners are ineffectual and have way too many meetings,' or 'The owners actually prevent me from doing my job,' or 'The owners have "Founders Syndrome" and just because they started this business, doesn't mean they know how to effectively manage it at its current level of growth; they should hire a consultant or someone to manage it for them.' This company actually lost many good people and found it almost impossible to keep people in a number of key positions. They have had to close certain aspects of the business and downsize the parts that still exist."

Disgruntled Employee
Blog Post

The greatest chance of business success and employee gruntledness can be achieved by taking a holistic approach. This part provides techniques for improving gruntledness and success at the same time by addressing employee behaviors, leadership behaviors, and business system characteristics. This holistic approach will improve workgroup morale and increase business results. This approach also improves the chances of success with implementing business initiatives such as mergers and acquisitions, offshore outsourcing, and information system implementation efforts.

Determining Your Gruntledness and Success Levels

Root cause analysis helps determine the causal factors behind disgruntledness and business performance problems. Your workgroup's gruntledness and success depends on three causal factor categories. As Part 2 demonstrates, employee behavior preferences have a lot to do with workgroup gruntledness and success. Part 3 shows how leadership behaviors can impact gruntledness and success. Part 4 shows how certain business system characteristics encourage different employee and leadership behaviors. So employee behavior preferences, leadership behavior preferences, and business system characteristics are the three causal factor categories for gruntledness and success problems, and within each of these factors, one or more leadership/employee activities or business characteristics may point to more specific causal factors.

Such problems are rarely attributed to a single causal factor, so don't be surprised at the number of causal factors uncovered. Once the causal factors are identified for your gruntledness and success levels, you can use techniques to address them and get to the root cause of the problem. To determine causal factors, you need to talk to your employees.

You can use the behavior matrices in Appendix A to create a list of questions for your employees to find out how they feel about employee behaviors in their workgroup and your leadership behaviors. You can also use the Business System Characteristics Matrix in Appendix A to create questions to get feedback from your employees about how they feel the business system influences employee and leadership behaviors.

To improve organizational culture or day-to-day operations, you can ask your workgroup members how they feel about the current state of the five employee activities, four leadership activities, and four business system components. Their response to what they feel is called the *current state*, which will identify the causal factors for employee morale and business success issues for your workgroup. You can then ask your workgroup what they feel needs to change (*desired state*) regarding certain behavior activities and business system characteristics. The desired state responses will determine the *critical success factors*; that is, the needed behaviors and characteristics that will improve gruntledness and business success. Improvement plans can then be developed to implement the critical success factors. Appendix A can also be used to define questions to help determine causal factors and critical success factors for business strategy implementation.

Causal Factors Applied to Different Scenarios

Employee morale and business success can be improved by addressing employee behavior, leadership behavior, and business system characteristic causal factors as necessary. Employee morale and business success problems can exist within a workgroup, between two workgroups, or between two people (interpersonally).

The three causal factor categories influence gruntledness and success levels within these three scenarios as shown in Figure 22.1.

Figure 22.1: Causal factor categories for gruntledness and success within scenarios

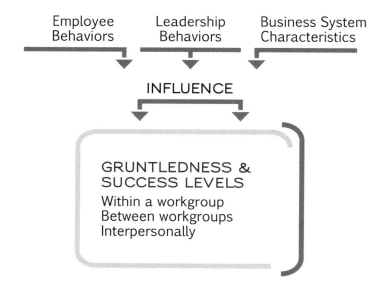

Each scenario comprises a specific behavior dynamic. Within a workgroup encompasses a *workgroup dynamic*. Between workgroups encompasses an *inter-workgroup dynamic*. Interpersonally encompasses a dynamic from person to person or an *interpersonal dynamic*.

The collective employee behaviors within a workgroup coupled with the workgroup leader's behavior preferences form a workgroup dynamic. The business system characteristics for that workgroup also influence whether the workgroup dynamic is more passive/authoritarian, independent/laissez-faire, interdependent/connective, or some other combination.

The collective behavior preferences for workgroup A coupled with the workgroup behavior preferences for workgroup B form an inter-workgroup dynamic. If one of the workgroups has a leadership role (which is often the case in customer/vendor situations), then the collective behavior preferences of the workgroup in a leadership role will influence whether that dynamic has more of a passive/authoritarian, independent/laissez-faire, or interdependent/connective dynamic. If the two workgroups are at the same peer level then the dynamics could be dominant/passive, independent/independent, interdependent/ interdependent, or some other combination. The business system characteristics that govern the two workgroups will further influence certain dynamics.

The behavior preferences of the people that you interact with at work coupled with your own behavior preferences form an interpersonal dynamic. If you or the other person that you are interacting with is in a leadership role, you may have a passive/authoritarian, independent/laissez-faire, or interdependent/connective dynamic. At the same peer level, your dynamic could be dominant/passive, independent/independent, interdependent/interdependent, or some other combination. Although business system characteristics do not influence interpersonal dynamics as much as the other scenarios, they can also be a factor in how you interact with another person, particularly if one of you is in a leadership role.

Improving Your Gruntledness and Success Levels

The next three chapters comprise a holistic approach to changing behavior preferences and organizational culture at a workgroup level, between workgroups, and at a personal level. Chapter 23 shows how causal factors influence workgroup dynamics and provides techniques for improving these dynamics. Chapter 24 shows how causal factors influence interactions between workgroups and provides techniques for improving inter-workgroup dynamics. Chapter 25 shows how employee and leadership behavior causal factors influence interpersonal dynamics and how to improve your interactions with others. Ultimately, these chapters are designed to help you improve your gruntledness and success at various levels.

23

Addressing Causal Factors for Workgroup Dynamics

"Back in the 70s there was a very successful radio station that had a strong manager [who was also a popular radio personality] on the air. But things weren't that great in 'Showbiz land.' The manager constantly criticized the staff, yelled at them, talked down to them, and was just plain annoying. He also had a habit of promising employees promotions and raises with no intention of keeping his promise.

One week, the manager was on vacation. Two people from the staff's morning team orchestrated a 'revolt' of sorts. They called the 'head guy owner' and said, 'We want you to fire him. We don't like him.'

The head guy said that they coudn't do that because he's responsible for the station's success. The morning team member then said that they had 20 people who were going to resign immediately. The owner then said, "Uh . . . uh . . . hold on. I'll fly out and we'll discuss this.

It was a testy meeting. Twenty people had their resignations in hand and stood their ground—they were ready to walk off.

In the meantime, the manager, who was on vacation, picked up a copy of the [local newspaper] at a sandwich shop. Right on the front page was a little headline near the bottom, '[Radio Personality] Ousted from KXXX.' That was news to HIM!

I love that story because the staff got the upper hand in firing their boss—something that many of us have wanted to do in our past jobs! Yep, morale zoomed up, and the station did fine after his departure."

Disgruntled Employee
Blog Post

Many workgroups have a dynamic with their leaders that either negatively impacts employee morale or business results, or both. This dynamic is what primarily forms the organizational culture for the workgroup. Most leaders and workgroups are not aware of how they can change their organizational culture to be more effective.

Let's look closer at what defines organizational culture. Organizational culture is marked by the series of interactions that occur between employees and their leader. These interactions are typically either passive/authoritarian, independent/laissez-faire, or interdependent/connective. Of course, other combinations can also occur, for example, dominant/authoritarian or passive/laissez-faire. When the leader and employees consistently interact one way, then a culture forms for the workgroup.

However, how the workgroup interacts with their leader can vary depending on the situation. Leaders and employees can interact one way regarding normal day-to-day operations and an entirely different way when implementing a business initiative.

The techniques in this chapter will help you as a leader change your workgroup's dynamics to improve employee morale and business results at the same time. This chapter will use the following approach to help improve workgroup dynamics:

- Determine causal and critical success factors for your workgroup's dynamics
- Address business system characteristics as a causal factor for your workgroup's dynamics
- Address your leadership behavior preferences as a causal factor for your workgroup's dynamics
- Address the collective employee behavior preferences as a causal factor for your workgroup's dynamics

Determining Causal and Critical Success Factors for Workgroup Dynamics

You probably already have a sense of whether your workgroup dynamics are primarily passive/authoritarian, independent/laissez-faire, interdependent/connective, or some other combination. During normal business operations, many workgroup dynamics work out just fine. The leader's preference for authoritarian, laissez-faire, or connective behaviors often set the tone for the workgroup. Employees respond accordingly with passive, dominant, independent, or interdependent behaviors.

Certain situations may occur that elicit different behaviors; but for the most part, the leader and workgroup members are used to working together in a certain way that gets the job done. The workgroup may not have the highest productivity or employee morale, but they deliver acceptable business results and have found a way to accept or at least cope with each other's behavior preferences.

However, when a business initiative comes along to improve business results, the workgroup dynamic may start to show signs of stress. The business system characteristics that encourage the workgroup dynamics may not work as effectively with the change. Interactions among workgroup members and between workgroup members and their leader may become more challenging and sometimes unpleasant. The workgroup may fail to meet anticipated business objectives. The workgroup that under normal circumstances worked fairly well together may now find itself falling apart.

If the workgroup dynamic becomes ineffective in times of change, you need to determine which of the three causal factor categories—employee and leadership behaviors and business system characteristics—are contributing to the problem at hand. Using the matrices in Appendix A, you can create questions for whatever activities and characteristics are pertinent to the issue you are trying to solve. You can then ask your workgroup members the questions to determine the causal factors. You can develop a survey of the questions if you want to provide some level of anonymity for the responses.

If you are a senior manager and have a workgroup with direct reports who each manage their own workgroup, don't just stop at discussing causal and critical success factors with your direct reports. You will also need to get feedback from each workgroup to get a better picture of what's going on, since the dynamic the senior manager has with his or her direct reports can greatly differ from the dynamic that the direct reports have with their workgroups.

Because workgroups typically do not have the time or resources to address every issue uncovered, it's important for you to focus on the questions that your workgroup feels need the most improvement. This means that only some of the employee behaviors, leadership behaviors, or business system characteristics need to be changed to fix employee morale and business success problems.

Addressing Workgroup Dynamics Causal Factor: Business System Characteristics

The most efficient way to change workgroup dynamics is to change the business system characteristics for the workgroup to ensure they encourage the most appropriate employee and leadership behaviors. This causal factor category has the widest influence on workgroup dynamics. Changing business system characteristics influences all leader and employee behaviors within an organization.

Implementing interdependent business system characteristics is often the best way to achieve both business strategy objectives and desired employee gruntledness levels. Interdependent business system characteristics help promote interdependent and connective behaviors within a workgroup. Without them, leaders may use authoritarian behaviors to deliver business results. Note that certain situations may require specific workgroup dynamics. For example, authoritarian and passive behaviors may be more appropriate for a workgroup responsible for maintaining a nuclear power plant or for employees with minimal work experience.

Discussions about your workgroup's desired state will indicate the exact business system characteristics your workgroup feels are critical for success. Desired state comments will also help determine which workgroup dynamic—passive/authoritarian, independent/laissez-faire, or interdependent/connective—is the most appropriate for the workgroup.

Meet Company Vision and Objectives—Improving Business System Characteristics Example

Ricardo's company announced a business vision and objective last year of growing company revenue and profit by 10%. The company is currently falling short of meeting this objective. Ricardo's workgroup identifies certain business system characteristics to be causal factors in not meeting the company's growth objective. Workgroup discussions indicate that employees feel that the business system characteristics are primarily independent and dependent in nature. Workgroup discussions also indicate that employees feel that the business system characteristics should be more interdependent. Specific causal factors are listed below:

- Unclear roles and responsibilities regarding growth objectives
- No measurable targets by workgroup for growth objectives
- Insufficient planning at lower workgroup levels regarding how to meet growth objectives
- Sales processes are insufficient in helping workgroups grow
- Insufficient data regarding progress towards growth objectives

IMPROVEMENT PLAN: Ricardo asks for volunteers to participate in a special task force to review current business system characteristics to see what can be done to improve them so that they are more useful in meeting the company's vision and objectives. Based on workgroup discussions, the task force comes up with the following recommendations:

- Redefine roles and responsibilities clearly, explaining how each role can increase revenue and profit
- Conduct a series of workshops at each level of the organization to determine each workgroup's objectives in meeting growth objectives
- Allow the next management level down to refine business objectives and detailed implementation plans for increasing revenue and profit
- Set up a new team to measure the effectiveness of sales processes in

meeting growth objectives, and determine improvements based on the process's measurable results

- Evaluate individual IT needs to ensure everyone has access to the required data to make informed decisions regarding revenue and profit growth

Addressing Workgroup Dynamics Causal Factor: Leadership Behaviors

If discussions indicate that some leadership activities are causal factors for your workgroup, then a review of specific leadership activities that your workgroup feels are most critical is warranted. The biggest lever that leaders have for improving workgroup dynamics is their own behavior. As leaders change their behaviors, members of their workgroup will start to interact with them differently. Changing leadership behaviors influences how all the employees behave within the workgroup.

Using more connective behaviors is often the best way to improve business results and employee morale. Connective behaviors encourage interdependent behaviors from employees. However, a change in leadership behaviors should be based on which leadership behaviors your workgroup feels are critical for success and which dynamics are most appropriate for the workgroup.

Meet Company Vision and Objectives—Improving Leadership Behaviors Example

Discussions with Ricardo's workgroup indicate that the workgroup feels several leadership behaviors are causal factors for not meeting workgroup objectives for company growth. Current state discussions indicate that most employees consider their leader's behaviors to be primarily laissez-faire. Workgroup members think that connective behaviors are a critical success factor for meeting the company's growth objectives. Specific causal factors are listed below:

- Leader is not involved enough with workgroup regarding growth objectives

- No incentive to meet growth objectives
- No assistance from leader on how to meet growth objectives
- Not enough information-sharing or listening to employee concerns

IMPROVEMENT PLAN: Ricardo works with HR to see what can be done to improve his behaviors so that he can be more helpful to workgroup members in meeting their objectives to support the company's growth vision. Using comments from workgroup discussions as a guide, Ricardo and HR come up with the following recommendations for Ricardo:

- Work more closely with workgroup members by providing direction and listening to feedback on how to implement growth strategies
- Recognize and reward individuals and team for meeting interim milestones towards overall growth target
- Hold individual coaching sessions for workgroup members who are having difficulty meeting personal objectives for business growth
- Hold "all hands" meetings more frequently, allowing equal time for communicating current results and listening to employee concerns on meeting growth targets

If you manage leaders of workgroups, you may encounter leaders within your workgroup who are very attached to their current behavior preferences. If you find someone who prefers certain leadership behaviors that cause employee morale problems or negatively impact business results, then you have three choices: Coach, support, or replace the individual.

Coaching these individuals can be very effective. One-on-one discussions about how they handled a situation and what they might have done to handle the situation more effectively can help them start choosing more appropriate behaviors. Follow-up discussions will ensure that leaders are making progress towards changing their behaviors.

Sometimes a person isn't open to coaching. In that case, it may be useful to team the manager up with another employee (either inside or outside the workgroup) who will provide what the manager lacks. For instance, if a manager prefers laissez-faire behaviors, it may be helpful to team that manager up with another person who will provide more guidance and work more closely with the team, helping the manager get the workgroup to behave more interdependently. If a manager prefers more authoritarian behaviors, placing a person with connective leadership preferences between the manager and the employees can help move the workgroup toward interdependent behaviors.

If the leader is too attached to certain behavior preferences, it may be necessary to make some organizational changes to change the dynamic of the workgroup. Some people are too closed-minded to accept different ways of doing things. If you want to change the workgroup dynamic, a necessary step may be to replace closed-minded managers with those who are more open to changing their leadership behaviors. Moving unwilling leaders to staff positions where their behavior preferences have limited impact on workgroup dynamics is one technique. Another is letting the person know that it would be better to find work elsewhere.

Addressing Workgroup Dynamics Causal Factor: Collective Employee Behaviors

If workgroup discussions uncover that some of the collective employee activities are causal factors, then it is helpful to discuss areas where the group should focus for improvement. Remember, all behavior preferences have a time and place. But interdependent behaviors are more useful in many more situations in the business world and are usually a critical success factor for improving business results and employee morale. However, the desired state discussions will indicate which employee behavior patterns your workgroup deems critical for success.

Meet Company Vision and Objectives—Improving Employee Behaviors Example

Ricardo's workgroup's discussions indicate that most of the workgroup members think that certain collective behaviors of their coworkers contribute to not meeting growth objectives. Current state discussions indicate that most employees consider their coworkers' behaviors to be passive in meeting growth targets. As indicated by desired state discussions, the workgroup feels that working more interdependently with its leader would help it to meet growth objectives. Specific causal factors are listed below:

- Apathy regarding growth objectives
- Lack of participation in discussion on how to meet growth objectives
- Discounting the significance of problems regarding growth objectives
- Lack of understanding on how each role contributes to growth objectives

Ricardo recognizes that as the leader, he has a lot to do to improve leadership behaviors and business system characteristics, but he also decides to focus on collective employee behaviors since the success of their growth objective depends significantly on employees changing their behaviors.

IMPROVEMENT PLAN: Ricardo meets with his workgroup members to determine what they should do to address employee behavior causal factors. He asks for volunteers to define a plan on how they can improve collective employee behaviors. The volunteers come up with the following recommendations:

- Work with leader to understand his vision on why it is important to meet growth objectives
- Reserve one weekly staff meeting to review growth results on a monthly basis, and decide the best ways to improve results; workgroup members need to voice their opinions more often during meetings and actively participate in making decisions regarding how to meet growth objectives
- Identify respectful ways to confront each other when workgroup members are discounting problems regarding growth objectives
- Document the problem interdependencies in meeting growth targets; document how each individual can provide support to others in meeting growth objectives

Changing Workgroup Dynamics Is a Learning Process and Takes Time

It is important to work on improving employee behaviors, leadership behaviors, and business system characteristics in concert, since the three influence each other so much. There are many ways to apply the concepts in this book to improve your workgroup dynamics. One way is to use the following process to help you improve the dynamics for your workgroup:

1. **Determine what objective you are trying to achieve.**
   a. To improve employee morale?
   b. To improve business results?
   c. To implement a business strategy?
   d. To improve employee engagement?

2. **Using the behavior and business system characteristics matrices in Appendix A as a guide, determine causal factors for your workgroup dynamics (current state).**
   a. What employee behaviors are contributing to current workgroup dynamics?
   b. What leadership behaviors are contributing to current workgroup dynamics?
   c. What business system characteristics could be encouraging these dynamics?

3. **Using the behavior and business system characteristics matrices in Appendix A as a guide, determine critical success factors to improve workgroup dynamics (desired state).**
   a. What behaviors do you need from workgroup members to be successful at meeting your objectives?
   b. What leadership behaviors are needed to engage employees in meeting your objectives?
   c. What business system characteristics would encourage these behaviors?

4. Develop with your workgroup an improvement plan to address the factors that your workgroup feels are the most important.

   a. Develop a business system improvement plan, focusing on the business system characteristics deemed critical for success.

      i. What business system components were you planning on changing to achieve your objectives?

      ii. What other business system components could help improve chances of success?

      iii. What characteristics could you add to the business system to improve employee and leadership engagement?

   b. Develop a leadership behavior improvement plan, focusing on the leadership activities deemed critical for success.

      i. What training classes are needed to encourage the right leadership behaviors?

      ii. Do any of the leaders need coaching or mentoring on more appropriate behavior choices?

      iii. Would a workshop be helpful in increasing leader understanding of workgroup dynamics regarding meeting your objective?

   c. Develop a collective employee behavior improvement plan, focusing on the employee activities deemed critical for success.

      i. What training classes are needed to encourage the right employee behaviors?

      ii. Do any employees need coaching or mentoring?

      iii. Would a workshop be helpful in increasing employee understanding of workgroup dynamics regarding meeting your objective?

   d. Review the business system, leadership behavior, and collective employee behavior improvement plans together, looking for interdependencies between them.

   e. Update the appropriate plan accordingly to address identified interdependencies.

5. **Develop a timeline for implementing the business system, leadership behavior, and collective employee behavior improvement plans.**

6. **Several months after implementation of the three improvement plans, check with your workgroup to determine the degree of improvement and what activities still need to be focused on.**

If you find that the workgroup dynamics aren't improving fast enough to improve employee morale or meet business objectives, then you may need to look further at the interpersonal dynamics that are occurring between workgroup members and leaders. Chapter 25 describes in detail how to improve interactions between two people, including an employee and a leader.

24

Addressing Causal Factors for Dynamics Between Workgroups

"I worked for a large IT company that supplied contractors, leased equipment, and technology services. Our service division had leased two large computers from the leasing division of the same company. The end of the lease came up and the service division decided to send the current hardware back and replace it with the newest generation of equipment. The day the new computers came in, my coworker Scott met the delivery people in the computer room to handle the paperwork. The new computers were installed and the old computers were boxed up and loaded on the truck. Scott signed the paperwork to show that all the work was completed.

Six weeks later, Scott received a call from a collection agency demanding that he pay up on the shipping charges for the return of the leased equipment. This was in the tens of thousands of dollar range. He was told that he had 10 days to get this resolved before the collection agency would file charges of theft of services against him. Then law enforcement could/would be sent out to arrest him. It took a while for Scott to figure out just what was going on. It turned out that the leasing division and the service division of the same company, could not come to an agreement on who would pay for the shipping charges. So the leasing division turned in the problem to a collection agency, who then went after Scott in the other division. Scott thought this would be a great cause to go to jail for, and then just let the company HR decide who would post bail for their own employee. Scott's managers made a few calls and by the end of the week the threatening calls had ceased. We never did find out who paid the shipping charges."

Disgruntled Employee
Blog Post

When two workgroups are working together, often one workgroup takes the lead role. In customer/vendor interactions, the customer will typically use authoritarian behaviors and the vendor will respond with passive behaviors. Many customers and vendors talk about having a partnership, but most aren't using interdependent and connective behaviors and don't realize a true partnership.

The same thing can happen when two workgroups within an organization work together. For example, IT departments often collectively use dominant and authoritarian behaviors because the workgroups that need IT supports often have nowhere else to go. The technical lingo that an IT department uses also contributes to their use of dominant and authoritarian behaviors. For example, one technologist said years ago that if you can't dazzle them with your brilliance, baffle them with bull.

The problem isn't that the other workgroup behaves inappropriately; it's that your workgroup reacts to the behavior inappropriately. So the focus shouldn't be on changing the other workgroup, the focus should be on changing your workgroup so that they don't respond with an equally inappropriate behavior.

The techniques in this chapter will help you as a leader change the way your workgroup interacts with another workgroup to improve employee morale and business results at the same time. This chapter will use the following approach to help improve inter-workgroup dynamics:

- Determine causal and critical success factors for the dynamics between two workgroups
- Address business system characteristics as a causal factor for inter-workgroup dynamics
- Address your workgroup's collective behavior preference as a causal factor for inter-workgroup dynamics
- Address the other workgroup's collective behavior preference as a causal factor for inter-workgroup dynamics

Determining Causal and Critical Success Factors for Inter-Workgroup Dynamics

The dynamic between your workgroup and another workgroup, whether it is a leader/follower relationship or a peer-level relationship, may be primarily passive/authoritarian, independent/laissez-faire, interdependent/connective, or some other combination of employee and leadership behaviors. In a leader/follower relationship, the lead workgroup's preference for authoritarian, laissez-faire, or connective behaviors often sets the tone for the inter-workgroup dynamics. The other workgroup behaves accordingly with passive, dominant, independent, or interdependent behaviors.

In a peer-level relationship, either workgroup can use passive, dominant, independent, and interdependent behaviors depending on the situation, and the other workgroup will behave accordingly. This is because the behaviors of one workgroup influence the behaviors of the other workgroup significantly. For example, if one workgroup is behaving passively, then the other workgroup may start behaving more dominantly. However, either workgroup can change the dynamic to something more appropriate.

Certain situations may occur that elicit different behaviors, but for the most part, the two workgroups are used to working together in a certain way and have developed a pattern on how to interact that generally "works." The two workgroups may not achieve all that they could from the partnership, but they work together in an acceptable way and can cope with each other's collective behavior preferences.

Once you determine the dynamics, you can begin to determine causal factors for a particular inter-workgroup dynamic. The interactions between the two workgroups may be effective during normal business operations but ineffective in times of change. Therefore, you need to determine the causal factors specific to the type of situation that you want to change.

Using the matrices in Appendix A, you can formulate questions to determine causal factors for inter-workgroup dynamics. You can then ask the members of your workgroup to get their impression of the dynamics and causal factors for both workgroups. It isn't recommended to ask the other workgroup, since the workgroup may not be willing to answer these types of questions. Also some workgroup relationships deem asking such questions imprudent (for example, a fragile vendor/customer relationship). In addition, without a facilitator to help lead a discussion, comments could lead to arguments about whose perception of the workgroups' dynamic is correct. The result could end up hurting the relationship more than helping it.

Asking questions to only your workgroup members to get their impression of the dynamics with the other workgroup is still very helpful. The only behaviors you can really change are those of your own workgroup anyway. How your workgroup perceives interactions with the other workgroup will help your workgroup figure out ways to change that dynamic. Of course, asking the other workgroup about their impression of the dynamic would provide even more information. If you choose to do so, you need to ensure that a facilitator or someone who has strong social skills is present to work through differences in perception.

The questions should look at the possible causal factors to determine your workgroup's behavior preferences, the other workgroup's behavior preferences, and the business system characteristics contributing to the current dynamics between the two workgroups. During discussions, you should focus on the questions that your workgroup feels are the most important to address. The discussions should also give you an indication of inter-workgroup dynamics for each of the employee and leadership activities. For example, you may find that in completing tasks together, the members of both workgroups interact with each other using interdependent behaviors. But you may find that when the other workgroup is providing direction, the dynamic is more passive/authoritarian.

You need to determine which dynamics your workgroup thinks could be improved, and in which activities. Only the dynamics for some of the employee or leadership activities and business system characteristics may need to be changed to address the issues that you have with the other workgroup. Desired state comments will determine which collective behaviors and business system characteristics are critical success factors.

Addressing Inter-Workgroup Dynamics Causal Factor: Business System Characteristics

The most efficient way to change inappropriate inter-workgroup dynamics is to change the business system characteristics for the two workgroups. When a business system characteristic is a causal factor, it has the widest influence on inter-workgroup dynamics. Changing business system characteristics for two workgroups influences the members' behaviors in both workgroups.

Before you can change the business system characteristics, you must take into consideration the relationship between the two workgroups. For example, workgroups in the same company will operate under the same business system characteristics; whereas two workgroups in two different companies may operate under two different sets of business system characteristics. So in the latter case, you will need to have a good understanding of both business systems. Another setup can be a formalized relationship between two companies with a written contract defining a business system to govern how the two companies will work together.

For example, suppose you have a customer and vendor relationship and each company uses their own business system. The two companies will probably have an independent/laissez-faire dynamic because each company has its own business system. If the vendor adopts the business system of the customer, then the dynamic between the two companies will have a greater chance of being passive/authoritarian because the vendor is dependent on the customer's business system. If a business system is defined to govern how the customer and vendor work together and it contains interdependent characteristics, then the dynamic between the two companies will more than likely be interdependent/connective.

Implementing interdependent business system characteristics is the best way to achieve both business strategy objectives and employee gruntledness. Interdependent business system characteristics help promote interdependent and connective behaviors between two workgroups. Without them, one workgroup may feel it needs to use authoritarian or dominant behaviors to deliver business results.

The business system characteristics that your workgroup feel are critical to success are the factors that you need to address. A discussion of critical success factors should take place within the workgroup or between both workgroups if both participated in the discussion. This will help determine which inter-workgroup dynamic is the most appropriate between the two workgroups.

Meet Company Vision and Objectives—Improving Business System Characteristics Example

Mary is working for a company that is a supplier of IT services. Mary has just taken over an account where the client feels her company is not living up to their expectations, even though it meets contractual obligations. Mary decides to conduct an inter-workgroup dynamic survey with her workgroup to uncover causal factors for the strained relationship her account team has with the client. Current state discussions show that the workgroup feels some of the business system characteristics are causal factors to not meeting client expectations. Workgroup members believe the business system characteristics are primarily dependent and independent in nature. Desired state discussions indicate that workgroup members feel that interdependent business system characteristics are critical success factors for improving the relationship with the client. Specific causal factors are listed below:

- Current roles and responsibilities limit employees to contractual obligations rather than broader client expectations
- Employees do not understand where to go for help when clients raise certain issues
- Vendor objectives to reduce cost seem to be in conflict with client objectives of having higher levels of service
- Processes seem to be overly defined, increasing the cost and time required to perform services

IMPROVEMENT PLAN: Mary works with her leadership team to review current business characteristics to see what can be done to improve them so that they are more useful in meeting the client's expectations. Using the responses as a guide, Mary and her leadership team come up with the following recommendations:

- Review roles and responsibilities between the two workgroups to remove any limitations that prevent her workgroup from meeting objectives and to clarify how to meet client expectations
- Review the organizational structure to see if it can be streamlined and communicate how the organizational structure can be used to support client expectations
- Compare vendor objectives with client objectives and identify ways to cost effectively meet client expectations for higher service levels
- Improve processes by removing bureaucratic and unnecessary steps and by clarifying needed steps to help meet client expectations

Addressing Inter-Workgroup Dynamics Causal Factor: Collective Behaviors for Your Workgroup

If the discussions uncover that some of your workgroup's collective behaviors are causal factors, then it is helpful to determine specific activities where the group can improve. Interdependent and connective behaviors are useful in many inter-workgroup dynamics and are usually a critical success factor for improving the working relationship between two workgroups. However, the desired state discussions will indicate which employee behavior patterns your workgroup deems critical for success. Also, discussing your workgroup's desired state behaviors is helpful in determining if they are appropriate for what you are trying to achieve.

Meet Company Vision and Objectives—Improving Collective Behaviors Example

The discussions with Mary's workgroup indicate that the workgroup thinks some of the collective behaviors in the workgroup contribute to negative dynamics with its client. Current state discussions indicate that while most employees consider their collective behaviors to be interdependent when interacting with the client, they feel that they would like to be less passive and even more interdependent when interacting with the client. Specific causal factors are listed below:

- Not speaking up in client meetings, particularly when the client seems upset
- Not completely understanding client opinions
- Not discussing a topic before a client meeting to understand and formulate a collective opinion beforehand
- Not proactively bringing up issues for discussion with the client

IMPROVEMENT PLAN: Mary holds a meeting with her workgroup to review the results of the survey and to have them define a plan on how they can improve their dynamics with the client. Her workgroup members come up with the following recommendations:

- Try to voice their opinions more in meetings with the client
- Ask the client questions to ensure they understand clients' opinions
- Ensure that they reach a collective agreement within the workgroup before discussing decisions with a client
- Bring up items in meetings with the client to make more decisions jointly

Addressing Inter-Workgroup Dynamics Causal Factor: Collective Behaviors for Other Workgroups

It is possible that the collective behaviors of the other workgroup are a significant causal factor for inter-workgroup dynamics. Focusing the inter-workgroup dynamic questions to a specific situation can help determine causal factors for why the other workgroup is behaving the way they are.

Suppose you are a supplier to another workgroup and your client uses dominant/authoritarian behaviors and micromanages your workgroup. A good question to ask is if your workgroup is giving the client reason to micromanage. If your workgroup isn't meeting its obligations to the client, then the answer is yes. If your workgroup has a preference for passive behaviors and it's just doing as it's told by the client, then you should expect the client to develop a preference for dominant or authoritarian behaviors when dealing with your workgroup.

After you work on changing your workgroup's collective behaviors from passive to something more appropriate such as independent or interdependent, you might find that the client still uses primarily dominant/authoritarian behaviors. If so, they've developed a preference for these behaviors in their interactions with your workgroup and it will take a conscious effort on their part to change these dynamics. However, there isn't anything that you can do to directly change the behavior preferences of another workgroup. All that you can do is work on changing the collective behaviors of your workgroup, which will change how your workgroup interacts with the other workgroup, and ultimately the dynamic.

Chapter 25 provides an approach for changing the dynamics between two people. These same techniques can be applied to changing the dynamics between two workgroups. After all, inter-workgroup dynamics are just a combination of a lot of interpersonal dynamics that occur between the members of your workgroup and the other workgroup.

Meet Company Vision and Objectives—Addressing Other Workgroup's Collective Behaviors Example

Since Mary doesn't want to highlight the relationship issues any further to the client, she decides to survey only her workgroup to see how it perceives the client's collective behaviors. Survey responses indicate that her workgroup thinks some of the client's collective behaviors contribute to the negative dynamics between the two workgroups. Current state responses indicate that the primary concern of her workgroup is the client's use of dominant behaviors. They also wish that the client would use more interdependent behaviors when interacting with her workgroup.

IMPROVEMENT PLAN: Mary holds a meeting with her workgroup members to review responses and discuss how their own behaviors may contribute to the client's use of certain behaviors. After comparing her workgroup's own behaviors to the perceived client's behaviors, the workgroup feels that the client needs to change their behaviors more than they need to change their own behaviors. Realizing that they can only change their own behaviors, they decide to use the techniques in Chapter 25 on interpersonal dynamics to encourage the client to use different behaviors. The responses help them realize that they need to apply those techniques in the following areas:

- Conflict resolution and conflict expectation are the activities that the workgroup has identified to be the biggest problem areas; the workgroup needs to figure out how to respond more appropriately when the client uses dominant behaviors during conflict
- The workgroup also would prefer that the client use less dominant behaviors in making decisions; the workgroup needs to figure out how to encourage more sharing of each other's opinions so that they can make more decisions jointly
- Regarding problem solving, the workgroup feels that the client overreacts to problems; the workgroup needs to respond to these client behaviors in a way that will encourage the client to be supportive

Changing Inter-Workgroup Dynamics Is a Learning Process and Takes Time

It is important to work on improving business system characteristics and your workgroup's collective behaviors in concert, since the two influence each other so much. There are many ways to apply the concepts in this book to improve the dynamics your workgroup has with another workgroup. One way is to use the following process to help you improve the dynamics between your workgroup and another workgroup. Note: Involve a facilitator to help with discussions between workgroups if both workgroups will be involved.

1. Determine what objective you are trying to achieve.
   a. To improve employee morale of one or both of the workgroups?
   b. To improve business results based on the interaction between the two workgroups?

c. To implement a business strategy that impacts both workgroups?

d. To improve engagement of both workgroups in meeting shared objectives?

2. **Using the behavior and business system characteristics matrices in Appendix A as a guide, determine causal factors for your inter-workgroup dynamics (current state).**

a. What behaviors does your workgroup use on a regular basis that could contribute to current inter-workgroup dynamics?

b. What behaviors does the other workgroup use on a regular basis that could contribute to current inter-workgroup dynamics?

c. What business system characteristics could be encouraging inter-workgroup dynamics?

3. **Using the behavior and business system characteristics matrices in Appendix A as a guide, determine critical success factors to improve inter-workgroup dynamics (desired state).**

a. What behaviors does your workgroup need to use to improve inter-workgroup dynamics?

b. What behaviors does the other workgroup need to use to improve inter-workgroup dynamics?

c. What business system characteristics would encourage these behaviors?

4. **Develop with your workgroup an improvement plan to address the factors that your workgroup feels are the most important.**

a. Develop a business system improvement plan, focusing on the business system characteristics deemed critical for success.

i. What business system characteristics could you change that would improve inter-workgroup dynamics?

ii. What characteristics could you add that would improve inter-workgroup dynamics?

   b. Develop a collective employee behavior improvement plan for your workgroup, focusing on the employee activities deemed critical for success.

      i. Are there any training classes that would help your workgroup improve their behavior choices?

      ii. Do any of your workgroup members need coaching or mentoring on more appropriate behavior choices?

      iii. Would a workshop be helpful in increasing your workgroup's understanding of inter-workgroup dynamics?

   c. Work with your workgroup to develop some techniques for changing its response to the other workgroup's behavior for activities that are identified as the most problematic.

   d. Review the business system and collective employee behavior improvement plans together, looking for interdependencies between them.

   e. Update the appropriate plan accordingly to address identified interdependencies.

5. Develop a timeline for implementing the business system and collective employee behavior improvement plans.

6. Several months after implementation of the two improvement plans, check with your workgroup to determine the degree of improvement and what activities still need to be focused on.

If you find that your interactions aren't improving with the other workgroup, then you may need to look further at the interpersonal dynamics that are occurring between your workgroup members and the members of the other workgroup. Chapter 25 describes in detail how to improve interactions between two people, including employees within two different workgroups.

25

Addressing Causal Factors for Interpersonal Dynamics

"A boss I had at the phone company decided that all of her employees were incapable of getting work done flawlessly, so she insisted on always reviewing every piece of work we did. She wanted us all to know how invaluable she was and how her department ran efficiently because of her and her alone. So it came as no shock to me when she called me over to her desk and threw a handwritten note at me then asked 'WHAT'S THAT?'

I looked at it and said, 'A phone message.'

She said, 'I mean what is this letter you wrote at the beginning of this word?'

I looked at the note and saw the word began with a G so I told her it was a G. She curtly told me that was not the way one wrote a G then proceeded to show me how to write a G. I told her that that may be the way she writes a G, but it's not the way I write my G. She insisted that I write my Gs her way. I looked at her with defiance, but told her that I'd try to change the way I write, but I couldn't guarantee I'd always remember because I've been writing my Gs this way for years. It wasn't long after this incident that she called me into a conference room and asked me what my problem was. I told her she was my problem, that she had no confidence in any of her employees, that she wasted our time and her time reviewing all of our work and picking on the littlest items like the way I made my Gs, and that I was fed up with her. Believe it or not we were able to work out our differences and learned to respect each other. When she finally retired she called me up and invited me to her retirement party. I felt that spoke volumes about how we had resolved our differences."

Disgruntled Employee
Blog Post

Most people would agree that the behavior of others also impacts our personal and workgroup gruntledness and success levels. It might seem that the workplace would be a lot nicer if managers, coworkers, vendors, and customers behaved more appropriately. However, the problem isn't that other people behave inappropriately; it's that we react to their behavior inappropriately.

For example, if someone inappropriately chooses dominant behaviors to interact with us, the problem isn't necessarily that person's inappropriate behavior choice. The problem is that we inappropriately choose passive behaviors in response. If we choose a different behavior pattern than passive, then we change how we interact with that person. For example, if we respond with a dominant behavior, for better or worse, we might start an argument with the other person, which is definitely a different dynamic than passively going along with the other person's dominant behavior.

We can also change how we initiate interactions to change the dynamics that we have with others. For example, if we typically use a dominant behavior in making a decision with another person, we can consciously choose to use an interdependent behavior instead. If we usually state our opinion before the other person, we can decide to hold back our opinion until we've elicited the other person's opinion on the topic.

So the focus shouldn't be on changing the other person, the focus should be on changing ourselves so that we don't respond with or initiate equally inappropriate behaviors. Much of what happens in our interactions with others is a result of coping strategies we use to deal with people with certain behavior preferences.

In an interaction, your behavior can influence another person's behavior, and that person's behavior can influence your behavior. If a person chooses dominant or authoritarian behaviors, the other person often chooses passive behaviors. The more a person chooses interdependent and connective behaviors, the more others choose interdependent and connective behaviors in return.

Complementary and Contradictory Interactions

In the late 1970s, I learned a helpful technique created by Dr. Eric Berne for interacting with people called Transactional Analysis (TA). Through TA concepts, I developed a way to analyze and improve workplace interactions. In the workplace, we either interact with each other in complementary or in contradictory ways.

A *complementary interaction* occurs between two people when one uses an expected behavior pattern in response to another's behavior pattern. For example, someone uses a dominant or authoritarian behavior and expects a passive behavior in return. If the other person responds passively, this completes a complementary interaction. This is a complementary *dependent* interaction because dominant behavior needs (or depends on) a passive behavior in response to maintain the status quo of the established dynamic. This interaction causes a certain amount of harmony—even if the person acting passively gets the short end of the stick. It is devoid of conflict, which works for people with a preference for passive behaviors who may feel that it is better to bow down than cause a rift.

With anyone you interact with on a regular basis, you probably have developed a consistent dynamic. For example, if someone prefers dominant and authoritarian behaviors, you may choose to use passive behaviors around that person. As a result, interactions with that person will often have a passive/dominant or authoritarian dynamic. Your interactions with that person are complementary.

A *contradictory interaction* occurs when a person uses an unexpected behavior pattern in response to another's behavior pattern. For example, someone interacts using a dominant behavior and expects a passive response, but the initiating person receives an interdependent response from the other person instead. Since the first person expected a passive response rather than an interdependent response, the result is a contradictory interaction.

If you use contradictory behaviors with a person, it will change the dynamic between you and the other person. The other person may back off and start treating you with respect or might get really upset. To change the dynamic for the better, you must change yourself and have the courage to respectfully confront the other person's inappropriate behaviors. The problem with your interactions with others is you; it is always you—no one else—until you change your behavior. The root cause of your problems with others is you.

The techniques in this chapter will help you change your dynamics with your coworkers, leaders, customers, and anyone else you encounter in the workplace. These techniques are often critical for improving workgroup dynamics because they can change the way leaders and workgroup members interact. They are also useful in improving inter-workgroup dynamics because they can change the way employees from two different workgroups interact. This chapter will use the following approach to help improve your interpersonal dynamics:

- Determine the causal and critical success factors for your dynamics
- Address inappropriate passive dynamics
- Address inappropriate dominant dynamics
- Address inappropriate independent dynamics

Determining Causal and Critical Success Factors for Dynamics

Asking yourself some questions to determine causal and critical success factors can help you improve your interactions with others. The first step is to better understand what dynamics you have with those that you interact with on a regular basis. To do this, you can ask questions about how you react to behavior during interactions and how the other person reacts to your behavior. Your responses regarding your own behavior will point to whether you behave passively, dominantly, independently, or interdependently while interacting. Your response to questions regarding the other person's behavior will indicate how you think he or she primarily behaves while interacting with you.

Note that sometimes your perception of the other person's behavior will say more about you than the other person. For example, if you desire the other person to use more passive behaviors and less dominant behaviors while interacting, it is possible that you have difficulty dealing with dominant behaviors, so you use passive behaviors as a way to cope with them. When you understand how you typically react to passive, dominant, independent, or interdependent behaviors, you can reflect on whether you've developed an ineffective coping strategy in response to these behaviors and see how your behavior impacts your gruntledness and success. Since you can only change yourself and not others, you may need to work on changing your behavior with people who use inappropriate behaviors. Improving the dynamics that you have with your coworkers, leaders, and others is done one interaction at a time.

Since your behavior preferences and the other person's behavior preferences contribute to the way that you interact, you need to determine how these two causal factors complement each other. The best approach is to have both of you answer questions to get an impression of each other's behavior preferences and normal ways of interacting. However, this approach isn't always prudent if the other person isn't open to changing the dynamics between you. If the person is open to it, then it's best to review responses using a facilitator to help resolve differences in opinions. Either way, you can still answer the questions yourself to gain further insight into the dynamics of your interactions with the other person.

You can use the Employee Behavior Matrix in Appendix A to develop questions to determine your common dynamics with a coworker. You can also determine critical success factors for improving your interactions by listing your desired state for the other person's behavior as well as your own. If one of you is in a leadership role, you can use the Leadership Behavior Matrix in Appendix A to develop some questions about leadership behaviors.

A review of current state responses will also give you an indication of the amount of complementary versus contradictory interactions you have with this person. The more contradictory interactions, the more likely you have a relationship with a lot of conflict and confrontation. However, complementary interactions don't necessarily mean that all is peaceful between the two of you. One of you may be biting your tongue a lot and experiencing internal turmoil. A conflict-free relationship is positive only if both parties use appropriate behaviors. For example, if you react passively to inappropriate dominant behavior, then things aren't really good between you; on the surface this complimentary relationship may appear fine, but in reality, it can be much more unhealthy than a relationship that has quite a bit of conflict in it.

Asking yourself questions about how you behave when performing each of the activities (employee and/or leadership) with another person will indicate the dynamic that occurs between the two of you in those specific activities. Looking at the dynamic for each of the activities can provide focus areas for improving the dynamic. You need to determine which dynamics are causing you stress or concern and in which activities. Only the dynamics for some of the employee or leadership activities may need to be changed to address the issues that you have with this person. The behavior activities that have been identified as the most problematic are the factors that need to be addressed.

Improving Dynamics with Contradictory Interactions

As with behaviors, contradictory interactions can be appropriate or inappropriate. It's common to use them inappropriately because of behavior preferences. For example, if you have a preference for dominant behaviors and use them as a coping strategy, you may often respond with a dominant behavior regardless of whether the other person uses a dominant, independent, or interdependent behavior. Your behavior preference can be the controlling factor in an interaction, and can lead to responding inappropriately for the situation.

You can use contradictory interactions appropriately as a technique to encourage different behaviors from another person. If a person frequently uses inappropriate passive or dominant behaviors, the way to deal with this situation is to start responding with independent or interdependent behaviors as appropriate. Your lead-by-example technique can result in the other person interacting more independently or interdependently towards you. However, if the individual has a firm preference for a certain behavior pattern, that person may not follow your example. In these cases, your contradictory responses may not be enough, so you'll need to stop the conversation and confront their inappropriate behavior rather than passively accept it.

If you interacted with a person in a way that left you feeling troubled, the Interaction Analysis Tool and the Revised Interaction Tool can help you figure out what dynamic was at play during the interaction and how to improve the dynamic. Figure 25.1 shows a sample tool that assesses an interaction for a particular situation.

As you can see, the first column describes the initiating person's behavior. (You can add more rows to describe the interaction.) The third column describes the responding person's behavior. You can be either the initiating person or the responding person. After you fill out the first and third columns of the tool, you can use the behavior matrices in Appendix A to fill out what employee or leadership activity and behavior pattern was used in the second and fourth columns.

Figure 25.1: Example Interaction Analysis Tool for a situation

Interaction Analysis			
Person A *Mary*		**Person B** *Randy*	
Person A's Initiating Behavior	Behavior Activity/Pattern	Person B's Responding Behavior	Behavior Activity/Pattern
"I need you to complete this report by Wednesday."	Providing direction/ Authoritarian – Provides direction without feedback	"I'll see what I can do."	Completing tasks / Passive – Uncommitted
"What do you mean you'll see what you can do? If this report isn't done on time, it will be the last thing you do for this company!"	Motivating/ Authoritarian – Motivates through negative consequences	"Ok, I'll get it done by Wednesday."	Completing tasks / Passive – Blindly follows direction

As shown in Figure 25.2, you can then use the behavior matrices to determine a contradictory response that would have changed the dynamic for the better. You can use the blank tools in Appendix B to assess an interaction.

After you complete the Interaction Analysis Tool, you will have a better understanding of the dynamic that caused you concern. Once you determine your dynamic, you can see what behavior pattern initiated the interaction—either passive, dominant, independent, or interdependent if initiated by a coworker—or authoritarian, laissez-faire, or connective if initiated by a leader. After you complete the Revised Interaction Tool, you will also see how different responses could have changed the dynamic. Most of the time, the "troubled" interaction will be a complementary passive/dominant interaction. But sometimes a contradictory interaction can cause a problem. So in that case, the solution would be to revise the interaction to be complementary.

Figure 25.2: Example Revised Interaction Tool for a situation

Revised Interaction			
Person A *Mary*		Person B *Randy*	
Person A's Initiating Behavior	Behavior Activity/Pattern	Person B's Responding Behavior	Behavior Activity/Pattern
"I need you to complete this report by Wednesday."	Providing direction/ Authoritarian – Provides direction without feedback	"I have numerous things on my plate right now. I would like to review them with you to see what priority you want to give this report."	Completing tasks/ Interdependent – Joint commitment (manager works with me to prioritize report with rest of my workload)
"It all needs to be done. If this report isn't done on time, it will be the last thing you do for this company!"	Motivating/ Authoritarian – Motivates through negative consequences	"I have a personal commitment tonight that I can't change. I don't think that's enough time to get everything done by their due dates. I understand that this report needs to be done Wednesday. I'll review things and let you know what I won't be able to complete on time as a result of working on this report."	Conflict resolution/ Independent – Confronts conflict

While it's too late for this particular interaction, working through how you could have better handled the situation prepares you for future interactions with this person. The next sections show examples of how to use contradictory interactions to encourage different behaviors from another person.

Addressing Inappropriate Passive-Initiated Interactions

The phrase "pushing a noodle uphill" describes what it is like to interact with someone with a preference for passive behaviors. In order to have an appropriate interaction with a person who is inappropriately using passive behaviors, it is important that you interact with the person in a way that encourages the individual's independent behavior. Before people can work together interdependently, both people must be able to stand on their own two feet. Therefore, independent behaviors may be more appropriate than interdependent behaviors. A passive/independent contradictory interaction encourages a person to use independent behaviors.

The following example of Tom and Jane shows how Tom can respond to Jane's passive behavior in a complementary dominant fashion or with a contradictory interaction by responding from an independent position.

Scenario

Tom is a project manager working with Jane, his customer. Jane is a month behind schedule in defining requirements. Jane now promises to deliver requirements by Friday so Tom's team can start working on implementing them. If Jane doesn't deliver by Friday, Tom's team will have to work weekends to complete the project on time.

Initiation of Interaction—Passive Example

Jane: It's only Wednesday, but it's been a rough week so far. I haven't had time to schedule the meetings that we need to define requirements. We had a retirement party for Larry, and planning it took up a lot of my time. It would really help me out if I could give you the requirements in two weeks. That won't impact the project end date that much, will it?

Complementary Interaction—Dominant Example

Tom: Certainly. No problem. Anything you can give us sooner would be appreciated. We'll have to work weekends, but we'll do whatever it takes to stay on schedule.

Contradictory Interaction—Independent Example

Tom: Sorry, but my team will have to work five weekends if we get the requirements two weeks late. We really need to hold to our planned date for requirements, or we will have to move out the project end date by two weeks, which will cost your company more money.

ANALYSIS: Jane's initial behavior is passive because she is already a month late in defining requirements. Jane is also about to miss her latest commitment to deliver requirements by Friday, which is another demonstration of passive behavior. Jane initiates a passive interaction, providing an excuse for potentially missing the Friday deadline and appealing to Tom to give her another two weeks. Jane feels she doesn't need to be responsible for meeting her commitments. She expects Tom to respond from a dominant behavior, making up the schedule impact for her.

In the complementary interaction, Tom does as Jane hopes: He responds with an overly responsible dominant behavior by rescuing Jane and enabling the irresponsible passive behavior of not meeting time commitments. His behavior could be a coping strategy to avoid conflict with Jane.

In the contradictory interaction, Tom doesn't respond as Jane expects. Instead, he responds from an independent perspective, pointing out the impact of late requirements on his team and appealing to Jane to either meet her latest commitment date or deal with the monetary consequences of pushing it out further.

The contradictory interaction of Tom responding with independent behavior encourages both Tom and Jane to take responsibility for their part.

Even if this interaction doesn't change Jane's passive behavior in this situation, at least in the future Jane will think twice before acting passively and expecting Tom to pick up the slack.

Addressing Inappropriate Dominant- and Authoritarian-Initiated Interactions

You may think that passive-initiated interactions are easy compared to the antagonistic interactions that you may have to deal with on a regular basis. In order to have an appropriate interaction with a coworker who is inappropriately using dominant behaviors, it is important that you interact with that individual in a way that encourages the person's independent behavior. A person with a preference for dominant behaviors frequently oversteps boundaries. Learning appropriate independent behavior first may be a prerequisite for them in using interdependent behaviors. A dominant/independent contradictory interaction will encourage this.

To have an interdependent interaction with a boss who frequently uses authoritarian behaviors, it is important that you interact with your boss in a way that encourages connective behaviors on the boss's part, such as asking your boss to coach you on the best way to handle a problem.

The following example shows how Catherine can respond to Anna's dominant behavior in a complementary passive way or choose to respond to Anna's dominant behavior with a contradictory independent behavior.

Scenario

Catherine recently started working in a clothing store. They just received a new shipment of clothes and Anna, one of Catherine's coworkers, asks her to stock the racks with the new shipment. Catherine stocks the racks according to size: one rack for small blouses, one for medium blouses, and another for large blouses.

Initiation of Interaction—Dominant Example

Anna (in front of customers): I wanted you to stock the racks by type of blouses—one rack for sleeveless blouses, one for short sleeves, and one for long-sleeved blouses. If you didn't know what you were doing, why didn't you ask?

Complementary Interaction—Passive Example

Catherine: Sorry, I'll ask next time.

Contradictory Interaction—Independent Example

Catherine: The clothes used to be sorted by size. I assumed that the new clothes would be stocked the same way. I would have gladly done it the way you wanted if you had mentioned it to me beforehand. In the future, if I make a mistake, I would appreciate it if you would mention this to me respectfully and in private.

ANALYSIS: Anna initiates an interaction using a dominant behavior by assuming a lead role and telling Catherine how she should have completed the task. She also uses a dominant behavior in relating to Catherine by criticizing her and not showing her respect.

In the complementary interaction, Catherine responds as Anna expects her to: From a passive position, she follows Anna's direction and accepts her criticism even though it's disrespectfully stated in front of customers. A passive coping strategy could be the cause of her passive behavior: Catherine fears dominant behavior, so she avoids conflict.

In the contradictory interaction, Catherine responds with independent behavior. She also confronts Anna's inappropriate dominant behavior by respectfully asking Anna to bring up issues in the future in a more respectful way.

Addressing Inappropriate Independent- and Laissez-Faire-Initiated Interactions

Most of us in the business world have heard the phrase "trying to herd cats" in reference to working with independent-minded people. Dealing with a person with a preference for independent behaviors is the same.

To have an interdependent interaction with a person with a preference for independent behaviors, it is important that you encourage that person to continue to interact with you or others. Allowing people to go off and work on their own doesn't lead to interdependent behavior.

To have an interdependent interaction with a boss who regularly uses laissez-faire behaviors, it is important that you interact with the boss in a way that encourages connective behaviors, such as asking your boss to give direction at a more detailed level or to work more closely with the team while implementing direction.

The next example shows how Jeremy can respond to Killian's behavior in a way that allows him to work alone or in a way that encourages collaboration. It is just a matter of whether Jeremy wants to encourage interdependent behavior or independent behavior. Either could be appropriate, depending on the situation.

Scenario

Jeremy, the department head of a business college, wants to revamp the college's course curriculum to be more modern. Killian, the associate dean, knows that Jeremy wants to set up a meeting to get input from the faculty on the course curriculum. He walks into Jeremy's office to talk to him about an alternative to the meeting.

Initiation of Interaction—Independent Example

Killian: There's no need to hold the meeting. I looked at leading university Web sites to see what they're offering. I've already come up with a proposed course curriculum for next year based on my research.

Complementary Interaction—Laissez-Faire Example

Jeremy: Excellent. This will save a great deal of time. Go ahead and finish your proposal.

Contradictory Interaction—Interdependent Example

Jeremy: While I am sure that your efforts will be very useful and save time, I also want the benefit of insight from the rest of the staff. I would like to hold the meeting anyway and brainstorm with the professors.

ANALYSIS: Killian initiates an interaction using an independent behavior hoping to kill any further interdependent interactions between Killian, Jeremy, and the faculty. Jeremy's complementary response to Killian's independent behavior allows Killian to continue using independent behavior. Jeremy's pattern of behavior could be based on not wanting to deal with conflict or being too busy to deal with Killian at the moment. When Jeremy responds to Killian's behavior with a contradictory interaction, he encourages Killian to use interdependent behavior.

Changing Interpersonal Dynamics Is a Learning Process and Takes Time

You may recall from the behavior chapters in Part 2 that dominant and passive behaviors are sometimes appropriate. Similarly, dominant and passive interactions are also appropriate at times. If you are working on a task with someone who is more knowledgeable than you, it is appropriate for that individual to interact with you in a dominant way, making more of the decisions, leading the effort, and being more involved in problem resolution. It is also appropriate for you to interact with that individual in a passive way by deferring decisions, following direction, and being less involved in problem resolution.

Every day at work you're on a playing field that presents many possibilities and all kinds of situations for improving your gruntledness and success. Whenever you interact with someone else, you have an opportunity to change the outcome—by changing your behavior.

One appropriate contradictory interaction will not change a relationship from dependent to interdependent; however, repeated attempts at appropriate contradictory interactions can eventually lead to changing the nature of the relationship. With each interaction, you get one step closer to appropriate interactions with the other person. You move towards interdependent and connective behaviors one person at a time, and one interaction at a time.

You may have developed coping strategies for dealing with dominant, passive, or independent behaviors. These coping strategies become difficult to let go of, so you may need to look further into the causal factors behind your coping strategies in order to improve your interactions with others. Part 6 will give you the opportunity to do so.

Of course, it is possible that the person with whom you interact is deeply rooted in coping strategies and refuses to interact with you in any other manner. In that case, you must decide whether you want to continue the relationship, or at least, determine how much you want to interact with the person.

Keep in mind, it took time to establish the current dynamics that you have with another person, and it will take time to change those dynamics to something more appropriate and pleasant. Learning to choose different behaviors and create contradictory interactions instead of complementary interactions also takes practice. Sometimes you'll be successful at it and other times you may resort to your previous behavior patterns. There are many ways to apply the concepts of this book to improve interpersonal dynamics. One way is to use the following process to improve stressful dynamics between you and another person:

1. **Determine causal and critical success factors for any interpersonal dynamics that are causing you stress.**
   a. Using Appendix A as a guide, choose relevant employee/leadership activities to create questions that will assess the interpersonal dynamics between you and another person.
   b. Answer the questions.
   c. Review your question responses to determine which activities are the most problematic.

2. **(Optional) Review the other person's causal and critical success factors for your interpersonal dynamics. Note: It is recommended that this be done with the assistance of a facilitator to help deal with any differences in opinion.**
   a. Have the other person answer the questions to get his/her perception of the interactions between you.

b. Review the other person's responses to determine which activities he/she thinks are most important to address.

c. Use questions i-ii to compare your current state responses to the other person's responses.

    i. How similarly do you view the dynamics between the two of you?

    ii. In what activities do you view the dynamics to be different?

d. Use questions i-ii to compare your desired state responses with the other person's responses.

    i. How similar are the desired dynamics between the two of you?

    ii. In what activities do you have different desired dynamics?

3. (Optional) Discuss differences in perception with the help of a facilitator.

a. Listen to the other person explain his/her feelings about the current and desired state dynamics for the activities where you see differently.

b. Discuss with the other person why you feel the way you do about the current and desired state dynamics for the activities where you see differently.

c. After you both understand where each other is coming from, document the activities where you have a shared understanding of the dynamics between you.

4. Develop an improvement plan to address the activities that are most problematic.

a. Develop an employee/leadership behavior improvement plan for yourself focusing on the activities that are the most stressful to you.

b. Find a coworker who witnesses you using this dynamic and who is willing to help you change the dynamic. This can be the person who is involved in the dynamic or someone else. Recommend that you do this with the continued assistance of the facilitator if you chose the person who is involved in the dynamic.

c. If the other person has participated in this exercise with you, discuss acceptable ways to interrupt old behavior patterns. This provides a non-threatening technique that each of you can use in case the two of you find yourselves reverting to the old dynamic.

5. Use the Interaction Analysis Tool and the Revised Interaction Tool to provide additional insight into troubling interactions and to fine-tune your skills in using contradictory interactions to improve your dynamics with others.

Sometimes these changes are dramatic, and you will see an immediate change in your relationship with the other person. Your sense of well-being and personal satisfaction will tell you that your interactions are improving. If you find that the interpersonal dynamics aren't improving fast enough for you personally, then your behavior preferences may be holding you back. Part 6 describes in detail the root causes for behavior preferences.

26

Why a Holistic Approach for Improving Gruntledness & Business Success Matters

"The first 'real job' I ever had was when I was 16. I was a secretary for a CPA firm that had three partners and approximately five accountants. The senior partner who started the firm was an incredible taskmaster and very cheap—so cheap the secretaries he hired were part-time work study students taking secretarial/book-keeping classes at the local high school. This boss was incredibly exacting and highly critical. He did not hesitate to raise his voice to not only me but to his junior accountants as well. His criticism was personal. For example, he would tell his junior accountants when they made a mistake that they were stupid, that he didn't know how they passed the CPA exam, etc. He expected me and other part-time high school students to be as productive as highly experienced executive sec-retaries. He would give dictation (this is in the age of shorthand) without regard to speed. We had to create statistical financial reports (balance sheets, income statements, statements of change in retained earnings, etc.) with no experience in that type of documentation. The tone of voice he would use was highly critical and so tinged with sarcasm that it was painful. I went home from work in tears many a night. The consequence of his behavior was incredibly high turnover in staff. His partners lasted only a few years; just long enough to gain the loyalty of a few clients and take them with when they left. When he retired, he was all alone. But, because everyone who worked there was so afraid of him, the quality of the work produced was, in the end, always high and his client base (other than those clients his partners stole from him) remained loyal."

Disgruntled Employee
Blog Post

I f your workgroup is successful and employee morale is high, it is a result of your employees' collective behaviors, your leadership behaviors, and the business system characteristics that govern your workgroup. From all the previous chapters, you should now have a clear picture of what gets in the way and stays in the way of high employee morale and business success within your workgroup, between workgroups, and in your dynamics with others personally. You should also understand the techniques of regaining your workgroup's happiness and success.

At a workgroup level, how gruntled are your workgroup members? Do they enjoy interacting with you and being a part of your workgroup? Do you have the reputation of being difficult to work with? Do interactions with you stress out the members of your team? Is employee morale high within your workgroup? Do workgroup members treat each other respectfully or is there tension? Do they work well with other workgroups?

How successful is your workgroup? Are you meeting all your business objectives, including financial objectives? How well does your workgroup implement business initiatives? Are you meeting the business objectives that were intended for the initiative? Are employees engaged in making your workgroup successful? Do you feel that your workgroup is delivering the highest business results that it can? Do you feel that you could get more contribution from your workgroup members? Could you be a more effective leader?

After answering the above questions, you may find that your workgroup has a different response for gruntledness versus success. For example, your workgroup may be fairly successful but have employee morale problems. Or employee morale could be high, but the workgroup is struggling to meet business objectives. If the answers to these questions aren't as positive as you would like, then using the holistic approach in Part 5 will help you identify and address the causal factors behind your business success and employee morale problems. These techniques apply to any type of formal leader— a project manager, team lead, first-level supervisor, or executive manager. They also apply to any employee in an informal leadership position.

The Root Cause of Business Success and Employee Morale Problems

Figure 26.1 on the following page shows that your workgroup's gruntledness and success are dependent on the dynamics within your workgroup and between workgroups. Whether or not the dynamics are conducive to gruntledness and success is dependant on the three causal factor categories: employee behaviors, leadership behaviors, and business system characteristics. Figure 26.1 also shows that the root cause behind these three causal factors is individual behavior preference.

Workgroup dynamics are based on the leader's individual behavior preferences and the collective behavior preferences of workgroup members. Inter-workgroup dynamics are based on the collective employee behaviors of both workgroups. Collective employee behavior preferences are based on the most prevalent individual behavior preferences of workgroup members. Workgroup and inter-workgroup dynamics are both influenced by business system characteristics. The business system characteristics are based on the individual behavior preferences of the executives who defined the system. Therefore, the collective employee behaviors, leadership behaviors, and business system characteristics are all based on individual behavior preferences.

So whether your goal is workgroup success or happiness, the root cause behind why you may not be achieving that goal is the same: individual behavior preferences. The conclusion to all this is that the root cause of workgroup gruntledness and success comes down to the personal behavior preferences of the executives, leaders, and members of the workgroup.

A Holistic Approach to Improving Workgroup Gruntledness and Success

Because employee morale and business success problems have multiple causal factors, the best way to improve them is to use a holistic approach that addresses each factor. With any system, if three things are broken, then the system won't run properly if you only fix one or two of the problems.

Figure 26.1: Workgroup gruntledness and success causal factor and root cause tree

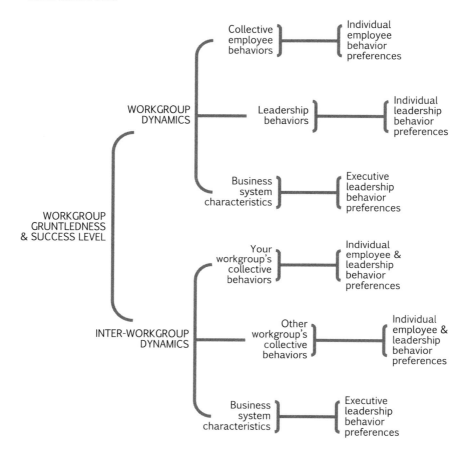

Most companies do exactly this. A business issue occurs, and they try to fix it with a process improvement or reorganization. They address only one or two of the business system components and never even consider leadership or employee behaviors as causal factors. Employee morale problems are addressed similarly. HR frequently tries to address employee morale problems by looking at leadership behaviors but neglects to see collective employee behaviors and business system characteristics as causal factors. For that reason, the techniques in Part 5 provide a holistic approach for addressing the collective employee behaviors, leadership behaviors, and business system characteristics in three different scenarios: workgroup dynamics, inter-workgroup dynamics, and interpersonal dynamics.

Changing the dynamics within your workgroup to be more collaborative between the leader and workgroup members means understanding how collective employee behavior preferences, leadership behavior preferences, and business system characteristics impact workgroup dynamics. Without a holistic approach, an attempt to change workgroup dynamics will not be effective or long-lasting. The dynamics might change during normal day-to-day interactions but deteriorate under stress or when a challenging business initiative comes along.

For example, if leaders don't address collective employee behaviors, they may become discouraged in trying different leadership behaviors and conclude that the old behaviors were more effective. If leaders don't address their leadership behaviors, employees can become frustrated that their new employee behaviors are getting challenged by their leaders. Even if both employees and leaders attempt to change the dynamics of their interactions, if business system characteristics aren't addressed, then organizational framework, management systems, processes, and information technology factors will encourage the old dynamics.

In short, a holistic approach is the only way to provide long-term business benefits and improve employee morale. The techniques in Part 5 are designed to identify all the causal factors that are contributing to the problem at hand. As you saw in Chapter 25, no matter whom you interact with and what behaviors they choose, you always have a choice on how you behave. You can change the dynamics—whether they're between you and your workgroup members, two workgroups, or you and an individual.

Your Behavior Preferences as the Root Cause

You may be a leader, manager, or employee at any level who wants to be more successful at leading a workgroup or organization, implementing business strategies, or changing organizational culture. Improving your own behavior preferences and gruntledness level is helpful before attempting to change things for others. Someone who is disgruntled is not going to be very good at leading the rest of the organization through change. Someone who often uses employee or leadership behaviors inappropriately isn't going to be successful at leading an organization, implementing business strategies, or changing organizational culture.

The common denominator in your workgroup dynamics, inter-workgroup dynamics, and interpersonal dynamics is you. While others may share the same situations as you do, often they will have different dynamics than you. The dynamic that you have with your workgroup leader can be completely different from the one someone else in your workgroup has with the same workgroup leader. The experience that you have in interacting with another workgroup can be very different from another person's experience with that same workgroup. And the interactions that you have with another person can be very different from a coworker's interactions with the same person. So if you're having a problem interacting with others within your workgroup, between workgroups, and at a personal level, the root cause is your behavior preferences. Even if you and others experience the same dynamics with others, the root cause of all your gruntledness and success problems in any scenario is your behavior preferences.

If you find your efforts aren't successful after trying the techniques in Part 5 to address employee morale and business success causal factors, you may need to dig deeper and find the root cause, which as previously stated, is your behavior preferences. Part 6 will provide techniques to help you identify and address causal factors for your behavior preferences. Part 6 will also show how your behavior preferences influence your personal happiness and success. Changing your behavior preferences will improve your interactions within your workgroup, between another workgroup, and on a personal interaction level. Not only will this positively improve your personal gruntledness and success levels, it will improve your workgroup's gruntledness and success levels.

Part 6

Addressing Causal Factors for Personal Success and Gruntledness

"Important, far-reaching change is often more possible than it seems. Work from the inside out, beginning where you have total autonomy and control (over change within yourself), next where you have authority over others, then where you have none but there exists the possibility of influence. . . . When you change yourself you alter the strength and intensity of the influence you exert."

Tom Watkins
Owner, professional coach, and mentor at EncourageMentors

27

A Holistic Approach to Addressing the Root Causes of Success and Gruntledness Problems

"Since my bosses' desks were right in the same room where I worked, they watched everything I did—and I mean EVERYTHING. If I said something to a customer that wasn't exactly what they would have said, I got talked to.

There was nothing I did or said that wasn't being scrutinized and it kept me on edge at all times. I was a nervous wreck. Consequently, I did start making true mistakes, and I felt like I was the most incompetent worker ever. Since this was a new feeling for me, I didn't know how to deal with it. I had trouble remembering the details of things that went wrong, simply because my brain would freeze. When I tried to defend my actions, my concerns were dismissed. Whenever I went to one of them to ask a question, I was often treated as though I was being a pain and they simply had too much important work to do to answer at that point. Unfortunately, when this happened, I never did get an answer, so things were left unresolved and I was still in the dark. I never once got a compliment from either boss. I was never told that I did something well, and there were things that I did well.

My belief is that if a boss treats an employee as though they are incapable, then that employee will not perform well. It's psychological warfare to get rid of employees and it's very effective. It damaged my self-confidence enough that I was fearful of making even the tiniest of mistakes in my succeeding jobs. This is a powerful weapon to use against someone. I always felt as though I was a strong, confident person in any job I had. This job shattered all that within me. Perhaps I allowed it, but I honestly didn't even know how to combat it. It was a new concept to me."

Disgruntled Employee
Blog Post

We can recover easily enough from an inappropriate behavior choice we made in one particular situation. But when we develop a preference for a behavior that we repeatedly inappropriately use, we cause real problems for ourselves, our workgroup, and our company. Since we and our behavior preferences are the root cause of all our success and gruntledness problems, the techniques in this chapter will start to address the factors that contribute to our behavior preferences.

Each of us brings to the workplace different perspectives shaped by—or sometimes still stuck in—our past. These perspectives are based on our past experiences. Our behavior preferences are often formed based on these experiences and how we dealt with them. Many of us let our preferences for passive, dominant, or independent behaviors keep us from experiencing happiness in the workplace and hold us back from being more successful at work. People who are unaware of their passive, dominant, or independent tendencies use more inappropriate forms of these behaviors. Those who are aware of their tendencies have the ability to use these behaviors more appropriately.

Changing our behavior preferences can also be a challenge. When our behavior preferences become coping strategies, we aren't very willing to change and give them up. Also, when we believe that people don't change, we typically resist change ourselves. However, when we are willing to change, we can end up being more gruntled and successful at work.

Author and motivational speaker Anthony Robbins says that change is nothing more than adding another choice. Part 6 will show that personal behavior is a choice just waiting to be changed. We will use a holistic approach to work on the following:

- Determine behavior preferences
- Determine causal factors for behavior preferences
- Address mental causal factors for behavior preferences
- Address emotional causal factors for behavior preferences
- Address physical causal factors for behavior preferences

Determining Your Behavior Preferences

The first step to choosing more appropriate behaviors is understanding your current behavior preferences and aversions. Once you accurately understand this, you will have the chance to reflect on whether you are making appropriate behavior choices. Changing behavior preferences is as simple as making better, more appropriate behavior choices one situation at a time.

You may already have some sense of what your behavior preferences are. However, it is possible that others perceive your behavior preferences differently than you do. To determine your behavior preferences, it is helpful to talk to someone who will give you honest feedback. The employee and leadership behavior matrices in Appendix A can be used to ask another person about his or her perception of your behavior preferences.

You can also use the matrices to conduct a *360-degree survey,* which will tell you if your self-assessment is aligned with how others perceive your behavior preferences. A 360-degree survey usually includes input from various members from your workgroup. Your peers, subordinates, and superiors will answer questions that help determine your behavior preferences for employee and leadership behavior activities. Note that 360-degree surveys are typically conducted by a facilitator to keep the participants' responses anonymous and to help you accept and understand the survey results.

You may find that you have a different behavior preference for each of the employee and leadership activities. For example, you may prefer independent behaviors when making decisions but prefer passive behaviors when resolving conflict. You may also find that you prefer authoritarian behaviors in providing direction but prefer laissez-faire behaviors when building team capabilities.

Causal Factors for Your Behavior Preferences

Focusing on the root of the behavior and not the behavior itself can light the path to better behavior choices. It may seem somewhat confusing to try to determine when a particular form of behavior is appropriate. So keep this in mind: Where you are coming from when you choose the behavior is more important than the behavior itself. Behavior choices can be explained by these causal factors:

1. **Mental Factors.** Whether or not you possess a mental skill that is needed for a particular work activity influences whether you choose passive, dominant, independent, or interdependent behaviors. Beliefs about yourself compared to your coworkers are also a key reason for certain behavior choices.

2. **Emotional Factors.** Emotions and fears and how you cope with them influence whether you develop a preference for passive, dominant, independent, or interdependent behaviors. The lack of certain emotional skills, especially in social situations, can lead to inappropriate behavior choices.

3. **Physical Factors.** Dietary choices influence the nervous system, which in turn influences behavior. Stress also affects the nervous system and can lead to inappropriate behavior choices.

As shown in Figure 27.1, employee and leadership behavior are caused by mental, emotional, and physical factors. These three causal factors influence employee and leadership behavior in a particular situation (regardless of appropriateness), which can lead to behavior preferences.

Since mental, emotional, and physical factors influence the behavior preferences of executive leaders, these three causal factors also influence business system characteristics. Executive leaders define the business system characteristics for a company or business unit. The behavior preferences of executive leaders influence the type of business system characteristics they choose. For example, a leader with a preference for authoritarian behaviors usually will embed more dependent characteristics into the business system.

Figure 27.1: Causal factors for employee and leadership behaviors

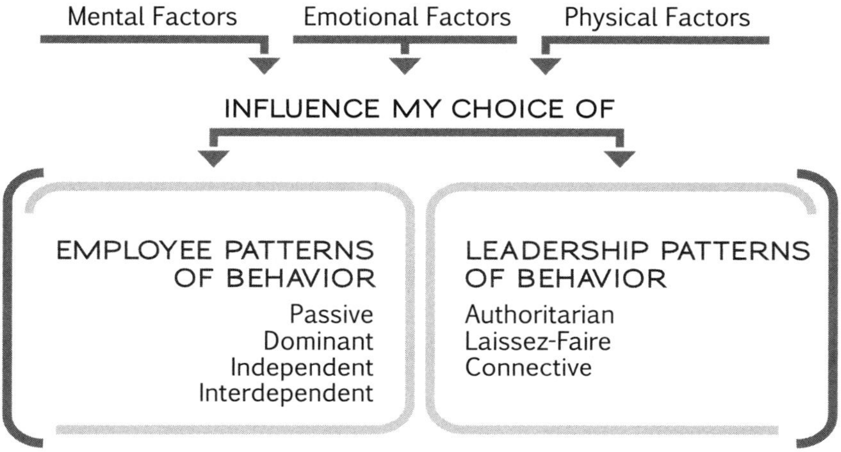

Mental Factors   Emotional Factors   Physical Factors

INFLUENCE MY CHOICE OF

EMPLOYEE PATTERNS
OF BEHAVIOR

Passive
Dominant
Independent
Interdependent

LEADERSHIP PATTERNS
OF BEHAVIOR

Authoritarian
Laissez-Faire
Connective

Getting Myself on the Path to Interdependence and Connective Behaviors

It took a great deal of effort for me to start to use more interdependent employee behaviors and connective behaviors. The journey began when I realized that my beliefs and mental skills were a key reason for the behaviors I chose and the behaviors I encouraged in others. For example, I often believed that I knew more than my coworkers, so I typically chose a dominant behavior, which caused my coworkers to use passive behaviors to the disadvantage of everyone.

Second, after reading Daniel Goleman's books on emotional and social intelligence, I became aware that a lack of certain emotional and social skills also influenced my behavior preferences. I also took the Hay Group's emotional IQ test; at that time, I scored the weakest in social awareness. If I had been more aware of the negative impact of my behavior on others, I would not have used dominant and authoritarian behaviors as much as I did. Before I had this insight, I believed that I was using these behaviors appropriately when in actuality I was not.

Third, over the years, I noticed the impact of food and stress on my behavior. Having functional hypoglycemia (low blood sugar) often led to my inappropriate dominant behaviors. Many of my coworkers cut short late-morning meetings with me rather than risk my unpleasant behavior resulting from being late for lunch. I also observed that what I ate had an impact on my behavior. If I ate any foods that contained sugar, I would be more irritable for the next day or two. Exercise had a calming effect on me. If I worked out, I was more able to deal with stress at work.

Once I realized these mental, emotional, and physical causal factors existed, I could see how to change my behavior. With this understanding and the ability to choose more appropriate behaviors, I was able to influence the dynamics of my workgroup. This was true whether I was a workgroup member or leader.

The next three chapters will cover why it is necessary to understand mental, emotional, and physical causal factors for personal and workgroup gruntledness and success.

28

Addressing Mental Causal Factors of Behavior Preferences

"I was involved in a company where the founder was creative and always thinking out of the box. This was great for looking forward and developing a strong belief in the future. The problem was that he was terrible at implementing his ideas. He would not delegate and would pull developers onto his latest brainstorm before an idea could play out. He couldn't/wouldn't even chase revenue because he was so focused on the latest idea. His company continues to limp along to this day."

Disgruntled Employee
Blog Post

Beliefs and mental skills are two mental causal factors that influence behavior. They affect how employees and leaders behave when performing work activities and influence how leaders and workgroup members interact with each other. They also are behind the dynamics with coworkers. Workgroup members who share common beliefs influence the dynamics between two workgroups. The beliefs and mental skills of upper management influence choices in business system characteristics.

This chapter explains how various beliefs and mental skills influence behavior choices in these different situations. It will also address mental causal factors of behavior preferences.

Beliefs Influence Our Behavior

The way that we were raised sets many of our beliefs as adults. These beliefs were set so long ago that we're often not consciously aware of them. Based on our upbringing and experiences, we arrive in the business world with a wide variety of beliefs on value, responsibility, and entitlement. These beliefs influence our behaviors, which impact work situations and, ultimately, influence business and personal success or failure. The following describes the three categories of beliefs that affect employee and leadership behaviors in the workplace: value, responsibility, and entitlement.

Beliefs Regarding Value

Our beliefs about our self-worth compared to others form our thoughts about how valuable we are and how valuable others are in a particular situation. The following summarizes these beliefs:
- I provide less value than others
- I provide more value than others
- I provide value on my own
- I provide value equal to others

Beliefs Regarding Responsibility

Our beliefs about our responsibilities compared to the responsibilities of others determine the role that we and others play in a situation. The following summarizes these beliefs:

• I am not responsible, or less responsible than others
• I am more responsible than others
• I am responsible
• I am equally as responsible as others

Beliefs Regarding Entitlement

Our beliefs about entitlement determine what we feel we are entitled to compared to what we think others are entitled to. The following summarizes these beliefs:

• I am not entitled
• I am entitled more than others or at the expense of others
• I am entitled
• I am equally as entitled as others

We may believe different things at different times. These differing beliefs influence the way we work. People who don't believe in their own value, don't feel responsible for a task, or don't believe they are entitled to something will behave much differently than people who believe they add value, are responsible, or are entitled. We may also generalize these beliefs across different types of situations. Appendix C contains four tables showing examples of how various beliefs about value, responsibility, and entitlement influence how employees and leaders behave when performing work activities.

Mental Skills Influence Our Behavior

Our mental skills also contribute to our beliefs about our value; therefore, strengths and weaknesses in our mental skills contribute to our behavior preferences. For instance, a weakness in a mental skill can lead to passive behaviors in situations where that particular mental skill is required. Or a limitation in a particular mental skill can lead to independent behaviors like choosing to struggle with a task alone rather than letting others observe our weakness. Strengths in a particular skill can lead to dominant behaviors when that mental skill strength surpasses the strengths of others involved in a situation.

Left- and right-brain thinking also contribute to behavior preference. Note that no one's thinking is only right-brain oriented or only left-brain oriented; everyone uses both sides. However while growing up, most of us develop either right-brain functions or left-brain functions more than the other. The following lists some common left- and right-brain mental skills:

Left-Brain Thinking	Right-Brain Thinking
Analytical	Creative
Detailed	Big picture/strategic
Logical	Intuitive
Based on facts	Based on feelings
Sequential	Simultaneous
Reasoning	Artistic

Strengths and weaknesses in right- or left-brain functions can influence behavior preferences. For example, if a task requires creativity and a person is limited in creative thinking, then he or she will probably behave more passively during that task.

Let's look at the mental explanations (beliefs and mental skills) for passive, dominant, independent, and interdependent behaviors.

Mental Explanations for Passive and Laissez-Faire Behaviors

Beliefs

Specific beliefs on value, responsibility, and entitlement are behind passive behavior. In a particular situation, for instance, if we believe that we provide less value than others, or we don't need to be responsible, or we're not as entitled as others, then we might choose to behave in a passive manner. If we regularly use passive behaviors, we may have generalized these beliefs.

These beliefs are also sometimes the basis for laissez-faire behaviors. As leaders, we may choose laissez-faire behaviors because we believe that we provide less value than our team members, we are less responsible for an activity than our employees, or our team members are more entitled than we are.

Passive behavior preferences can be based on beliefs that we formed as we were growing up. The following lists some examples of how our current passive beliefs might have been formed:

- If we believe that we provide less value than others, a childhood influence (such as parents, siblings, friends, teachers, etc.) may have frequently undermined, criticized, and judged us
- If we believe that we don't have to be responsible, our parents or siblings may have taken more responsibility in our care than necessary and may not have encouraged us to be responsible for taking care of ourselves
- If we believe that we're not as entitled as others, a childhood influence may not have respected us and crossed our personal boundaries mentally, emotionally, or physically, and no one stood up for us when this happened

Mental Skills

A weakness in left- or right-brain mental skills can contribute to a belief that we provide less value than others, which can cause us to prefer passive or laissez-faire behaviors. For instance, if we have a weakness for analysis and need to make a decision, perform a task, or resolve a problem that requires logic, financial analysis, or technical evaluation, we will probably react passively. If we have a weakness in strategic thinking, we may choose a passive or laissez-faire behavior when an activity requires conceptualizing abstract ideas, seeing the big picture, or creating something new. If we have a weakness in detailed thinking, we may avoid detailed decision making, be less responsible when completing detail-level tasks, or defer problem resolution on issues that are administrative in nature.

My Personal Experience with Mental Factors behind My Passive and Laissez-Faire Behaviors

While growing up, people frequently violated my mental and emotional boundaries, so I generalized the belief that I was not entitled to be treated with respect. I was taught to respect people in positions of authority such as my parents, other adult relatives, teachers, nuns, and policemen, whether they were right or wrong.

I went to Catholic grade school and remember a couple bad encounters with nuns that went unnoticed. In first grade, I lied to a nun that I didn't feel well so that I could get out of finishing my lunch; when she found out, she grabbed me by the shoulders and roughly shook me. In seventh grade, I rolled my uniform skirt up too short and a nun slapped me on the legs with a ruler. My parents never questioned the nuns' behavior; the assumption was that I deserved what I got. My parents accepted the authority of the nuns at the school regardless of what they did.

These beliefs influenced my behavior as an adult. I felt that if I wanted to keep my job, I would have to accept disrespectful behavior from others. When interacting with people speaking from a position of authority, I sometimes believed that it was best to just do what they told me to do.

Throughout my career, when I encountered people with certain mental strengths that were greater than mine, I tended to choose passive behaviors because I believed that I provided less value than they did. I remember one woman that I worked with many years ago who was more analytical than I. I experienced self-esteem problems for awhile when working with her until I was able to appreciate how my own strengths complemented her abilities.

In many workgroups I managed, I believed the employees provided more value than I did from a technical perspective; in many cases, they had more experience than I. I also believed that it was my team members' responsibility—more than mine—to deliver what was requested. They worked long hours to get the job done. I believed the employees should be entitled to certain rewards since they, not I, had delivered business results. In situations where I held these beliefs, I used more laissez-faire behaviors.

Mental Explanations for Dominant and Authoritarian Behaviors

Beliefs

In a particular situation, if we believe that we provide more value than others, are more responsible than others, are more entitled than others, or are entitled at the expense of others, we may choose to behave in a dominant manner. If we regularly use dominant behaviors, we may have generalized these beliefs.

These beliefs are also sometimes the basis for authoritarian behaviors. As leaders, we may choose authoritarian behaviors because we believe that we provide more value than our team members, we are more responsible for an activity than our employees, or we are more entitled than our team members.

Dominant behavior preferences can be based on beliefs that were formed while growing up. The following list shows some examples of how our current dominant beliefs might have been formed:

- If we believe that we are superior to others, our parents may not have corrected our improper dominant behavior. If we believe that we provide more value than others, our parents may have treated us as if we were more important than others
- If we believe that we are more responsible than others, we may have had to take care of others
- If we believe that we are entitled to something at the expense of others, we may have had to take on more responsibility than others and because of this, received more privileges than others

Mental Skills

In a particular situation, if we're better than others at left-brain thinking, then we may believe we provide more value than others in activities that require more left-brain thinking, such as financial analysis or technical problem solving. Since much of what goes on in the business world requires left-brain thinking, then a high left-brain mental ability can easily lead us to a more generalized belief that we provide more value than others. This will lead us to choose dominant or authoritarian behaviors more often. Tending to be more authoritative and critical of others because of above-average analytical skills may provide a basis for the belief: I provide more value than others in many situations.

My Personal Experience with Mental Factors behind My Dominant and Authoritarian Behaviors

I grew up as a "Miss Know It All," and that attitude didn't end when I started working in the business world. Early successes at outsmarting my parents and siblings led me to a generalized belief that, intellectually, I provided more value than most people. In addition, being the oldest child, I took care of my siblings and developed a generalized belief that I had to be more responsible than others. I didn't learn appropriate boundaries while growing up, so I ended up with a generalized belief that I was entitled to certain behaviors that really weren't socially acceptable.

Feeling that I was more responsible than others and entitled to voicing my opinion vehemently led me to have emotional outbursts at work. I held onto my opinion and had difficulty considering other perspectives. I often told people the solution to a problem rather than listen to what they had to say. Because I believed I was more responsible than others, I did more work than I should have. I didn't realize that doing the majority of the work wasn't really cooperation.

One of my bosses at the first company where I worked gave me a good performance appraisal but then pushed the written appraisal aside and told me that, while the quality and quantity of my work was good, it was a pain to work with me. I often argued my points arrogantly in meetings, discounted others' opinions, overreacted, and several times either burst into tears in meetings or stormed out of the meeting in anger if the decision didn't go the way I wanted. His comments had a profound effect on me, and I settled down quite a bit after that.

Several jobs later, my boss told me that he was really glad I worked for him, but he didn't think he would want two of me. I had started using dominant behaviors more appropriately but still more than my boss wanted.

As I became more experienced as a leader, I behaved more appropriately; however, in many situations I still believed that I provided more value than the employees who worked for me. As a result I used authoritarian behaviors.

When cost-cutting strategies, such as downsizing and offshoring, became common, it was difficult to get my workgroup to go along with the business strategies and deliver intended results. At times, my workgroup showed minimal interest in doing what was requested. The more challenging the business objectives, the more useful my analytical and strategic mental skills were, so because of these mental skills, I felt entitled to do whatever it took to deliver business results. My detailed thinking contributed to my controlling tendencies. These particular mental skills also led me to use more authoritarian behaviors.

While we were getting the business results that our company desired, the employee morale within my workgroup was not as high as it was when I used to use more laissez-faire behaviors. I wasn't enjoying my work as much either. One of my managers during that time told me that it was a good thing I was moving onto another assignment. He felt that the time for ruling with an iron-fist had passed, and it was more beneficial to the workgroup to have a more pleasant person in charge.

Mental Explanations for Independent and Laissez-Faire Behaviors

Beliefs

If we believe that we provide value on our own, we need to be responsible for ourselves, or we're entitled to certain rights, we may choose in a particular situation to behave in an independent manner. If we regularly use independent behaviors, we may have generalized these beliefs.

These beliefs are also sometimes the basis for laissez-faire behaviors. As leaders, we may choose laissez-faire behaviors because we believe that employees provide value on their own, team members can be responsible on their own, or employees are entitled to be rewarded for their efforts.

Independent behavior preferences can be based on beliefs that were formed while growing up. The following lists some examples of how our current independent beliefs might have been formed:

- If we believe that we provide value on our own, childhood influences may have encouraged us to pay attention to our own judgment
- If we believe that we need to be responsible for ourselves, childhood influences may have encouraged us to take care of ourselves
- If we believe we are entitled to certain things, childhood influences may have protected us and taught us how to take care of our personal boundaries

Mental Skills

If we lack certain mental skills, we can develop a tendency for independent or laissez-faire behaviors. For example, we may have sufficient mental strengths to work alone; but if we have a weakness in an area, we may shy away from interdependent or connective behaviors that could expose our weakness when we're in a group setting.

People with strengths in right-brain skills are often considered free spirits and independent thinkers. In the primarily left-brain business world, they are also sometimes considered "out in left field." When leaders and coworkers ostracize them for their unique mental skills, it can lead to independent or laissez-faire behavior choices.

My Personal Experience with Mental Factors behind My Independent and Laissez-Faire Behaviors

While growing up, I was extremely independent. I always stayed on top of things so that no one could accuse me of being a slacker. My tendency to use independent behaviors continued in the workplace. In many work situations, I believed that I provided value on my own, so I didn't worry about what others had to say.

Also, with the boundary issues I developed while growing up, it took time for me to realize that I was entitled to proper work and life boundaries and people treating me with respect. However, this realization drove me to the opposite extreme, which led to more independent behaviors. I became very confrontational, even belligerent, when people crossed my boundaries at work. One time, one of my bosses embarrassed me in front of my peers by pointing out problems within my workgroup. I called my boss on the phone and yelled at her about how inappropriate it was to give me feedback in a public setting. I stayed out of her sight for the next few weeks until I was able to find another job assignment elsewhere in the company.

My mental skills were a good match for the work that I was doing, so this also triggered me to choose independent behaviors many times. I often preferred to work alone and figured out new tasks on my own. I made decisions on my own often outside the scope of my responsibilities. I would rather ask for forgiveness than ask for permission. I'd often coach others to not ask questions that they didn't want to hear the answers to.

One of my first management assignments was for a workgroup with twenty employees who were about the same age as I was. Since they were my peers, I used laissez-faire behaviors because I believed they, like I, were responsible and entitled to work independently. I trusted them, so I believed I could be lax concerning their whereabouts. One day I needed to contact an employee who was chronically missing. When I couldn't reach him after several calls, I did some investigating. I found out that he was running his own landscaping business during company time.

Because of my beliefs, I assumed incorrectly that everyone had the same work ethic that I did and would work responsibly. This belief also backfired because, although my workgroup members felt the business strategies were fun to implement and they were gruntled for the most part, we often missed our deadlines and went over our estimated budgets. I believed that everyone was responsible enough on their own to meet business objectives, but this wasn't true.

Mental Explanations for Interdependent and Connective Behaviors

Beliefs

If we believe that we provide value equal to others, we're jointly responsible, or everyone is entitled to the same rights, we may choose in a particular situation to behave in an interdependent or connective manner. If we regularly use interdependent behaviors, we may have generalized these beliefs.

These beliefs are also sometimes the basis for connective behaviors. As leaders, we may choose connective behaviors because we believe that team members provide value equal to ours, we each are equally responsible for an activity, or we each are equally entitled.

Interdependent behavior preferences can be based on beliefs that were formed while growing up. The following list shows some examples of how our current interdependent beliefs might have been formed:

- If we believe that we provide value equal to others, a childhood influence may have encouraged us to voice our opinion and listen to the opinions of others
- If we believe that we need to be jointly responsible in certain situations, parents may have encouraged us to share in household responsibilities
- If we believe that everyone is entitled in certain situations, a childhood influence may have respected us, not crossing our personal boundaries inappropriately, and taught us to behave similarly

Mental Skills

Those who become competent in all mental skills typically have the ability to work interdependently in more situations. As previously stated, a weakness in a certain mental skill may lead to passive behaviors when a work activity requires that particular mental skill. The more competent you are in all mental skills, the more you'll be able to contribute to a work activity and collaborate with others. As leaders, if we have some degree of competence in both left- and right-brain mental skills, we'll have the mental ability to use connective behaviors in more situations. If we are weak in certain mental skills, in some situations we may not have the mental skills to work collaboratively with coworkers or workgroup members.

Just being able to recognize our and others' mental strengths and weaknesses ultimately helps us to figure out ways to collaborate. We can work interdependently with coworkers if we accept others' relevant, unique mental skills and contribute our own. Most activities require several mental skills to complete them successfully. For example, a technical problem may require analytical thinking, logic, and creativity. One person may be good at analytical and logical thinking and another person at creativity. Rather than discounting each other's mental strengths, appreciating the differences can lead to collaboratively finding a better solution.

My Personal Experience with Mental Factors behind My Interdependent and Connective Behaviors

Growing up in a family that primarily used passive and dominant behaviors, I didn't have a good model for interdependent behaviors. Most of what I know about interdependent behaviors I had to figure out on my own. Luckily, even at a young age, I was often able to recognize inappropriate behavior based on having interdependent beliefs. When I was a teenager, I remember my father getting laid off from his job; he was out of work for several months. My mother, who was a registered nurse, refused to get a job to help out with the family finances. I remember confronting her about this and telling her that she was a part of a team and should get a job to help relieve some of the financial stress on my dad. She replied that it was his responsibility as the man in the family to provide for us financially. She refused to get a job, so my dad ended up taking a job that he didn't want and wasn't a good fit for him. Recognizing and confronting others' inappropriate behaviors and beliefs was the first step for me, but it would take a while for me to start recognizing my own inappropriate behaviors.

When I entered the workforce, I used to feel that I wasn't responsible for any unpleasant dynamics that occurred between others and me. I thought they should change their behaviors since I wasn't the one behaving inappropriately. Then in the 1980s, I started reading self-help books and took several seminars from Anthony Robbins that provided techniques on how to change beliefs. I started to recognize that no one was accepting responsibility for the unpleasant dynamics in my relationships, and I had to accept that I had an equal part in those dynamics: If the other person used inappropriate dominant behaviors with me, then I used inappropriate passive behaviors with that person. I began to realize that we were doing the best we could at the time. Accepting equal responsibility for our interactions permitted me to choose interdependent behaviors, regardless of how others chose to initiate interactions. Also, believing that we were both equally entitled to respect allowed me to confront their inappropriate behavior, but respectfully.

Changing my beliefs also helped me work interdependently with clients. I remember one of the clients I supported was a high-tech company. The people that I interacted with were much more knowledgeable about technology than I was. In the past, this would have been challenging for me. But because I changed my beliefs, I could handle collaborating with people with different mental skills. As a result, I was able to develop an interdependent relationship with them.

I also started taking dance lessons in the 1980s. As a left-brained programmer, I was able to memorize dance steps like the best of them. However, it took about five years of lessons before I started hearing dance rhythms. After about ten years of dance lessons, I was musically inclined, which had a huge impact on my career. Dancing improved my right-brain functions, which allowed me to be more creative at work. I doubt that I would have been able to write this book if dancing hadn't converted me from a primarily left-brained techie nerd to a more whole-brained person with a balance between creative, right-brain and analytical, left-brain functions.

Changing my beliefs and developing more right-brain mental skills helped me use more connective behaviors. As a result, the workgroups I worked with accomplished extraordinary things. We implemented extremely challenging business-transformation efforts and delivered outstanding business results before, during, and after transformation initiatives.

Interestingly enough, my contribution as their leader wasn't all that visible. No one stood out as being the one to take credit for the results. What we accomplished was the result of a team effort based on the beliefs that we all provided equal value, we were all responsible for the results, and we were all entitled to be recognized for the results we delivered.

Addressing Mental Causal Factors

Changing Limiting Beliefs

Your beliefs are based on certain events, the people with whom you interacted, and the results that you achieved. Some beliefs become generalized and limit your behavior. It is a good idea to take some time and reflect on what your generalized beliefs might be in common stressful situations and see if these beliefs are negatively impacting your success and gruntledness at work. Doing so will help you identify your *limiting beliefs*. Limiting beliefs hold you back from behaving in a certain way that will give you the best results. For example, if you believe that you aren't very good at problem solving, then you may behave passively and limit the role you take in solving problems.

If you want to change your limiting beliefs, you need to look at your experiences from a different perspective. To see your experiences in a different light, it's helpful to ask yourself questions. The first step is to choose a belief that limits you and think of an event that has occurred that supports this belief. Then ask, "What negative results have occurred because of my belief?"

You can compare the results that you have obtained from this limiting belief to possible results that you could achieve if you changed your belief. Ask, "What could be a possible positive result if I changed my belief?"

Imagining a situation that is counter to your limiting belief starts to erode the influence of this belief. For example, you may believe that you can't rely on others to help out, and if you want something done correctly, you must do it yourself. The result may have been you did the job correctly, but you missed your deadline. Imagining a positive situation where letting others contribute to a task turns out well might help you realize that you could accomplish more if you allow others to contribute.

The next step is to look at the events that happened to you and use them to re-evaluate your beliefs. Ask, "Have I obtained a better result that was contrary to my belief?" For example, you may have generalized the belief that certain people don't provide value—but then they do something out of the ordinary that demonstrates their value after all. Recognizing that this event is contrary to your generalized belief is the next step to changing this limiting belief.

Additionally, you can look at the people you associate with at work and see if they are contributing to a limiting belief on your value, responsibility, or entitlement. For example, if people frequently criticize you, then you may have generalized the belief that you don't provide value. When other people are a factor, it's important to ask, "Am I letting their behavior influence how I feel about myself?" Recognizing how others' behaviors influence your beliefs will help you tremendously in changing any limiting beliefs you might have.

In addition to the above techniques, you can use the Belief-Changing Tool shown in Figure 28.1 to help you change limiting beliefs on value, responsibility, or entitlement. A blank Belief-Changing Tool is provided in Appendix D.

Improving Mental Skills

All of us have inherited from our parents a certain set of mental skills. Our experiences in life enhance these mental skills. The activities we do and our career choices continue to develop our mental skills—some skills more than others.

As discussed in earlier sections, a weakness or strength in our mental skills contributes to our beliefs about our value, compared to other people's value. Mental skills are a key influencer of our behavior choices.

You can improve your mental skills in areas where you are weak and try different activities that use that part of your brain. For instance, to increase creativity, take up a musical instrument, sign up for dance lessons, or learn to paint. To increase organizational skills, organize something that's currently a "mess," such as track personal finances according to a budget, clean

Figure 28.1: Example of the Belief-Changing Tool

Briefly describe a common situation where you think those that you interacted with didn't behave appropriately.
There are lots of meetings where I voice my opinion and people react very negatively, criticizing me. Most recently, I mentioned that the way they are reporting their inventory numbers is incorrect.
Which of the beliefs on value, responsibility, or entitlement may be behind their behavior?
They basically told me that I was out to lunch and that there wasn't anything wrong with the inventory report. (They provide more value than I do.)
Which of the beliefs on value, responsibility, or entitlement may be behind your behavior?
I had reviewed the inventory report prior to the meeting and know that I am right and they are wrong. (I provide more value than they do.)
How did you communicate this belief?
I probably stated my opinion strongly as if it were the only right answer.
How would the interdependent form of this belief sound?
We both provide value.
How might you have interacted differently if you had believed something else?
There might be a problem with the inventory report and that I would be glad to review it with someone to confirm.
How might have others responded if you had interacted differently?
They probably would have been willing to look into the inventory report.
How do you reinforce this limiting belief?
I often go home and tell my wife about how stupid the people are that I work with.
What can be done to help you change your limiting belief?
Ask my wife to let me know when I complain about how stupid my coworkers are.
What could you do differently to get better results from similar situations in the future?
State my opinions less forcibly—more as a possible option instead of the only way to do something.

out a closet, or organize a desk. Increasing weak mental skills can be as simple as doing the things that you avoid on a regular basis.

Many companies provide a variety of techniques to help people strengthen their mental skills and appreciate the mental skills of others. Herrmann International, for instance, provides the Herrmann Brain Dominance Instrument survey over the Internet. After the survey is complete, the company will send personal profile information, which comes with exercises that help improve areas of weakness.

In addition, Ned Herrmann's *The Whole Brain Business Book* has chapters on communication, supervision, delegation, training and development, strategic planning, organizational change, creativity, decision making, and problem solving.[65] The book provides numerous suggestions and alternatives that can be very helpful in improving mental skills in many business situations.

Understanding Mental Causal Factors: Why It Matters

To understand how to change our behaviors to interact in interdependent, connective ways with others in the workplace, we first have to understand ourselves. The need to do this cannot be understated; without changing our beliefs or mental skills, there isn't much hope for changing our behaviors in the long term.

Beliefs

The following summarizes how beliefs affect us and our coworkers:
- Passive beliefs limit our contribution at work
- Dominant beliefs limit the contributions of others
- Independent beliefs limit the synergies that could be gained from working with others
- Only interdependent beliefs allow us to gain the most from our own and others' efforts and allow us to gain synergies from collaborating with others

If we generalize the beliefs that the value we provide isn't as great as others or that we're not as responsible as others, we won't be as successful at work as we could be. Nor will we contribute as much to our organization's success as those who believe that they provide value and are as responsible as others. If we generalize the belief that we're not entitled to respect, we won't confront others' inappropriate behavior. Being the victim of inappropriate dominant or authoritarian behavior won't leave us feeling very gruntled.

If we generalize the beliefs that others don't provide as much value as we do or that others are not as responsible as we are, then we won't allow others to contribute as much as they can. When executive leaders generalize these beliefs, they tend to build in dependent characteristics into the business system. This further limits the contributions that employees can make to business success. If we generalize the belief that we are entitled to more than others or at the expense of others, we may have momentary gratification when we get what we want, but once we admit the impact that our behavior has on others, this generalized belief can eventually cause remorse, which will impact our gruntledness.

If we generalize the beliefs that we provide value best on our own and are more responsible on our own, then we limit our achievement to what we are capable of on our own. We will miss the joy and success that comes from collaborating with others. When executive leaders encourage these beliefs in their employees and build independent characteristics into the business system, this further limits employees' opportunities to work together and reap the benefits and synergies of collaboration.

If we generalize the belief that we provide value equal to the value others provide, we'll be successful in more situations since we'll benefit from our own and others' contributions. The same goes if we have generalized the belief that we are equally responsible as others. If we generalize the belief that everyone is equally entitled to success, then we'll have more opportunities to experience the joy of team accomplishments. We'll also be much happier since we won't have to deal with feelings of remorse or feelings of having been a victim or an abuser. Executive leaders who generalize these beliefs tend to embed more interdependent characteristics into the business system. As a result, employees are encouraged to work together more cooperatively and collaboratively.

Mental Skills

It's important to recognize our own strengths and weaknesses and appreciate others' mental strengths. Probably the most unrecognized preconceived judgments that exist today are the judgments we make against people who don't think the same way as we do.

If we are big-picture thinkers, we might tend to discount more detailed thinkers, dismissing them as having their heads in the weeds. But how is any direction or business strategy to be implemented without someone working through the details?

If we are detailed thinkers, we might tend to discount the big-picture thinkers, dismissing them as having their head in the clouds. But without their insight, we might develop a detail-level plan that misses the point. It is important to ensure that detail-level plans are on target for the problem or task.

If we prefer analytical thinking, we might tend to discount intuitive or feeling-based thinkers, dismissing them as warm-and-fuzzy types. In doing so, we'll miss their insight on whether our analysis feels right and how to get employees to emotionally accept our data.

If we are intuitive or feeling-based thinkers, we might tend to discount analytical thinkers, dismissing them as cold and calculating. But supporting intuition with facts will always strengthen our position. Analytical thinking helps ensure ideas, strategies, and problem identification are based on factual data, which leads to more accurate decisions.

Having an appreciation for our own and others' mental skills can also impact our gruntledness levels. Without this appreciation, a big-picture thinker may become frustrated communicating ideas to a detail-level thinker and vice versa. The same goes for analytical-based thinkers communicating with intuitive and feeling-based thinkers. Frustrations can escalate to heated arguments simply over a difference in thinking styles.

Both left-brain and right-brain mental skills are critical for success as an employee or leader. While it is difficult to improve our mental weaknesses, it is possible to do so. But even with improvement in our mental weaknesses, there will always be people who excel in those areas. Learning to appreciate others' mental strengths is an important step to working more interdependently.

29

Addressing Emotional Causal Factors of Behavior Preferences

"I was part of a team working with two others in my group. The other two people had worked there several years before I started and were not welcoming or at all happy to have another member. They were rude and unable to communicate like normal human beings. For example, in meetings they would berate me and make me feel stupid. They were relentless in their torment. They even talked badly about me to our manager who took a laid back approach and just told them to leave me alone. They had no social skills, and as a result, I was miserable every second I was in their company for the first three years at my job. I tried to avoid them any way I could by canceling meetings where we would be alone because I knew they'd rip me up for the entire meeting, and it was two against one. I often left work those days hating my job and mostly them. Fortunately, I [actually] loved my job and was able to avoid them enough that I outlasted their bullying and emotional abuse. The jerks are gone, and I still have my great job that I love!"

Disgruntled Employee
Blog Post

Emotions and how skilled we are at using them socially are two emotional causal factors that influence behavior. If we have fear-based emotions or lack certain emotional and social skills, we will try to deal with our fear or compensate for what we lack by using coping strategies. Coping strategies are behaviors we use to help us manage our fears and deficiencies. For example, we may choose a passive behavior as a way to deal with not having the emotional skill of being assertive. Or if we fear someone's dominant behavior, we may choose an independent behavior to deal with that behavior instead of confront our fear.

So whether we choose a passive, dominant, or independent coping strategy depends on our fears and the emotional and social skills we are lacking. These emotional causal factors also affect how we as employees and leaders behave when performing our activities. Workgroup members who share common fears also influence the dynamics between two workgroups.

This chapter will look at explanations for the emotions and emotional and social skills that influence employee and leadership behaviors. It will also discuss ways to address emotional causal factors.

Emotions Influence Our Behavior

We can break down the emotions that we experience at work into two categories: positive and negative. Positive emotions make us feel good; these include acceptance, affection, compassion, empathy, gratitude, happiness, hope, and love. Negative emotions make us feel bad; these include anger, anxiety, disgust, disappointment, doubt, embarrassment, fear, frustration, guilt, hostility, hysteria, jealousy, judgment, regret, remorse, sadness, shame, and worry.

Negative emotions are all based on some degree of fear. For instance, anger is based on a fear that what someone did will have negative consequences. Anxiety is based on a fear that something negative will happen. Disappointment is based on the fear that we let someone down. Doubt is based on the fear that we might not be correct. Embarrassment is based on the fear that we might look stupid. Frustration is based on the fear that we might not get something we want.

304

Our negative emotions are often behind our passive, dominant, and independent behavior choices. When we are not fearful and are feeling positive emotions, we are more likely to choose interdependent behaviors.

Emotional and Social Skills Influence Our Behavior

In addition to mental causal factors, emotional and social skills are behind preferences for particular behavior patterns. The way we were brought up, as well as our interpersonal experiences since then, provide us with a set of emotional and social skills. We need a set of emotional skills for managing our emotions (internal state), and we need a set of social skills for interacting with people (external state). An important part of changing behavior preferences is first understanding our emotional and social skills to see if they contribute to our behavior preferences. The following lists show a few common emotional and social skills that are often required in work activities.

Emotional Skills	Social Skills
Be assertive	Respect differences
Be self-aware	Be sensitive toward others
Have an appropriate level of self-esteem	Cooperate with others
Have self-control	Include others
Be self-reliant	Accept others
Take initiative	Communicate clearly

A lack of certain emotional or social skills can be the cause of passive, dominant, or independent behavior preferences. Someone who demonstrates preferences for authoritarian or laissez-faire behaviors may also lack certain emotional or social skills. To be able to use interdependent and connective behaviors more frequently, it is necessary to be proficient in emotional and social skills.

Appendix E contains four tables showing examples of how a lack or possession of certain emotional and social skills when performing work activities impact employee and leadership behaviors.

Coping Strategies

We use our emotional and social skills to find ways to handle unpleasant situations. But if we have a limitation in certain emotional and social skills, it can lead us to use a coping strategy rather than confront our fears. Typically, we use coping strategies to deal with difficult people who are inappropriately using dominant or authoritarian behaviors. But some of us use coping strategies to deal with people who are inappropriately using passive or independent behaviors.

A workgroup can also exhibit collective behavior preferences based on coping strategies. Certain behaviors become so common within a workgroup that many workgroup members resort to the same coping strategy. For example, one very independent workgroup that was accustomed to laissez-faire management developed a "wink-and-nod" coping strategy whenever a leader tried to use authoritarian behaviors, whether appropriate or not. Employees would nod in agreement to what the leader was saying but would look at another workgroup member and wink. This meant they were going to ignore the leader's direction and decide what to do on their own.

This behavior was based on the fear that the leader's interfering would reduce their independence. Their preference for independent behaviors led to the "wink-and-nod" coping strategy whenever someone tried to get them to use passive behaviors.

Emotional Explanations for Passive and Laissez-Faire Behaviors

Emotions

If we fear that others will hurt us mentally, emotionally, or physically, we may choose to behave in a passive manner. This fear can be expressed in many different emotions. For example, we may worry about being reprimanded for making a mistake, we may be anxious about doing something on our own, or we may be embarrassed to speak up. Fear of rejection or criticism can also lead to passive behaviors.

Emotional and Social Skills

When we lack certain emotional or social skills, it can lead us to have a preference for passive behaviors. For instance, if we lack emotional skills such as being able to express our emotions appropriately or being assertive, it can lead us to use passive behaviors such as keeping our opinions to ourselves, letting others get their way, or deferring decisions.

Passive Coping Strategies

Some of us who encountered verbally or physically abusive adults while growing up learned passive coping strategies for surviving in an abusive environment. We learned to ignore our own thoughts and feelings and deny what was really happening. We also learned to be hyper-vigilant of others' moods and emotions so that we could avoid those people when they were in a bad mood or feeling negative emotions.

Lacking certain emotional or social skills can also lead us to use passive coping strategies. For example, in the workplace, if we feel that standing up to inappropriate dominant or authoritarian behaviors will result in our fears coming true—such as being reprimanded, laid off, or marked down on the next performance review—we will use passive coping strategies to avoid those outcomes. For instance, rather than dealing with a stressful situation, we may cope by seeking emotional support from our coworkers, family, or friends, and complain to them about the situation and play the victim. Or we may cope by deciding that this type of stress is just part of the working environment and accept the situation as something that we have to learn to live with.

Sometimes we use denial as a coping strategy, acting as if the stressful situation isn't really happening to us. At other times, we may attempt to correct the stressful situation; but if it is not resolved immediately, we cope by deciding to give up and quit trying. We might also turn our attention to other work activities or even non-work activities as a way to not think of the stressful situation. Some of us resort to alcohol or drugs to cope with workplace stress.

These passive coping strategies are emotionally based and don't address the stressful situation in an active and productive way. None of these coping strategies will solve the problem that caused the stressful situation. Passive coping strategies only limit the emotional impact of the stressful situation to something that is tolerable.

My Personal Experience with Emotional Factors behind My Passive and Laissez-Faire Behaviors

In the beginning of my career, I was weak in several emotional skills including assertiveness and self-reliance. As a result, I used passive behaviors when interacting with those who used dominant and authoritarian behaviors. I was afraid of getting in trouble if I confronted their inappropriate behaviors. I had several bosses with a preference for authoritarian behaviors and their behaviors kindled a fear that I might lose my job if I didn't do as they directed. As a result, I often ended up doing things that I wasn't comfortable with.

Sometimes I talked to other leaders about the situation, hoping that they would solve my problem for me. I complained to HR about my bosses' behavior in an attempt to get HR to change their behavior. But my usual way of dealing with long-term unpleasant situations was to quit rather than stand up for myself and insist that I be treated with respect. We all have a fight-or-flight instinct. My flight instinct is much greater than my fight instinct. I'll put up with the situation to a point; and then when I'm really upset, I'm out of there. This is a coping strategy that I developed early in life and used numerous times in my personal and work relationships.

Early in my career, I was also afraid of conflict and this impacted my behaviors as a leader. I had several employees that had a preference for passive behaviors and used them inappropriately most of the time. One employee would miss half his work day to play video games. After several warnings, it became apparent that it was time to fire him, but I didn't have the emotional skills to confront my fear of conflict. So I talked another person into firing him for me. However, as I progressed in my career, I had many more opportunities to strengthen my emotional skills since similar situations came up again and again.

Emotional Explanations for Dominant and Authoritarian Behaviors

Emotions

If we fear that others will let us down in some way, or if we don't trust others, we may choose to behave in a dominant manner. This fear can be expressed in many different emotions. For instance, we may worry that others will make mistakes or cause a mess without our help. Or we may dread that others will get what we want unless we fight for it.

Emotional and Social Skills

If we lack certain emotional or social skills, we may use dominant behaviors more frequently. For example, if we haven't developed social skills in respecting differences and cooperating with others, we may prefer dominant behaviors more often. If so, we'll have more difficulty paying attention to others' opinions, resolving conflict equitably, and protecting others' boundaries. In such cases, we may handle problems and tasks without being sensitive to others. Also, if we lack the ability to follow direction, we may not be able to work with others as a team member and may insist on always leading.

Dominant Coping Strategies

Some of us who encountered verbally or physically abusive adults while growing up learned how to use dominant coping strategies through their example. We may have been taught that we will lose something unless we put ourselves before others. The adults around us may not have taught us how to be more sensitive to others.

Fears and a lack of certain emotional and social skills can also cause us to use dominant coping strategies. For instance, we may deal with a stressful situation by venting our feelings. Rather than holding in emotions, we let them out by letting the person causing our stress know that we are upset.

If we use dominant coping strategies, we also may confront stressful situations in a hostile manner. We may decide not to live with stress as part of our working environment and refuse to accept that we have to learn to live with some situations. Some people say that they don't get headaches; they give them. Rather than accepting stressful situations, they project the stress onto someone else. They don't solve the stressful situation; they just work to remove the stress from their lives by giving it to others.

Dominant coping strategies are emotionally based and do not address the stressful situation in a positive way. Anger doesn't solve the problem that caused the stressful situation; it only projects the problem onto someone else to deal with it.

Like passive coping strategies, dominant coping strategies limit the personal emotional impact of a stressful situation. While passive coping strategies turn the emotional impact into something tolerable, dominant coping strategies remove the emotional impact by transferring the stress onto someone else. If we really want to address the situation that is causing the stress, we have to look at the missing emotional or social skills that may be causing our dominant coping strategy.

My Personal Experience with Emotional Factors behind My Dominant and Authoritarian Behaviors

I often felt that I knew more than others and that others let me down, which contributed to my preference for dominant behaviors. I also often feared that others would make mistakes if I wasn't involved. As I grew older and acquired more experience, this fear only increased.

I became more and more judgmental about inappropriate passive behaviors, particularly when people didn't pay attention to details or analyze situations enough to accurately understand the facts. Someone shooting from the hip and making up answers or giving loosely based opinions sent me off the deep end. It made me angry when people weren't responsible enough to do things right.

As a result of these fears, I used authoritarian behaviors as a coping strategy. I frequently took over other people's responsibilities when I was afraid that they wouldn't live up to my expectations. In one situation, I attended a class that two of my employees were teaching. When I realized that they were having difficulty explaining the material to the students, I just took over the class without consulting them and taught the material myself. I didn't realize until much later in my career that my dominant and authoritarian behavior was a problem.

Emotional Explanations for Independent and Laissez-Faire Behaviors

Emotions

If we fear that others may hurt us mentally, emotionally, or physically or that others will let us down, then we may choose to behave in an independent manner. This fear can be expressed in many different emotions. For example, we may worry that if we work with others, we'll accomplish less, or that we won't get what we're entitled to.

Emotional and Social Skills

A lack of certain emotional and social skills can be the reason behind independent behaviors. For example, if we are missing the social skills of being sensitive to others or including others, we may find it easier just to work alone. If we are unable to effectively express our thoughts and feelings to others, we may isolate ourselves rather than interact with others.

Independent Coping Strategies

While growing up, we may have experienced the pain of boundary violations from dominant or passive interactions, which lead us to use independent coping strategies. For example, while growing up, some of us may have encountered a person in a position of authority who was mentally, emotionally, or physically abusive. Or we may have encountered someone who primarily used passive behaviors and came to depend on us to take care of him or her mentally, emotionally, or physically. In either case, we may have decided the best way to handle the situation was to keep to ourselves, and we may have developed some rigid boundaries as a coping strategy to protect ourselves.

At work, rather than trying to resolve stressful situations caused by others, we may decide to work more by ourselves. We may solve the problem on our own by removing ourselves from the situation as much as possible.

Conversely, we may attempt to correct a stressful situation by taking action to get rid of the problem. We may change our own actions to improve the stressful situation.

Independent coping strategies are an improvement to passive and dominant coping strategies. Passive and dominant coping strategies only limit or project the emotional impact of the stressful situation. Independent coping strategies tend to be more action-based and may address the stressful situation completely or to some extent.

However, when another person is contributing to a stressful situation, an independent coping strategy like isolating ourselves usually doesn't solve the problem; the other person won't have a clue that his or her actions are causing stress. If we really want to address the complete situation that causes our stress, we have to look at whether missing emotional and social skills causes an independent coping strategy and keeps us from talking to others who are contributing to the stressful situation.

My Personal Experience with Emotional Factors behind Independent and Laissez-Faire Behaviors

From the beginning of my career, I preferred working for managers with a preference for laissez-faire behaviors because they would, for the most part, let me work independently. I was afraid that I wouldn't be able to do what I wanted, so I'd rarely ask management for direction and rarely provide status. I sought out these managers and usually started looking for another job when I was transferred to a manager with a preference for authoritarian behaviors. I had dealt with enough authoritarian behaviors while growing up, and I coped with such behavior by seeking out laissez-faire managers.

One of my managers told me that my greatest problem was that I didn't promote myself. The truth was I didn't want feedback on anything I did, so I avoided telling management what I was doing even if it was positive.

I expected my managers to trust me with what I was doing, and I minimized interactions with them. I was happiest when I worked remotely from my managers and had infrequent meetings with them. As I moved up the corporate ladder, I felt that one of the main benefits of being promoted was the opportunity to do my own thing.

Emotional Explanations for Interdependent and Connective Behaviors

Emotions

Overcoming our fears is a necessary part of becoming more gruntled. The less we fear, the better we feel. We're not focused on our fears when we feel positive emotions of acceptance, affection, compassion, empathy, gratitude, happiness, hope, joy, and pride. All of these feelings can be associated with gruntledness. When we feel these positive emotions, it is easier to use interdependent behaviors.

Emotional and Social Skills

The more emotional and social skills we have, the easier it will be to use interdependent behaviors. For example, if we have an appropriate level of self-esteem, we will be more capable of using independent and/or interdependent behaviors more often. If we respect differences or if we're able to express emotions appropriately and with self-control, we'll be more capable of using interdependent behaviors. If we're able to cooperate, we'll be more likely to use interdependent behaviors.

Interdependent Strategies

If we encountered more interdependent and connective behaviors while growing up, we may have learned to deal with situations by our parents' example. Some of us didn't have this privilege and as a result, we had to learn through trial and error a better way of relating to others and working through our fears.

In the workplace, it is much more effective for gruntledness and success outcomes to use interdependent behavior strategies instead of using dependent or independent coping strategies. Interdependent strategies are not coping strategies; coping strategies try to reduce the emotional consequences of stressful events or minimize stressful events, whereas interdependent strategies eliminate the underlying condition causing stress. How can we do that?

Using interdependent strategies, we can take action with others to try to get rid of the problem causing our stress. We can come up with a plan to alleviate the stressful situation, and we can decide together how to eliminate competing activities until we work through the stressful situation.

Rather than coping by talking to others for emotional support, we can talk to the person we see as the cause of our stress. Talking about this person to others for emotional support does nothing to eliminate the stress. Talking to this person directly about the situation can do wonders for eliminating the stress.

Interdependent strategies are action-based and address a stressful situation head on. For instance, if we find that we contributed to the cause of a stressful situation, we must recognize that we need to change our behavior and talk to the other contributors directly to resolve the stress. If we really want to address the complete situation that is causing the stress, we have to be sure we have the necessary emotional and social skills to interact properly with others in an interdependent or connective way.

My Personal Experience with Emotional Factors behind Interdependent and Connective Behavior

I eventually realized that I had to deal with other people's dominant behavior preferences because people with dominant behavior preferences kept coming back into my life. I first overcame my fears, then relied on myself to change the abusive dynamics between others and me. It took many hours of counseling, self-help seminars, and books to overcome my more debilitating fears. By confronting others on their inappropriate behaviors, I moved away from my passive coping strategies and used more interdependent behaviors. As a result, the people that I interacted with also changed their behaviors, and I learned that I was a much more powerful person than I realized.

Confronting managers and coworkers who behaved inappropriately often caused conflict. To keep my self-esteem intact, I sometimes had to ignore their criticism and judgments. Although their criticism was often harshly and inappropriately stated, I would still search for an essence of truth in what they said so that I could try to improve.

Next, I also had some dominant coping strategies that I needed to give up. I realized that while my dominant behaviors addressed the immediate situation, they didn't improve or correct the situation in the long term and did nothing to prevent future occurrences. I came to realize that people using passive behaviors were doing the best they could. They had mental, emotional, and physical factors that they were often unaware of that caused them to use a passive coping strategy.

I had to work on several of my emotional skills in these situations. I took the Hay Group's Emotional Intelligence test to understand where I needed to improve. I had to work on expressing my emotions appropriately and develop much more self-control. I found myself biting my tongue more often and not saying anything until I carefully thought through whether it was my responsibility and whether it would be helpful. I started reminding myself that everyone makes mistakes and that, again, everyone was doing the best they could at the time, regardless of how inappropriate their behavior was. With this in mind, I was able to stay calmer and be more open-minded before confronting those involved in the situation.

Working with my coworkers helped me give up my independent coping strategies. I realized early on that working together with someone actually increased my effectiveness. I came to appreciate conflict, and rather than fear it, saw it as an opportunity to learn from others. Reading Thomas Crum's *The Magic of Conflict* really helped in that respect.[66]

Developing my emotional skills then helped me to overcome my fear of working interdependently with my boss or coworkers. Having an appropriate level of self-esteem allowed me to take criticism in stride, realizing that I still added value. It also allowed me to not be intimidated by other people's strengths. In addition, working on my social skills helped me let go of my independent coping strategies. Becoming more socially aware and appreciating others' contributions helped me work more interdependently with others rather than preferring to work by myself.

Dancing also improved my emotional causal factors. My dance instructors made us watch ourselves dance on videotape. It was a humiliating experience that taught an over-confident me self-awareness and more appropriate levels of self-esteem. The dance instructors also taught dance etiquette: You can't turn anyone down who asks you to dance, and you always thank the person for the dance no matter how horribly they danced. The dance instructors also insisted that people rotate partners in group lessons so that everyone had a chance to dance with everyone else. These few rules helped me be more sensitive towards others (particularly new, struggling dancers), include others, and accept others.

Dancing really helped me overcome my preference for dominant behaviors. Because the male leads on the dance floor, I had to learn to follow my dance partner's lead, which was a challenge for me. Dancing got me more in touch with my emotional and feminine side. It also helped me overcome my tendency to resort to independent behaviors. When I started entering dance competitions, I realized that it wasn't just about my dancing skills; it was about how well we danced as a team. Dancing taught me a lot about interdependent behaviors and how to cooperate with others.

Addressing Emotional Causal Factors

Overcoming Fears

Fears limit your behavior in situations. You may not do or say certain things because at some level, whether conscious of it or not, you are afraid of the outcome. Your current fears come from what you have experienced, such as negative emotional events, social conditioning, and inappropriate learning.

The first step is to clearly identify what you fear. The next step is to clearly identify the coping strategy that you use to address your fear. To overcome your fears, you may need to think differently about them. When faced with a situation that causes you some fear, you may imagine the worst possible outcome if you confront the situation. But usually the possibility of the worst-case scenario is small. A more realistic outcome from confronting the situation will often occur. Not confronting the situation also has an outcome—more of the same.

You can use the Emotional Improvement Tool shown in Figure 29.1 on the following page to help you overcome any fears you may have on a regular basis. A blank Emotional Improvement Tool is provided in Appendix F.

Improving Emotional and Social Skills

Many companies have tools that can help you assess your emotional and social skills. They identify any weaknesses that you might have and identify how these weaknesses contribute to your workplace coping strategies and behavior preferences.

The Hay Group, for example, offers an Emotional and Social Competency Inventory (ESCI) 360-degree assessment on their Web site (www.hay-group.com). It will send scores in the four areas of Emotional Intelligence: self-awareness, self-management, social awareness, and relationship management. The package comes complete with suggestions on how to master skills and provides improvement plans for each of the four areas.

Understanding Our Emotional Causal Factors: Why It Matters

Renowned motivational writer and speaker Dale Carnegie in 1936 wrote in his book, *How to Win Friends and Influence People,* "When dealing with people let us remember we are not dealing with creatures of logic. We are dealing with creatures of emotion."[67] Our emotional capabilities have a major impact on our behavior preferences.

Figure 29.1: Example of the Emotional Improvement Tool

Briefly describe a common situation where you think those that you interacted with didn't behave appropriately.
In situations with people behaving dominantly, I feel as if I can't express my opinion without being dominant. Usually I just keep my opinion to myself. If everyone is belligerently stating their opinion, then they don't hear me unless I also state my opinion in the same way. The few times that I do state my opinion, I usually get a "why are you so upset?" reaction.
What fear might be causing you to behave this way?
Fear of being embarrassed for expressing my opinion whether it is right or wrong. Fear of looking stupid in front of others.
What coping strategy do you normally use?
I use passive behaviors and keep my opinion to myself.
How does this coping strategy limit you?
I feel like I've been relegated to the side and that I'm not really a valued member of the team.
What do you do that makes this fear come true?
I state my opinion just as forcibly as the rest of them, which usually makes them attack my opinion. I might even state my opinion more forcibly than others just because I've reached the limit of my patience with keeping things to myself.
Is there anything you can do to minimize the chances of this fear coming true?
I could state my opinion in a way that has less chance of evoking criticism (and other dominant behaviors).
If this fearful situation does occur, is there something you can do to make yourself feel better afterwards?
I could talk to the person that criticized me and say that I'm reluctant to share my opinions in the future because of the way they react.
Is there a way that you can confront these types of situations in small doses?
I could start voicing my opinions in meetings with just a few people instead of the whole team.
What behavior do you usually use when you get into these situations?
Passive and occasionally dominant. When I finally voice my opinion, I usually do so very dominantly because it appears to be the only way to be heard.
What behavior should you use instead?
Interdependent—state my opinion in a way that respects their opinions also. I could also confront disrespectful behavior by others by simply making a request for us to be more respectful when something disrespectful is said.

Fears

The 32nd President of the United States, Franklin D. Roosevelt said, "The only thing we have to fear is fear itself," which is profound considering how much trouble fear gets us into. Our fears are often the root cause of our passive, dominant, or independent behavior preferences.

If we fear that we are not good enough and might be reprimanded for a mistake, or fear that we will look stupid if we try something new, then we won't put much energy into our work activities. Consequently, without a full commitment to whatever we are doing, we will not be as successful as we could be. If we hold back because of our fears, it will also impact our workgroup's and organization's success.

Also, if we fear that others will let us down or make mistakes unless we help them, then we will put more energy into our work activities than we should. This might seem like an acceptable way of dealing with others' passive behaviors, but eventually it can cause burnout and resentment.

If we fear that we will be less successful or accomplish less if we work with others, then we'll refuse to work with others. However, when we are faced with a task that requires a joint effort, the result of our independent effort will not be as great as it could have been. Our own personal success will be less because we did not benefit from others' contributions. Our workgroup or organization will also suffer from our unwillingness to collaborate.

Often our decisions and actions are emotionally based. If the emotion we feel is based on some fear, then we are not going to make the best possible choices. Fears that cause passive behaviors limit our value at work. Fears that cause dominant behaviors may increase our value, but limit the value of others. And fears that cause independent behaviors limit the value and synergies that we can gain by working with others.

In general, fears blind us from what's really going on. For example, when we have fear while making a decision, we only see what might impact us the most emotionally rather than what is more appropriate for the situation at hand. Additionally, our fears also inhibit our ability to trust others.

Trust allows coworkers to rely on each other and encourages interdependent and connective behaviors.

Fear does not move organizations forward. Organizations need innovation and innovation depends on an environment that encourages taking risks. An environment of fear creates an unwillingness to step out and take a risk that might end up as a mistake. But not taking the risk could be a bigger mistake. Fears can also be behind resistance to change. Adaptability to change is a critical characteristic for gruntledness and success with today's rapidly changing business environment.

Coping Strategies

Coping strategies limit what employees can accomplish individually at work, but a leader's coping strategies have more of an impact on workgroup success. For example, when leaders use authoritarian coping strategies, they will encourage employees to use passive behaviors. But a leader won't be able to pick up the slack for all the employees who are using passive behaviors in the workgroup; despite the leader's efforts, the workgroup will still fall short. As long as the workgroup is encouraged to behave in this manner, it will not be as productive as a workgroup that is encouraged to contribute more. A leader's authoritarian behaviors and coping strategies negatively impact workgroup success.

Coping strategies can violate personal boundaries in the workplace. For example, an employee using passive coping strategies can pull someone with a preference for dominant behaviors across a boundary, hoping the dominantly preferred employee will rescue the employee from the situation. Conversely, people using dominant coping strategies can push themselves across a boundary to deal with employees who use passive behaviors.

Not caring, being indifferent, being apathetic, not participating in meetings, being late for meetings, being irresponsible, using passive-aggressive tactics, and not listening, are all passive coping strategies. Criticizing, being judgmental, being selfish, controlling others' actions, making decisions for others, manipulating people, being impatient, using sarcasm, interrupting people, causing public humiliation, and being arrogant are all dominant coping strategies. Both passive and dominant coping strategies show disrespect to people, cross boundaries, and impact others' gruntledness.

Finding the courage to confront boundary violations is difficult but necessary. We can begin to do this by improving our emotional and social skills, which in some cases means learning how to confront others who either dominantly or passively cross our personal boundaries. Addressing dominant and passive boundary violations and ensuring that others treat us with respect will also do a lot to improve our gruntledness at work.

If we use a passive, dominant, or an independent coping strategy, then all we accomplish is minimizing the pain from inappropriate behaviors and boundary violations. Until we learn how to confront inappropriate behaviors and boundary violations, we can't really be happy when we work with others. Only interdependent strategies allow us to gain the most synergy from working with others and to experience the joy of teamwork.

30

Addressing Physical Causal Factors of Behavior Preferences

"In one of my teaching jobs, my stress level was at a peak. I had an assistant principal who had decided somewhere along the way that I didn't have good classroom management and that my communication with parents was poor. This started innocently enough with a couple of chronic parent complainers early in the year, but it quickly snowballed into one of the most stressful years of teaching I ever encountered. Keep in mind that I had a history of excellent classroom management and good parent communication, so I was treading in unfamiliar waters when I started getting questioned about every little thing that went on in my classes. Because of my fears and stress, I did begin to make some of the very mistakes that I was worried about. Of course, this created more stress and more meetings with the vice principal. It soon began to affect my health. I seemed to have a cold every month, I got the flu, and my back went out for days; I could barely walk. I slept fitfully and always felt tired during the day, which contributed to a less-than-stellar performance at work. If that wasn't enough, [my] tooth fell apart, and it had to be pulled! Now I can't say for sure, but I think I probably ground my teeth at night due to the stress, and I weakened it or damaged it. . . . Stress at work is a great disabler. It is powerful and can be very destructive."

Disgruntled Employee
Blog Post

Just as mental and emotional factors affect behavior choices, so do certain physical factors. Diet and stress affect the nervous system which, in turn, affects employee and leadership behaviors. Physical causal factors can influence whether we choose passive, dominant, authoritarian or any of the other behavior patterns in a particular situation and sometimes even as a behavior preference.

To take a holistic approach to improve our gruntledness and success, we must look at everything that could negatively impact it. Physical factors could be at the root of the problem for many of us.

This chapter will first explain how our nervous system and neurotransmitters relate to our behaviors. Then it will cover how our dietary choices and stress influence our behavior. Last, it will discuss ways we can improve physical causal factors that negatively impact our behaviors. Please note that since I am not an expert in this subject, Dr. Lindy Vaughn contributed her knowledge to the content in this chapter.

Neurotransmitters Influence Our Behavior

The nervous system is the primary communication system in the human body that lets the brain and the body "talk" to each other. *Neurons*, which are nerve cells, receive information and pass messages through the nervous system. The nervous system uses chemical substances called *neurotransmitters* to communicate messages between neurons, organs, muscles, or glands. Neurotransmitters break down into two categories:

- Neurotransmitters that stimulate the brain and facilitate the transmission of messages
- Neurotransmitters that calm the brain and impede the transmission of messages

When neurotransmitters become unbalanced, they impact the nervous system and negatively affect our health and behavior. Stress, poor sleep, sugar, poor dietary choices, drugs, alcohol, and caffeine can cause neurotransmitter levels to be out of balance.

Neurotransmitter imbalances directly relate to behavioral problems such as anxiousness, attention problems, aggression, irritability, low mood, fatigue, low energy, lack of focus, hyperactivity, and memory disorders. These behavioral problems can manifest themselves as passive, dominant, laissez-faire, and authoritarian behaviors.

Neurotransmitters can also affect sleep patterns, which indirectly impact behavior. For instance, if we don't get enough sleep, we may be chronically fatigued and develop a preference for passive behaviors because we just don't have the energy to behave otherwise. Or we may get cranky from lack of sleep and develop a preference for dominant behaviors.

Neurotransmitters can also affect concentration and memory. If we lack concentration or are forgetful, we may have difficulty being responsible, which may become passive behavior. The following lists some of the neurotransmitters that calm the brain:

- Serotonin – stabilizes mood and promotes contentment; well-being neurotransmitter
- Gamma-Amino Butyric Acid (GABA) – calms the body down, reduces anxiety, and promotes sound sleep; nature's tranquilizer
- Taurine – inhibits hyperactivity and anxiety, promotes sound sleep and calmness

If these neurotransmitters are too high, we may be overly relaxed, have impaired reactions, and may be apathetic. We might also experience low energy, fatigue, low motivation, or low mood. If these neurotransmitters are too low, we might suffer from insomnia, anxiousness, irritability, aggressive behavior, chronic impulsiveness, reduced inhibition, nervousness, panic attacks, restlessness, or hyperactivity. The following lists neurotransmitters that stimulate the brain and body:

- Norepinephrine – stimulates alertness, motivation, concentration, memory, and emotional stability; well-being neurotransmitter
- Epinephrine (adrenaline) – supports energy and mental focus
- Acetylcholine – supports learning and memory and is partly responsible for concentration and focus

- Glutamate – supports learning and memory
- Dopamine – alleviates depression and helps focus, motivation, assertiveness, learning, attention, emotion, pleasure, and satisfaction

When these neurotransmitters are too high, we may experience anxiety, aggression, hyperactivity, mania, sleep problems, ADHD, obsessive tendencies, or restlessness. When these neurotransmitters are low, we may experience low energy, fatigue, decreased focus, low motivation, low mood, or cognitive decline.

If neurotransmitter imbalances cause depression, low mood, chronic fatigue, low energy, low motivation, focus issues, attention problems, sleep problems or poor memory, then we may use more passive behaviors. If neurotransmitter imbalances cause aggression, anxiety, irritability, impulsivity, hyperactivity, mania, ADHD, obsessive tendencies, restlessness, or paranoia, then we may use more dominant behaviors. Appendix G provides tables that show how imbalanced neurotransmitter levels relate to passive, dominant, laissez-faire, and authoritarian behaviors.

Dietary Choices Influence Neurotransmitter Levels

The body breaks down proteins from food into amino acids to generate the neurotransmitters, hormones, and enzymes it needs to function. With a healthy diet, the body receives the amino acids it needs. The brain becomes malnourished when it doesn't receive proper nutrition, which will affect emotions and behavior.

We need the amino acid tryptophan, the precursor to serotonin, which has a calming effect on the body. We also need the amino acid tyrosine, the precursor to dopamine and norepinephrine, to energize our bodies. Food sources for tryptophan include brown rice, whole grains, and sweet potatoes. Food sources for tyrosine include fish, poultry, meat, soy products, legumes, nuts, and seeds.

Bad dietary choices contribute to neurotransmitter imbalances. Foods that contain *simple carbohydrates* (such as canned fruits, cakes, biscuits, chocolate, candy, soft drinks, and fruit juice) or processed foods (such as white bread, crackers, and instant rice) have a *high glycemic index*, which means they rapidly break down and put high levels of *glucose* (or sugar) into the bloodstream. Eating such foods will spike levels of glucose, tryptophan, and serotonin neurotransmitters for a short while, which will then be followed by low blood sugar and low serotonin levels. This will give us a temporary boost, and then can leave us feeling tired and cranky.

Caffeine is a stimulant that initially increases neurotransmitters that elevate mood for the short term. However, with prolonged use, these neurotransmitters become depleted. Many people start the day by stimulating their nervous system with caffeine and end the day by calming their nervous system with alcohol. These short-term impacts to neurotransmitter levels can eventually damage the nervous system in the long term.

My Personal Experience with Dietary Choices

I figured out the connection between diet and behavior in my twenties because I had problems with low blood sugar. I found that if I had not eaten in a while, I would use more passive behaviors since my brain was malnourished. I would get "spacey" and have a hard time formulating words, so I would sit quietly in meetings not talking much and allowing others to take the lead. However, if someone said something that irritated me, I would react with anger and use inappropriate dominant behaviors since my brain didn't have the nutrition it needed for proper neurotransmitter function. Once I figured this out, I decided that it was my responsibility to bring half a sandwich to meetings that might run over into lunch or suppertime to help ensure that I would not use inappropriate behaviors.

I also learned to pay attention to what I ate and how I felt afterward. I realized that sugar had a very negative effect on my blood sugar and neurotransmitters and caused many inappropriate behaviors. I kept a food diary and soon realized that the next couple of days after I had a cookie, I would either be in tears or be angry with someone. I found out through trial and error that I had to be very careful with what I ate if I wanted to be more pleasant at work.

Chronic Stress Influences Neurotransmitter Levels

Many jobs today require that we work fifty, sixty, seventy, or more hours a week, and during that week we run from one meeting to the next and fight one issue after another. Even commuting to the office each day provides many opportunities on the freeway for our neurotransmitters to get out of balance. When one stressful event after another stimulates our neurotransmitters, they can become depleted, so we stay in a constant state of stress. Our bodies don't have a chance to return to normal, so we create an imbalance in our neurotransmitter levels.

Today's business strategies of downsizing, offshoring, revenue growth, and process reengineering all have heavy time demands and short time-frames, which adds to our stress. Moreover, some leaders and organizational cultures don't tolerate mistakes or normal productivity, which also contributes to our stress. Our passive, dominant, or independent behavior preferences may allow us to cope with stressful environments for years. However, using our behavior preferences as coping strategies will eventually catch up with us. Our neurotransmitter levels can become so out of balance that our bodies are not able to function normally. We may not be able to handle a stressful situation as calmly as we did before. Or we may develop some health issues that are directly related to being chronically stressed.

My Personal Experience with Chronic Stress

A few years ago, I learned the hard way about how chronic stress affects neurotransmitter levels. I had been working in a high-stress environment for about a year, implementing a very aggressive business-transformation initiative for a client. Somewhere along the way, I tore my rotator cuff (shoulder joint) and had to have surgery. I ended up with frozen shoulder as a result of post-operative scar tissue. To treat the frozen shoulder, I had two additional medical procedures, which had limited success, so my physical therapist started working on my shoulder to tear up the remaining scar tissue. The physical therapy was extremely stressful to my body, which had already reached burn-out stage due to the work stress.

By this time, my body had endured more than it could handle and I started reacting in very strange ways at work. I cried in front of a client who said "no" to one of my requests. I got very upset and yelled at people with whom I normally would have been much more patient. After one yelling episode, I started having chest pains. Four hours later, I figured I should go to a hospital because I feared I might be having a heart attack. Thankfully, it ended up that I was having an anxiety attack.

Shortly afterwards, my doctor assessed my neurotransmitter levels, which were extremely out of balance. The chronic stress of my job, coupled with the stress of physical therapy, had completely worn out my nervous system. Fortunately, my doctor was able to balance my neurotransmitter levels with amino acid supplements. These days I watch my diet more carefully and exercise regularly.

Personal stress can also impact us at work. I was working in New Jersey on September 11, 2001 and was able to see the World Trade Center towers from my office window. I watched the towers fall that day from my desk. A week or so later, letters containing anthrax were sent from the same post office that delivered to my house. Shortly after that, I had several episodes of breaking out into hives as soon as I walked into my office building.

The first time it occurred, I had to go to a meeting. I sat in front of my team with an extremely bright red face. One of my coworkers in a teasing tone asked if I had stayed in a tanning booth too long. I told him that I was having a panic attack. He then asked me what I was panicking about, to which I replied, "Terrorists."

We all had a pretty good laugh about it even though it was a rather unpleasant situation that impacted my work. I was afraid to set client meetings first thing in the morning, in case I would break out into hives.

So I went to see a doctor who recommended that I go on anti-depressants to help me get over my anxiety. Because I didn't want to take drugs, she suggested that I try bio-feedback. I used bio-feedback techniques for 6 months, which calmed me down and stopped me from breaking out into hives. I continue to use those techniques to calm myself down whenever I'm in a stressful situation.

Dancing also had a positive impact on reducing my stress. I used to dance for ten or more hours a week, and it always put me in a more positive mood—no matter what was going on at work. Dance lessons also taught me how to let go of stress. I typically took private dance lessons right after work, so if something stressful happened at work, I brought that stress into the lesson. I quickly found out that stressing out about work instead of focusing on new dance steps was a waste of money. If I was going to get the best value out of my lesson, I would have to let go of the stress.

Addressing Physical Causal Factors

Better Dietary Choices

Not eating properly can lead to too much energy and feeling hyper, jittery, or nervous. This set of physical effects can lead to dominant behavior choices. For others, not eating properly can lead to having little energy and feeling drowsy and lethargic. This set of effects can lead to passive behavior choices.

Eating more foods "as nature intended" and less processed foods has a significant effect on your blood sugar levels. Eating more protein and *complex carbohydrates* (such as vegetables) and avoiding simple carbohydrates (such as processed food) will keep your blood sugar levels from spiking and falling, which is good because this change in levels can negatively impact your behavior.

Complex carbohydrates differ from simple carbohydrates in that they contain fiber, which takes time to digest. As a result, the sugar in complex carbohydrates is released slowly into the bloodstream and keeps serotonin levels up longer than a simple carbohydrate like a chocolate bar would. Other examples of foods with complex carbohydrates include yams, brown rice, spinach, peas, beans, and lentils. Complex carbohydrates and proteins don't have as much of an immediate impact on mood or behavior, and they have a much more beneficial effect on neurotransmitters in the long term.

Proper neurotransmitter function is also dependent on omega-3 fatty acids. Low-fat diets that are low in omega-3s can have a negative impact on neurotransmitters and affect emotion and behavior. Diets that contain nuts, seeds, fish, and flax oil provide the omega-3 fatty acids that our bodies need. Also, if we are deficient in certain vitamins such as folic acid, B12, and B6, certain neurotransmitter levels will be too low, leading to low mood and depression. Certain foods such as legumes, seeds, and leafy green vegetables contain folic acid. Animal products and protein-rich foods contain B12 and B6. These foods raise serotonin levels as well as other neurotransmitters.

Additionally, it's important to pay attention to your metabolism to determine your dietary choices. How you metabolize food is primarily based on your heredity. The book, *The Metabolic Typing Diet,* discusses the hereditary factors that influence metabolism.[68] Depending on your metabolic type, you may find that you do better eating more protein than carbohydrates, while others feel better eating more carbohydrates than proteins. You can take a metabolic typing survey online at www.metabolictypingonline.com.

You can use the Behavior and Diet Diary Tool shown in Figure 30.1 on the next page to help you determine if your dietary choices are contributing to your behavior preferences. A blank Behavior and Diet Diary Tool is also available in Appendix H. The following list explains each of the Behavior and Diet Diary Tool columns:

- Noting the date and time of the inappropriate behavior can help you pinpoint whether low blood sugar may be a cause of your behavior
- Describing the inappropriate behavior can help you determine which of the behavior patterns you typically use when under stress
- Writing down how you were feeling emotionally, mentally or physically at the time of the inappropriate behavior (tired, low energy, irritable, didn't sleep well, high energy, sad, depressed, happy, angry, excited, etc.) can also provide some insight into the cause of your inappropriate behavior
- Noting any foods that you ate today or yesterday helps to determine if certain foods led to your inappropriate behavior

Figure 30.1: Example of the Behavior and Diet Diary Tool

Date/Time of Inappropriate Behavior	Description of Inappropriate Behavior	Emotional/Mental/ Physical State	Foods Eaten Recently
Oct 4 2:30 pm	Hung up phone on coworker when whining about their job	Irritability	Turkey sandwich and candy bar
Oct 12 9:15 am	Was somewhat harsh on employee that asked me for the umpteenth time for an exception to the process	Irritability	Skipped breakfast since early morning meeting provided continental breakfast with sweet rolls
Oct 12 11:45 am	Had a difficult time forming sentences and communicating my thoughts	Mental fog	Nothing since the continental breakfast at 7am — didn't get lunch until almost 1pm
Oct 12 3:30 pm	Left work early and went home and took a nap even though I had work that needed to be done	Fatigue	Pizza
Oct 18 1:15 pm	Told my friend at work about my fantasies of telling off my boss	Anger covered up by sarcasm	Hamburger and fries

Another excellent source of nutritional information is Dr. Joseph Mercola. Dr. Mercola has the world's highest ranked Web site for natural health. His nutrition plan can be found at www.mercola.com, which includes a free nutritional typing test.[69]

Improving the Way You Deal with Chronic Stress

You can do several things to address chronic stress. Exercise is at the top of the list. Endorphins are released when you exercise. Endorphins release neurotransmitters that inhibit pain signals to the brain. These neurotransmitters also aid in the reduction of stress.

During times of exercise, you also activate norepinephrine and epinephrine, which helps you be more alert, motivated, and focused. Exercise also increases serotonin, which helps lift your mood, reduces stress, and increases the feeling of well-being. So exercise improves mood, decreases anxiety, improves sleep, and improves resilience in the face of stress.

In addition to exercising, the following lists ways to alleviate stress at work and relax your mind and body:

- **Improve Your Work/Life Balance.** Going home earlier and setting some boundaries around working evenings and weekends can provide the needed downtime to deal with workplace stress.
- **Make a Game Out of It.** If people are irritating you in a meeting, you can reduce the stress from the meeting by making a game out of the interaction. For example, you can turn the behavior matrices in Appendix A into a bingo-like game and track other people's behavior during meetings.
- **Breathe Deeply.** Taking deep breaths can do wonders for alleviating stress.
- **Tense up Your Hands and Then Release the Tenseness.** This helps with releasing built-up tension due to anxiety or frustration.
- **Talk to the Person Causing You Stress.** Remember that interdependent and connective strategies are action-based. If you are in a stressful situation that causes you to work less interdependently, connect with the person who seems to be causing the stress and talk together about how to resolve the problem.

You can also find some excellent articles on stress management with or without exercise on Dr. Mercola's Web site.[70]

Understanding Our Physical Causal Factors: Why It Matters

Obviously, we need to be in good health to perform at our most effective level at work. When our neurotransmitters are out of balance, our health suffers. Neurotransmitter imbalances not only impact our health, they also impact our behavior, which impacts our success at work. When imbalances cause depression, low mood, chronic fatigue, low energy, low motivation, focus issues, attention problems, sleep problems, or memory problems, we use more passive behaviors. When imbalances cause aggression, anxiety, irritability, impulsiveness, hyperactivity, mania, ADHD, obsessive tendencies, restlessness, or paranoia, we use more dominant behaviors.

Here are other examples of how neurotransmitters impact our success at work:

- **Chronic Fatigue.** Chronic fatigue can cause the following issues: attention lapses, slowed reaction times, safety issues, calling in sick, poor customer service, and low level of energy.
- **Migraine Headaches.** Serotonin is known to be a factor in migraines. A study found that businesses spend $12 billion on direct costs of migraine and another $12.5 billion on indirect costs.[71] Indirect costs include absenteeism (one workday per employee per migraine, on average) and reduced efficiency if the employee continued working during a migraine.
- **Depression.** This physical condition often results in increased absenteeism, decreased work productivity, and low energy levels due to sleep disturbance. In one study, a majority of employees suffering from depression reported their condition kept them from being selected for more exciting projects and from getting a promotion. 48% reported their coworkers avoided them.[72] Obviously, this would have a major impact on a workgroup's success.

If we try to change passive or dominant behaviors to more independent and connective behaviors when neurotransmitter imbalances are the cause of our behavior, we will fail. Try as we might to change our behaviors, this is one mountain that will be impossible to climb.

The good news is that we have more control over our neurotransmitter levels than most people realize. Antidepressants and other drugs don't have to be the answer to behavioral problems. As discussed, many of us get our neurotransmitter levels out of balance with our dietary choices or stress. So we can put them back into balance with better dietary choices and exercise. It may be daunting to hear that once again diet and exercise are the answer to our problems. Of course, they won't address every problem, but they will help bring neurotransmitter levels back into balance, which could be at the root of changing inappropriate behaviors.

31

Why Addressing Causal Factors of Behavior Preferences Matters

"I discovered that stress at work often led me to behave in the very way that I was fearful of behaving, thus causing more stress. Confused yet? Let me explain. In one job, I was being carefully watched and scrutinized. I was fearful that I would make a stupid mistake or say something that was inaccurate to a customer. Inevitably, this is exactly what would happen. Then my stress level would go up a notch, and I would find myself making more mistakes and saying more inappropriate or inaccurate things. And the cycle would continue. In one case, it actually led to my eventual dismissal. The stress I was feeling seemed to freeze my brain into a negative and self-destructive mode that I couldn't seem to get out of on my own. A word of encouragement from my boss would have probably helped me calm down, get a grip on my emotions, and get my brain running appropriately again, but when that didn't happen for me, the cycle got worse, and I became what I feared and worried about the most—incompetent."

Disgruntled Employee
Blog Post

I f you are happy and successful at work, it is a result of your behavior choices. If you are unhappy or unsuccessful at work, it is also a result of your behavior choices.

On a personal level, how happy are you? Do you enjoy going to work each day and being a part of your workgroup? Are the people in your workgroup difficult to work with? Do interactions with certain people stress you out? How do you feel about working with your workgroup leader? Is this another source of stress for you or do you enjoy working with him or her?

How successful do you feel at work? Do you feel that you are working at your highest potential? Do you feel stalemated in your career? Could you contribute more than you do?

If the answers to these questions aren't as positive as you would like, then using the holistic approach in Part 6 will help you identify and address the causal factors behind your behavior preferences and ultimately change them to improve your personal gruntledness and success. This is true no matter what your level is—a single contributor, team leader, middle manager, or executive manager.

The Root Cause of Personal Gruntledness and Success Problems

As you now know, your behavior preferences stem from your beliefs, mental skills, fears, emotional and social capabilities, dietary choices, and stress levels. Figure 31.1 illustrates how personal gruntledness and success levels are based on personal behavior preferences and interpersonal dynamics. Your interpersonal dynamics are based on your behavior preferences and the others' behavior preferences. The figure also shows how your personal behavior preferences and others' personal behavior preferences are caused by mental, emotional, and physical factors.

Figure 31.1: The root cause of all gruntledness and success problems

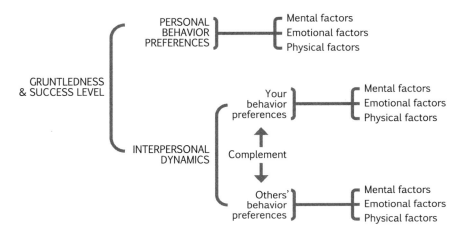

As you learned in Part 5, workgroup dynamics, inter-workgroup dynamics, and interpersonal dynamics are all based on certain employee and leadership behavior preferences and business system characteristics. Part 5 concluded that the root cause of workgroup gruntledness and success came down to the personal behavior preferences of the leaders and members of the workgroup. Mental, emotional, and physical causal factors are behind all behavior choices and behavior preferences. As a result, these three factors are the root cause of business success and employee morale issues.

The impact you have on organizational and workgroup success and employee morale also depends on your position within your organization. If you are a key individual within your workgroup, the causal factors for your behavior preference may have more of an impact on your workgroup than your coworkers' behavior. If you are a leader, then these causal factors greatly influence your workgroup dynamics and possibly inter-workgroup dynamics. If you are an executive leader or in a position to change business system characteristics, then the causal factors behind your behavior preferences influence every employee and leader of every workgroup that uses that business system.

It is important to note that the extent to which mental, emotional, and physical causal factors influence our behavior varies, as follows:

- One or more of the causal factors may influence our behaviors in one particular situation
- One or more of the causal factors may influence our behaviors for certain types of situations
- One or more of the causal factors may influence our behaviors across different types of situations

It is when one or more of the causal factors influence our behaviors across different types of situations that we develop a preference for certain behavior patterns.

Causal Factors for a Particular Situation

It is possible that these causal factors influence our behavior differently depending on the situation at hand. For example, suppose a new employee gets stuck while using the company's computer system, so he asks a co-worker for help. He believes that the coworker provides more value in this situation than he does. But after he learns from his coworker and is able to handle this issue on his own, he no longer has that belief. So in terms of value beliefs, for a particular situation, we can sometimes feel like we provide less value than others, and in other situations believe that we provide more value than others. Again, for a different situation, we can sometimes believe that we provide value on our own, and in other situations feel that we provide value equal to others.

Causal Factors for Certain Types of Situations

It is likely one or more of the causal factors are influencing your behavior for certain types of situations. Using beliefs for another example, an employee who has been working for a small retail store the longest believes that her seniority gives her priority in choosing time off. Each holiday season, she points this out to her supervisor who lets her choose the days she wants off before her coworkers. She doesn't ask for preferential treatment in any other situation—only during the holidays. So in terms of entitled beliefs, in certain types of situations, we can believe we're not entitled and in other types of situations, we can feel we are entitled or even feel we're more entitled than others. On the other hand, we can feel equally entitled to others in another type of situation.

Causal Factors Across Different Types of Situations

Sometimes, mental, emotional and physical factors influence our behaviors across many different situations. When specific causal factors (e.g., beliefs, mental skills, fears, emotional skills, etc.) become more widespread or common, we can develop a preference for passive, dominant, independent, or interdependent behaviors. For example, the more we believe that we don't provide much value, we're not as responsible as others, or we're not as entitled as others, the more often we will use passive behaviors. The more we believe that we provide more value than others, are more responsible than others, or are more entitled than others, the more often we will use dominant behaviors.

A Holistic Approach to Improving Personal Gruntledness and Success

Because behavior has multiple factors, the best way to change your behavior preferences is to use a holistic approach that addresses each factor. For that reason, the techniques in Part 6 provide a holistic approach, which first goes to the root of behavior to help you understand your behavior preferences, and then moves you towards choosing better behaviors.

Adopting more interdependent and connective behaviors means understanding how mental, emotional, and physical causal factors impact your behavior. Without a holistic approach, an attempt to change your behavior will not be effective or long lasting. You may change your behavior in a few situations but probably won't have much success with long-term behavior changes.

For example, if you don't change your beliefs and don't understand your own mental skills and appreciate the mental skills of others, you'll continue to interact with others as you currently do. If you don't address your fears, you'll hold on to your old coping strategies. By learning new emotional and social skills and overcoming your fears, you'll improve your ability to make better behavior choices in every situation. If you don't understand how your dietary and lifestyle choices affect your neurotransmitter levels and how they in turn affect your behaviors, you won't see the whole picture as to why you behave the way you do, so you won't be able to tackle that factor affecting your behavior.

In short, a holistic approach to any kind of change has vital benefits. It reduces or eliminates rework, leverages synergies, helps to maintain focus and direction, and results in greater chances for sustainability. These benefits do not occur when people take a piecemeal, non-holistic approach.

Your behavior preferences may be based on one, two, or all three causal factors. More than likely all three play a role in your behavior preferences. But whatever the factors are, they must be addressed. No one can become successful or gruntled if one of the three factors isn't addressed properly.

If you are having difficulty changing your interactions with another person, go back and see what mental, emotional, and physical causal factors are still contributing to your behavior preferences, and hence, your dynamics with certain people.

As you saw in Part 5, no matter who you interact with and what behaviors they choose, you always have a choice on how you behave. You can change the dynamic—whether it is with your boss, coworker, or customer.

You can also use the Causal Factors for Behavior Preferences Tool in Appendix I as a checklist to see what mental, emotional, and physical factors may be at the root of your behavior preferences in certain types of situations. Over time, completing several of these tools can give you some idea of the causal factors behind your behavior preferences. Changing your personal behavior preferences by addressing their causal factors is within your control.

Expanding Your Circle of Influence

In *The 7 Habits of Highly Effective People,* Stephen Covey describes our Circle of Concern and Circle of Influence.[73] Stephen Covey explained that we all have issues that we focus our attention on: our *Circle of Concern.* However, we have no control over many of those issues. But the issues we can control are within our *Circle of Influence.*

Individually, to worry about issues outside of our Circle of Influence leads to disgruntledness and decreases our effectiveness. Worrying about issues outside of a workgroup's Circle of Influence decreases employee morale and workgroup success. Once we've addressed issues within our Circle of Influence, we are in a better position to expand our level of influence to some of the other issues within our Circle of Concern. This is especially true when considering behavior preferences. If we can change our behavior (Circle of Influence), then we can change outcomes that used to be out of our control (Circle of Concern).

Figure 31.2 shows what is in your Circle of Influence as an employee and as a leader. It also shows how you can expand your Circle of Influence to issues in your Circle of Concern.

Figure 31.2: An approach to improve gruntledness and success

	Your Circle of Influence	Expanding Your Circle of Influence
Employees/ Leaders	• Improve your personal behavior preferences	• Improve your interpersonal dynamics
Leaders	• Improve workgroup dynamics	• Improve inter-workgroup dynamics

Personally, it is within your Circle of Influence to change your behavior preferences. The techniques for changing personal behavior preferences allow you to make more appropriate employee and leadership behavior choices to improve your gruntledness and chances of personal success.

As an employee or leader, you can expand your Circle of Influence by improving the interactions between you and others by changing your behavior.

The techniques for changing your interactions with others can improve your chances of success and gruntledness when working with others.

As a leader, it is within your Circle of Influence to change your workgroup's dynamics. The techniques for improving workgroup dynamics can help leaders influence employee behaviors, improve their own leadership behaviors, and align business system characteristics to encourage the desired dynamics.

As a leader, you can expand your Circle of Influence by improving your workgroup interactions with other workgroups. The techniques for improving interactions between workgroups can help leaders align behaviors and business system characteristics between workgroups. This can help workgroups collaborate successfully when implementing business strategies and make working together more enjoyable.

A Holistic Approach to Improving Workgroup Gruntledness and Success

Parts 5 and 6 provide techniques on improving workgroup dynamics, inter-workgroup dynamics, interpersonal dynamics, and personal behavior preferences. Figure 31.3 places each of these scenarios in a quadrant to illustrate how they can be used together as a holistic approach to improve workgroup success and gruntledness.

You can address your workgroup gruntledness and success problems starting in any of the quadrants. Suppose the biggest pain point that you have right now is your workgroup's interaction with another workgroup (lower left quadrant). You might start at that quadrant and apply the techniques described in Chapter 25.

However, you probably won't be as successful if you don't also address the other quadrants. For example, you may think that the other workgroup is the problem, but what you don't realize is that your workgroup has inappropriate responses to the other workgroup.

Figure 31.3: Holistic continual improvement for workgroup gruntledness and success

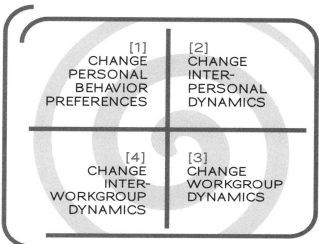

Your workgroup dynamics can very easily be the problem, so you need to change your workgroup dynamics first before trying to change your interactions with another workgroup (lower right quadrant). The problem with your workgroup's dynamics is primarily based on the interactions that you as a leader have with workgroup members. So it is appropriate for you to work on interpersonal dynamics first between you and your employees (upper right quadrant). But to be effective at that, you need to be able to change your own behavior preferences (upper left quadrant).

Figure 31.3 also shows a spiral through the process, representing the several iterations of the four quadrants that you'll need to undergo before you achieve optimum results.

Improving your behavior preferences, interpersonal dynamics, work-group dynamics, or inter-workgroup dynamics is a learning process and takes time. As I learned from Anthony Robbins, learning has four different stages. The following lists the four stages of learning:

1. **Unconscious Incompetence.** When you aren't aware that you are bad at something.

2. Conscious Incompetence. When you become aware that you are bad at something.

3. Conscious Competence. When you make a deliberate attempt to be good at something.

4. Unconscious Competence. When you are good at something without even thinking about it.

Initially, at the unconscious incompetence stage, you aren't even aware that your behavior preferences are inappropriate. Asking questions can help you move from unconscious incompetence to conscious competence. But sometimes it takes time to recognize your behavior preferences and how they play a key role in your interactions with others.

As a leader, it might also take a while to accept that your workgroup's dynamics aren't as effective as they could be and how your leadership behavior preferences contribute to those dynamics. It may also take a while to accept that your workgroup's collective behavior preferences are contributing to unhelpful dynamics with other workgroups.

Learning a new way to behave or interact takes you to the conscious competence stage. You may fail to make the right choice at this stage, but at least you're trying. Remember: You have a chance to choose again and hopefully make a better choice next time. The behavior matrices can also help you make more appropriate behavior choices and get you to the conscious competence stage. Embedding interdependent characteristics into your business system encourages the use of interdependent behaviors, which helps all employees get to an unconscious competence level of appropriate behavior choices.

Solving Gruntledness and Success Problems

This book provides a process for solving gruntledness and success problems. Recognizing that there is a problem is the first step. Part 1 discusses how bad the business environment is today: Business strategies frequently fail or aren't as successful as they need to be, and poor employee morale and engagement plagues most organizations.

Understanding causal factors for gruntledness and success problems is the next step. Parts 2 through 4 describe and show how the three possible causal factors—employee behaviors, leadership behaviors, and business system characteristics—impact business results and employee morale at a workgroup level and impact personal success and gruntledness.

Part 5 presents techniques for addressing the three causal factors and implementing critical success factors in different situations—workgroup dynamics, inter-workgroup dynamics, and interpersonal dynamics. Implementing these techniques will have a positive effect on business results and employee morale. Part 5 also concludes that the root cause of your gruntledness and success issues, whether as an employee or a leader, is your behavior preferences. Therefore in order to further improve business results and employee morale, it may be necessary to address the causes of your behavior preferences.

Part 6 provides a holistic approach to improving your behavior preferences by addressing their possible cause—mental, emotional, and physical factors. Addressing the causal factors of your behavior preferences gives you the greatest chance of improving your personal gruntledness and success. As a leader, it will improve your chances of raising employee morale and the success of your workgroup. As an executive leader, it will help you implement more appropriate business system characteristics that can improve the gruntledness and success of all the workgroups within your organization.

All of this might seem daunting, but you can't improve if you don't change what's wrong. Insanity is commonly defined as "doing the same thing but expecting different results." You can solve any business success and employee morale problems if you change your approach to a holistic approach that actually gets to the root cause of your problems—you. You have a choice to continue interacting the way you currently do with your coworkers, supervisors, and customers, or you can try something different. You have the power to transform your relationships with others and make a difference at your organization no matter your level. Choosing differently makes things better for yourself and for those you work with.

You may think that you are powerless, your coworkers aren't worth your time or attention, or that nothing can be done about your "boss from hell." You may think that your leaders expect the impossible and that what you have been tasked to do isn't achievable. But amazing things can happen when you work interdependently with others. When you address the mental, emotional, and physical causal factors behind your behavior preferences, you will be able to work more collaboratively with others. In doing so, you will find that your ability to influence what is going on in the workplace increases exponentially.

You may experience setbacks, but remember that personal growth takes time. Keeping the four stages of learning in mind will help you see how far you've come in changing your behavior preferences and what work you still have to do. The workplace is full of challenges, but these challenges are really just opportunities for personal growth. If you screw up, don't be hard on yourself. You will have many more opportunities to choose differently the next time.

You may ask yourself how you, one person with little influence, can possibly make a difference in your workgroup or organization. Here's how: Changing your behavior preferences changes the way that you interact with others. Changing the dynamics of your relationships with others starts to show them more effective ways of getting things done, which will be a model for success that others will follow. It is possible to have a workplace environment where people exceed business objectives and are happy at the same time. It starts with you. And happiness is contagious.

Imagine a work environment where you look forward to going to work and you leave at the end of the day with a sense of accomplishment and feeling good about what you contributed. Imagine a workgroup that works hard together, enjoys each other's company, respects each other's opinions, and resolves issues and conflicts easily. Imagine working for a company where all workgroups pull together to accomplish a common set of goals, see other departments as their internal customer, and work to make things run smoother. Imagine employees seeing how they can be of service to each other. Imagine working with other companies, brainstorming ways to solve customers' problems or creating better products and services, and providing better customer service.

Wouldn't it be great if instead of trudging through your work each day, you danced through it? Working with your coworkers and leaders in partnership can be a joyful waltz if you're open to making a change.

I read about a phenomenon that I believe describes how we can make these imagined scenarios reality. The phenomenon is called the "butterfly effect" and describes the initial occurrence and recurrence of events and their subsequent chain of events:

> "The phrase refers to the idea that a butterfly's wings might create tiny changes in the atmosphere that ultimately cause a tornado to appear (or prevent a tornado from appearing). The flapping wing represents a small change in the initial condition of the system, which causes a chain of events leading to large-scale phenomena. Had the butterfly not flapped its wings, the trajectory of the system might have been vastly different."[74]

Don't make the mistake of thinking you should do nothing to improve your workgroup or your company just because you think you can only do a little. The butterfly effect is an explanation for how small variations can produce large variations in the long-term.

Be a butterfly at your company! Flap your wings: Change your own behavior first and start a chain of events that will improve your gruntledness and change your company's organizational culture. If enough of us flap our wings together, we can change the climate of the business world to one that leads to more gruntledness and success in the workplace.

My wish is that you will find personal happiness and success at whatever you do in the workplace at whatever level you are in your organization. I look forward to hearing from readers who are willing to share their experiences in implementing the methods in this book to help me improve upon them and help create more gruntled employees in the business world.

Appendices

"In nature, action and reaction are continuous. Everything is connected to everything else. No one part, nothing, is isolated. Everything is linked, and interdependent. Everywhere everything is connected to everything else. Each question receives the correct answer."

Svami Prajnanpad
A Bengali sannyasin

Appendix A: Causal and Critical Success Factors

Employee Behavior Matrix

EMPLOYEE ACTIVITIES	PASSIVE BEHAVIORS	DOMINANT BEHAVIORS	INDEPENDENT BEHAVIORS	INTER-DEPENDENT BEHAVIORS
Decision Making				
Participation	Defers to others	Makes decisions for others	Makes own decisions	Makes joint decisions
Opinions	Keeps opinions to self	Disregards others' opinions	Considers only own opinion	Considers own & others' opinions
Completing Tasks				
Responsibility	Less responsible	More responsible	Personally responsible	Jointly responsible
Work Style	Follows direction	Leads	Works alone	Collaborates & cooperates
Resolving Problems				
Reaction	Discounts significance	Overreacts to significance	Appreciates significance	Appreciates problem inter-dependencies
Ownership	Defers action to others	Solves problems for others	Solves own part	Supportive of others
Conflict Resolution				
Approach	Avoids conflict	Uses conflict to an advantage	Confronts conflict	Resolves conflict equitably
Expectations	Approaches conflict expecting others to win	Approaches conflict expecting to win regardless of cost to others	Approaches conflict expecting to win	Approaches conflict expecting everyone to win
Relating to Others				
Attitude	Self-deprecating	Arrogant	Closed-minded	Open-minded
Respect	Does not respect self	Does not respect others	Insists on respect	Respects self & others
Boundaries	Allows boundary violations	Crosses personal boundaries	Protects personal boundaries	Protects everyone's boundaries

Leadership Behavior Matrix

LEADERSHIP ACTIVITIES	AUTHORITARIAN BEHAVIORS	LAISSEZ-FAIRE BEHAVIORS	CONNECTIVE BEHAVIORS
Providing Direction			
Setting Direction	Provides direction requesting minimal feedback	Provides minimal direction or allows team to set direction	Works with team to define/refine direction
Implementing Direction	Closely involved during implementation	Disengaged during implementation	Supports team during implementation
Motivating Employees			
Motivation Techniques	Motivates through negative consequences	Motivates through empowerment	Motivates through compelling vision with measurable objectives
Recognition	Recognizes those who follow direction	Recognizes individual accomplishments	Recognizes collective accomplishments
Building Team Capabilities			
Hiring/Promoting	Hires/promotes followers	Hires/promotes best individual performers	Hires/promotes team players
Addressing Weaknesses	Points out weaknesses	Expects employees to improve on their own	Coaches & mentors employees
Communicating			
Communication Style	Talks more than listens	Listens without much comment	Listens as much as talks
Communication Flow	Limits communications	Allows free-flowing communications	Coordinates communications

Business System Characteristics Matrix

BUSINESS SYSTEM COMPONENTS	DEPENDENT CHARACTERISTICS	INDEPENDENT CHARACTERISTICS	INTERDEPENDENT CHARACTERISTICS
Organizational Framework			
Roles & Responsibilities	Limited	Unclear	Helpful
Organizational Structure	Cumbersome	Not clearly defined	Supportive
Management Systems			
Management Plans	Top-down	Decentralized	Aligned
Management Reviews	Upper management only	Decentralized	Aligned
Processes			
Workflow	Bureaucratic	Flexible	Supportive
Enforcement	Strictly enforced	Unenforced	Institutionalized
Information Technology			
Data Architecture	Controlled data	Decentralized data	Shared data
Technology	Limited access	Uncontrolled access	Planned access

Appendix B: Interaction Tools

Interaction Analysis Tool

Interaction Analysis			
Person A		**Person B**	
Person A's Initiating Behavior	Behavior Activity/Pattern	Person B's Responding Behavior	Behavior Activity/Pattern

Revised Interaction Tool

Revised Interaction			
Person A		**Person B**	
Person A's Initiating Behavior	Behavior Activity/Pattern	Person B's Responding Behavior	Behavior Activity/Pattern

Appendix C: Belief Explanations

Examples of Belief Explanations for Passive and Laissez-Faire Behaviors

Belief:	When I believe that I provide less value than others
Activity	**then as an employee I may...**
Decision Making	- put more weight on others' opinions than on my own
Completing Tasks	- follow direction of others who are more competent than I when completing tasks
Resolving Problems	- defer problem resolution to others more competent than I
Conflict Resolution	- avoid conflict since I do not feel capable of winning

Belief:	When I believe that I provide less value than my team
Activity	**then as a leader I may...**
Providing Direction	- allow my workgroup members to set direction instead of doing it myself
Motivating Employees	- empower employees to handle things on their own
Building Team Capabilities	- expect employees to improve on their own since I'm not sure I can help them out
Communicating	- listen to what employees have to say; not voice my opinion

Belief:	When I believe that I am not responsible
Activity	**then as an employee I may...**
Decision Making	- defer decisions to those who are responsible
Completing Tasks	- take less responsibility if a task is assigned to me
Resolving Problems	- defer problems to those who are responsible
Conflict Resolution	- avoid conflict since others are responsible for either causing or resolving the conflict

Belief:	When I believe that I am not as responsible as my team
Activity	**then as a leader I may...**
Providing Direction	- allow my workgroup members to set direction and implement it since they are responsible for the results
Motivating Employees	- recognize individuals who were responsible for delivering results
Building Team Capabilities	- hire or promote the best individual performers who will take responsibility for results
Communicating	- let those responsible determine what needs to be communicated

Belief:	When I believe that I am not entitled
Activity	**then as an employee I may...**
Decision Making	- defer decisions to those who are entitled
Completing Tasks	- defer to those who are entitled to lead a task
Resolving Problems	- defer to those who are entitled to lead the resolution
Conflict Resolution	- accept a losing position as inevitable

Belief:	When I believe that I am not as entitled as my team
Activity	**then as a leader I may...**
Providing Direction	- provide little direction since I don't believe I am entitled to tell employees what to do
Motivating Employees	- empower employees and only provide positive recognition since I don't believe I should say anything negative
Building Team Capabilities	- expect employees to figure things out on their own since I don't believe I am entitled to point out their weaknesses
Communicating	- allow employees to determine communications since I don't believe I'm entitled to communicate my opinions as their leader

Examples of Belief Explanations for
Dominant and Authoritarian Behaviors

Belief:	When I believe that I provide more value than others
Activity	**then as an employee I may...**
Decision Making	- put more weight on my own opinions and abilities than others'
Completing Tasks	- take on more responsibility since I am better at this task than others
Resolving Problems	- be overly involved since I am better at resolving problems than others
Conflict Resolution	- approach conflict expecting to win regardless of cost to others since I'm right and others are wrong

Belief:	When I believe that I provide more value than my team
Activity	**then as a leader I may...**
Providing Direction	- provide direction without listening to others' points of view and micromanage implementations since employees may do it incorrectly
Motivating Employees	- criticize employees who make a mistake or do not follow my direction
Building Team Capabilities	- criticize employees who don't do things the way I would do them
Communicating	- communicate my point of view but not listen to others

Belief:	When I believe that I am more responsible than others
Activity	**then as an employee I may...**
Decision Making	- make decisions for others since I am more responsible
Completing Tasks	- take on more responsibility even if a task is not assigned to me
Resolving Problems	- overreact to problems caused by others
Conflict Resolution	- put in more effort to resolve conflict

Belief:	When I believe that I am more responsible than my team
Activity	**then as a leader I may...**
Providing Direction	- provide overly detailed direction to employees who I believe are not as responsible as I am
Motivating Employees	- motivate through negative consequences, threats, and punishment to get others to do things my way
Building Team Capabilities	- hire/promote followers since others won't do the right thing on their own
Communicating	- communicate from a position of authority and limit communications since I am more responsible than others

Belief:	When I believe that I am more entitled than others
Activity	**then as an employee I may...**
Decision Making	- make decisions that others should make
Completing Tasks	- lead efforts even when others have been assigned the task
Resolving Problems	- solve problems for others
Conflict Resolution	- control conflict to my advantage

Belief:	When I believe that I am more entitled than my team
Activity	**then as a leader I may...**
Providing Direction	- provide direction through orders; I am in a position of authority
Motivating Employees	- use threats and criticism since I must look better than those working for me
Building Team Capabilities	- criticize others since they are not entitled to being treated respectfully when they make a mistake
Communicating	- talk but not listen to others since I am more entitled to my opinion as their leader

Examples of Belief Explanations for
Independent and Laissez-Faire Behaviors

Belief:	When I believe that I provide value on my own
Activity	**then as an employee I may...**
Decision Making	- be comfortable with making decisions on my own
Completing Tasks	- be comfortable working alone
Resolving Problems	- be comfortable resolving my own problems
Conflict Resolution	- be comfortable confronting conflict

Belief:	When I believe that employees provide value
Activity	**then as a leader I may...**
Providing Direction	- provide little direction or allow the workgroup members to set direction
Motivating Employees	- motivate by empowering employees
Building Team Capabilities	- allow employees to figure out how to improve on their own
Communicating	- listen to employees' perspectives without commenting

Belief:	When I believe that I am responsible
Activity	**then as an employee I may...**
Decision Making	- make my own decisions
Completing Tasks	- complete my work on my own
Resolving Problems	- resolve my own problems
Conflict Resolution	- confront conflict in situations where it affects me

Belief:	When I believe that employees are responsible
Activity	**then as a leader I may...**
Providing Direction	- not follow up with employees since they will do the right thing
Motivating Employees	- empower employees since they know what needs to be done
Building Team Capabilities	- hire/promote the best performers who will get the job done
Communicating	- listen to employees' perspectives since they are responsible

Belief:	When I believe that I am entitled
Activity	**then as an employee I may...**
Decision Making	- make decisions because I'm entitled to make them
Completing Tasks	- complete tasks assigned to me as I see fit
Resolving Problems	- resolve problems as I see fit
Conflict Resolution	- confront conflict and insist on being treated fairly in its resolution

Belief:	When I believe that employees are entitled
Activity	**then as a leader I may...**
Providing Direction	- provide little direction even in times of a business crisis
Motivating Employees	- motivate through empowerment even if employees make bad decisions
Building Team Capabilities	- allow employees to improve on their own since criticizing might make them feel bad
Communicating	- listen to employee opinions rather than communicate an unpopular business perspective

Examples of Belief Explanations for
Interdependent and Connective Behaviors

Belief:	When I believe that I provide value equal to others
Activity	**then as an employee I may...**
Decision Making	- be comfortable making decisions jointly with others
Completing Tasks	- be comfortable cooperating and collaborating with others
Resolving Problems	- be comfortable resolving problems with others
Conflict Resolution	- appreciate both others' and my own perspective
Belief:	**When I believe that my team and I provide equal value**
Activity	**then as a leader I may...**
Providing Direction	- define direction collaboratively with others
Motivating Employees	- reward all team members who contributed to a task
Building Team Capabilities	- hire team players
Communicating	- ensure that all points of view are heard
Belief:	**When I believe that we are equally responsible**
Activity	**then as an employee I may...**
Decision Making	- make decisions jointly with others
Completing Tasks	- assume joint responsibility with others for a task
Resolving Problems	- be supportive of others in resolving problems
Conflict Resolution	- work equally with others in resolving conflict
Belief:	**When I believe that my team and I are equally responsible**
Activity	**then as a leader I may...**
Providing Direction	- follow up with employees to see if they need my support
Motivating Employees	- recognize collective accomplishments
Building Team Capabilities	- allow my team members to coach or mentor me
Communicating	- ensure all perspectives are heard
Belief:	**When I believe that we are equally entitled**
Activity	**then as an employee I may...**
Decision Making	- ensure all opinions are heard when making a joint decision
Completing Tasks	- ensure all have the opportunity to contribute to the task at hand
Resolving Problems	- ensure all are supportive of others in resolving the problem
Conflict Resolution	- ensure that conflict is resolved equitably
Belief:	**When I believe that my team and I are equally entitled**
Activity	**then as a leader I may...**
Providing Direction	- collaboratively work with others to decide direction
Motivating Employees	- motivate through a compelling vision since employee happiness is equally important to business results
Building Team Capabilities	- coach and mentor employees since it is an effective way to get business results and treat employees respectfully
Communicating	- listen and consider employees' perspectives as much as upper management's perspective

Appendix D: Changing Beliefs

Belief-Changing Tool

Briefly describe a common situation where you think those that you interacted with didn't behave appropriately.
Which of the beliefs on value, responsibility, or entitlement may be behind their behavior?
Which of the beliefs on value, responsibility, or entitlement may be behind your behavior?
How did you communicate this belief?
How would the interdependent form of this belief sound?
How might you have interacted differently if you had believed something else?
How might have others responded if you had interacted differently?
How do you reinforce this limiting belief?
What can be done to help you change your limiting belief?
What could you do differently to get better results from similar situations in the future?

Appendix E: Emotional and Social Skills Explanations

Examples of Emotional and Social Skills Explanations for Passive and Laissez-Faire Behaviors

Emotional Skill:	When I am missing the emotional skill of appropriate level of self-esteem (low self-esteem)
Activity	**then as an employee I may...**
Decision Making	- be uncomfortable making decisions on my own and discount my own opinion
Completing Tasks	- be uncomfortable completing tasks on my own and prefer to follow others
Resolving Problems	- be uncomfortable resolving problems on my own
Conflict Resolution	- be uncomfortable confronting conflict
Activity	**then as a leader I may...**
Providing Direction	- provide little direction or allow the workgroup members to set direction
Motivating Employees	- empower those who have more self-confidence than I
Building Team Capabilities	- expect employees to improve on their own since I would be of little use to them
Communicating	- allow employees to communicate their perspectives since theirs are usually better than mine
Emotional Skill:	**When I am missing the emotional skill of taking initiative**
Activity	**then as an employee I may...**
Decision Making	- procrastinate on making decisions or wait until someone else makes the decisions
Completing Tasks	- take less responsibility in completing tasks and be somewhat uncommitted in doing my work
Resolving Problems	- defer problems to others or discount the significance of a problem
Conflict Resolution	- avoid conflict rather than make the effort to address it
Activity	**then as a leader I may...**
Providing Direction	- provide little direction and be disengaged during implementation rather than get involved with my team members
Motivating Employees	- reward those who take care of things for me
Building Team Capabilities	- hire or promote those who will take care of things for me
Communicating	- listen to employees and allow free-flowing communications rather than work with my team to ensure coordinated communications

Examples of Emotional and Social Skills Explanations for Dominant and Authoritarian Behaviors

Emotional Skill:	When I am missing the emotional skill of appropriate level of self-esteem (low self-esteem)
Activity	**then as an employee I may...**
Decision Making	- think more highly of my opinion and discount others' opinions
Completing Tasks	- take on more tasks than I should, thinking that I am better at this than others
Resolving Problems	- solve problems that are others' responsibilities
Conflict Resolution	- be overly confident that I am right when conflict occurs
Activity	**then as a leader I may...**
Providing Direction	- provide detailed direction since I know better than employees
Motivating Employees	- reward good followers who appreciate that I know more than they do
Building Team Capabilities	- hire or promote followers who appreciate that I know more than they do
Communicating	- communicate from a position of authority since I know more than others
Social Skill:	**When I am missing the social skill of being sensitive to others**
Activity	**then as an employee I may...**
Decision Making	- make decisions for others even when I shouldn't
Completing Tasks	- insist on leading tasks even when others should
Resolving Problems	- overreact to problems
Conflict Resolution	- use conflict to control situations so that I win
Activity	**then as a leader I may...**
Providing Direction	- provide direction through orders and micromanaging, unaware of the impact it has on my workgroup members
Motivating Employees	- motivate through threats and punishments, unaware of the emotional impact on employees
Building Team Capabilities	- criticize and point out weaknesses inappropriately
Communicating	- talk without listening, unaware that others have something to say

Examples of Social Skills Explanations for
Independent and Laissez-Faire Behaviors

Social Skill:	When I am missing the social skill of cooperating with or including others
Activity	**then as an employee I may...**
Decision Making	- be uncomfortable making joint decisions with others and considering others' opinions
Completing Tasks	- be uncomfortable cooperating and collaborating with others on tasks
Resolving Problems	- be uncomfortable resolving problems with others
Conflict Resolution	- not appreciate others' perspectives
Activity	**then as a leader I may...**
Providing Direction	- be uncomfortable defining direction collaboratively with workgroup members
Motivating Employees	- not recognize joint accomplishments as much as personal accomplishments
Building Team Capabilities	- not coach or mentor workgroup members when needed
Communicating	- not ensure that both my opinion and employees' opinions are communicated and understood
Social Skill:	**When I am missing the social skill of accepting others**
Activity	**then as an employee I may...**
Decision Making	- not pay attention to others' opinions
Completing Tasks	- not see how others can contribute to a task that I am working on
Resolving Problems	- not see how others can help resolve a problem better than I can on my own
Conflict Resolution	- not see others' positions in the conflict
Activity	**then as a leader I may...**
Providing Direction	- not see how direction can be improved with others' contributions
Motivating Employees	- not see the need to motivate workgroup members differently depending on their behavior preference
Building Team Capabilities	- not coach or mentor employees in a way that is helpful to them
Communicating	- not try to understand workgroup members' perspectives

Examples of Social Skills Explanations for
Interdependent and Connective Behaviors

Social Skill:	When I have the social skill of accepting others
Activity	**then as an employee I may...**
Decision Making	- pay more attention to differing opinions
Completing Tasks	- accept that others may have a different way of completing a task
Resolving Problems	- accept others' opinions on the cause and resolution of problems
Conflict Resolution	- accept that there is more than one side to an issue
Activity	**then as a leader I may...**
Providing Direction	- accept workgroup members' feedback on my direction
Motivating Employees	- accept that different employees may be motivated in different ways
Building Team Capabilities	- accept that employees may need to be coached or mentored differently
Communicating	- accept that employees may hear things differently and may need different communication methods
Social Skill:	When I have the social skill of respecting differences
Activity	**then as an employee I may...**
Decision Making	- voice disagreements to opinions respectfully
Completing Tasks	- cooperate with others on tasks more easily
Resolving Problems	- work with others on problem resolution respectfully
Conflict Resolution	- resolve conflict equitably for all since I respect others' perspectives
Activity	**then as a leader I may...**
Providing Direction	- appreciate workgroup members' contribution of collaboratively defined direction
Motivating Employees	- reward team accomplishments, understanding the importance of others' contributions as well as my own
Building Team Capabilities	- hire or promote team players, understanding that all members perform an important role in a highly effective workgroup
Communicating	- respect workgroup members' opinions

Appendix F: Improving Emotions

Emotional Improvement Tool

Briefly describe a common situation where you think those that you interacted with didn't behave appropriately.
What fear might be causing you to behave this way?
What coping strategy do you normally use?
How does this coping strategy limit you?
What do you do that makes this fear come true?
Is there anything you can do to minimize the chances of this fear coming true?
If this fearful situation does occur, is there something you can do to make yourself feel better afterwards?
Is there a way that you can confront these types of situations in small doses?
What behavior do you usually use when you get into these situations?
What behavior should you use instead?

Appendix G: Physical Explanations

Relation of Neurotransmitter Imbalances and Passive and Laissez-Faire Behaviors Examples

Physical Causal Factors:	When neurotransmitter imbalances cause depression, low mood, chronic fatigue, low energy, low motivation, focus issues, attention problems, sleep problems, or poor memory
Activity	**then as an employee I may...**
Decision Making	- not feel up to expressing my opinion or making decisions
Completing Tasks	- not have the energy, motivation, confidence, or focus to complete tasks
Resolving Problems	- not be able to think clearly enough or focus properly to effectively resolve a problem
Conflict Resolution	- not have the energy or confidence to confront conflict
Activity	**then as a leader I may...**
Providing Direction	- not have the energy to lead my team effectively
Motivating Employees	- not feel very motivated myself, which my employees may pick up on
Building Team Capabilities	- not notice when team members need coaching
Communicating	- not have the energy or confidence to voice my own opinion

Relation of Neurotransmitter Imbalances and Dominant and Authoritarian Behaviors Examples

Physical Causal Factors:	When neurotransmitter imbalances cause aggression, anxiety, irritability, impulsivity, hyperactivity, mania, ADHD, obsessive tendencies, restlessness, or paranoia
Activity	**then as an employee I may...**
Decision Making	- be more aggressive and overconfident in stating my opinion on decisions
Completing Tasks	- be more impatient, overconfident, and take over when completing a task
Resolving Problems	- overreact to problems
Conflict Resolution	- not have the patience to understand others' positions to resolve conflict equitably
Activity	**then as a leader I may...**
Providing Direction	- come across more overly confident with my direction than intended
Motivating Employees	- be more insistent on meeting objectives and irritable if we don't
Building Team Capabilities	- be less patient with employees' mistakes
Communicating	- communicate overconfidently and from a position of authority

Appendix H: Improving Diet

Behavior and Diet Diary Tool

Date/Time of Inappropriate Behavior	Description of Inappropriate Behavior	Emotional/Mental/ Physical State	Foods Eaten Recently

Appendix I: Causal Factors for Behavior Preferences

Causal Factors for Behavior Preferences Tool

Instructions: Think of a common situation that provides you some discomfort, and then select one of the four options in each row below that best describes you in the situation.				
	Passive	**Dominant**	**Independent**	**Interdependent**
Mental Causal Factors	What is going on with me emotionally that may have caused me to react this way?			
Belief on worth	I provided less value than the other person	I provided more value than the other person	I provided value on my own	I provided value equal to the other person
Belief on responsibility	I was less responsible than the other person	I was more responsible than the other person	I was responsible	I was equally as responsible as the other person
Belief on entitlement	I was not as entitled as the other person	I was entitled more than the other person	I was entitled	I was equally as entitled as the other person
Mental skills	The other person had better mental skills than I	I had better mental skills than the other person	I had the necessary mental skills	We both had the necessary mental skills
Emotional Causal Factors	What is going on with me emotionally that may have caused me to react this way?			
Emotions	The other person used dominant behaviors that made me uncomfortable	The other person used passive behaviors that made me uncomfortable	I was more comfortable working alone than with the other person	I was comfortable working with the other person
Emotional & social skills	I didn't have the emotional skills to deal with the other person's dominant behavior	I didn't have the emotional skills to deal with the other person's passive behavior	I didn't have the social skills to relate to the other person	I had the emotional and social skills to relate well to the other person
Physical Causal Factors	What is going on with me physically that may have caused me to react this way?			
Energy level	I was physically tired, feeling low emotionally, or mentally unfocused	I was highly energized, feeling manic, or was mentally over-focused	I had normal energy, felt normal emotionally, or had normal focus	
Diet	What did I eat that may have caused me to feel this way physically?			
Stress	What was stressing me out that may have caused me to feel this way physically?			

Notes

1   "Human Resource Statistics." *Entrepreneur.com*. Entrepreneur Media, Inc., 13 Mar. 2006. Web. 5 Jan. 2012.
<http://www.entrepreneur.com/article/printthis/81978.html>.

2   "2008 World of Work." *UsRandstad.com*. Randstad, 1 Oct. 2009. Web. 1 Dec. 2011.
<http://us.randstad.com/content/aboutrandstad/knowledge-center/employer-resources/World-of-Work-2008.pdf>.

3   "Employee Engagement Report 2011." *BlessingWhite.com*. BlessingWhite, Inc., Jan. 2011. Web. 6 Feb. 2011.
<http://www.blessingwhite.com/content/reports/BlessingWhite_2011_EE_Report.pdf>.

4   "Employee Engagement What's Your Engagement Ratio?" *Gallup.com*. Gallup, Inc., 2008, 2010. Web. 2 Sep. 2009.
<http://www.gallup.com/consulting/121535/Employee-Engagement-Overview-Brochure.aspx>.

5   "Closing the Engagement Gap: A Road Map for Driving Superior Business Performance." *Towersperrin.com*. Towers Perrin, 2008. Web. 18 Mar. 2011.
<http://www.towersperrin.com/tp/getwebcachedoc?webc=HRS/USA/2008/200803/GWS_Global_Report20072008_31208.pdf>.

6   "2008-09 Employee Hold'em National Workforce Engagement Benchmark Study." Web. 29 Aug. 2009.
<http://employeeholdem.com>.

7   Amble, Brian. "Getting to the Heart of the Disengagement Gap." *Management-issues.com*. Management-Issues Ltd., 16 Jan. 2008. Web. 21 Aug. 2009.
<http://www.management-issues.com/2008/1/16/research/getting-to-the-heart-of-the-disengagement-gap.asp>.

8   Catlette, Bill, and Richard Hadden. *Contented Cows Give Better Milk*. Germantown: Saltillo Press, 2001. Print.

9   "Giving Them What They Want: The Returns Are Huge." *Sirota.com*. Knowledge@Wharton, Apr. 2005. Web. 29 Mar. 2007.
<http://www.sirota.com/pdfs/Giving_Employees_What_They_Want_The_Returns_Are_Huge_April_2005.pdf>.

10   "Closing the Engagement Gap: A Road Map for Driving Superior Business Performance." *Towersperrin.com*. Towers Perrin, 2008. Web. 18 Mar. 2011.
<http://www.towersperrin.com/tp/getwebcachedoc?webc=HRS/USA/2008/200803/GWS_Global_Report20072008_31208.pdf>.

11   "Employee Engagement What's Your Engagement Ratio?" *Gallup.com*. Gallup, Inc., 2008, 2010. Web. 6 Feb. 2011.
<http://www.gallup.com/consulting/121535/Employee-Engagement-Overview-Brochure.aspx>.

12   "2008-09 Employee Hold'em National Workforce Engagement Benchmark Study." Web. 29 Aug. 2009.
<http://employeeholdem.com>.

13   Mankins, Michael C., and Richard Steele. "Turning Great Strategy into Great Performance." *Harvard Business Review* July-Aug. 2005: 3. Print.

14   Zook, Chris and James Allen., "Growth Outside the Core." *Harvard Business Review* Dec. 2003: 3. Print.

15   Barmford, J., D. Ernst, and D.G. Fubini. "Launching a World-Class Joint Venture" *Harvard Business Review* Feb. 2004: 1. Print.

16   "Dangerous Liaisons, Mergers and Acquisitions: The Integration Game." *Haygroup.com*. Hay Group, 2007. Web. 3 Sep. 2009.
<http://www.haygroup.com/au/downloads/details.aspx?ID=15965>.

17   "The Morning After – Driving for Post Deal Success." *Kpmg.com*. KPMG International, 2006. Web. 6 Feb. 2011.
<http://www.kpmg.com/CN/en/IssuesAndInsights/ArticlesPublications/Pages/Driving-for-post-deal-success-200602.aspx>.

18   Tinlin, Andy, and Alberto Verga. "Seven Catalysts for Merger Integration Success." *Accenture.com*. Accenture, 28 July 2009. Web. 6 Feb. 2011.
<http://www.accenture.com/us-en/Pages/insight-seven-catalysts-merger-integration-success-summary.aspx>.

19   "M&A Transactions and the Human Capital Key to Success – Global Report." *Aon.com*. Hewitt Associates LLC, 2009. Web. 1 Dec. 2011.
< http://www.aon.com/attachments/thought-leadership/Hewitt_Global_MandA_Survey_Findings.pdf >.

20   LIFS. "Outsourcing Cost Savings Exaggerated." *Littleindia.com*. Little India, 2 June 2007. Web. 1 Dec. 2011.
<http://www.littleindia.com/business/1789-outsourcing-cost-savings-exaggerated.html >.

21   Alter, Allan. "Offshore Success Is Uneven, Says Kearney Study." *globalromania.com*. Global Romania, 9 May 2007. Web. 31 Aug. 2009.
<http://globalromania.com/News/Articles/1249.aspx>.

22   "2005 Global IT Outsourcing Study." *Stormdetector.com*. DiamondCluster, 2005. Web. 12 Sep. 2009.
<http://www.stormdetector.com/essays/DiamondCluster2005OutsourcingStudy.pdf>.

23   Morgan, Timothy Pricket. "Deloitte Says Outsourcing Doesn't Always Pay." *itjungle.com*. Guild Companies, Inc., 2 May 2005. Web. 31 Aug. 2009.
<http://www.itjungle.com/tfh/tfh050205-story04.html>.

24   Wang, Eric T.G., Cathy Chia-Lin Lin, James J. Jiang, and Gary Klein. "Improving Enterprise Resource Planning (ERP) Fit to Organizational Process Through Knowledge Transfer." *International Journal of Information Management* 27.3 (2007): 200–212. Print.

25   Koch, Christopher. "Supply Chain: Hershey's Bittersweet Lesson." *Cio.com*. CXO Media Inc., 15 Nov. 2002. Web. 6 Feb. 2011.

<http://www.cio.com/article/31518/
Supply_Chain_Hershey_s_Bittersweet_Lesson>.

26   Worthen, Ben, "Nestlé's Enterprise Resource Planning (ERP) Odyssey."
Cio.com. CXO Media Inc., 15 May 2002. Web. 6 Feb. 2011.

<http://www.cio.com/article/31066/
Nestl_eacute_s_Enterprise_Resource_Planning_ERP_Odyssey>.

27   Morrison, Rodger, Mike Schraeder, and Paul M. Swamidass. "Employee Involvement, Attitudes and Reactions to Technology Changes." *Highbeam.com*. Journal
of Leadership & Organizational Studies, 22 Mar. 2006. Web. 2 Nov. 2007.

<http://www.highbeam.com/doc/1G1-142301157.html>.

28   Wiley, Jack W. "The Effects of Mergers and Acquisitions on Employee
Engagement." *Kenexa.com*. Kenexa Research Institute, 2009. Web. 17 Mar. 2011.

<http://www.kenexa.com/getattachment/309e96a3-261e-4a1f-9254-
6c6a359bf041/The-Effects-of-Mergers-and-Acquisitions-on-Employe.aspx>.

29   Barr, Stephen. "Survey Has a Lot to Mull For Homeland Security." High-
beam.com. *The Washington Post*, 12 June 2005.Web. 2 Nov. 2007.

<http://www.highbeam.com/doc/1P2-28338.html>.

30   Hammer, Michael, and James Champy. *Reengineering the Corporation*. New
York: HarperCollins Publishers, 1993. Print.

31   "The State of Employee Engagement 2008." *Slideshare.net*. BlessingWhite,
Inc., 2008. Web. 21 Aug. 2009.

<http://www.slideshare.net/PingElizabeth/2008-employee-engagement-overview>.

32   "Why Business Can't Ignore Bullying." *Walesonline.co.uk*. Media Wales
Ltd., 16 July 2007. Web. 17 July 2007.

<http://www.walesonline.co.uk/business-in-wales/business-features/2007/07/16/
why-business-can-t-ignore-bullying-91466-19463652/>.

33   "Human Resources Statistics." *Entrepreneur.com*. Entrepreneur Media, Inc.,
13 Mar. 2006. Web. 1 Dec. 2011.

<http://www.entrepreneur.com/article/81978 >.

34   "2008 World of Work." *Randstad.com*. Randstad, 1 Oct. 2009 Web. 1 Dec.
2011.

<http://us.randstad.com/content/aboutrandstad/knowledge-center/employer-
resources/World-of-Work-2008.pdf>.

35   Hewitt. "M&A Transactions and the Human Capital Key to Success –
Global Report." *Aon.com*. Hewitt Associates LLC, 2009. Web. 1 Dec. 2011.

<http://www.aon.com/attachments/thought-leadership/Hewitt_Global_MandA_
Survey_Findings.pdf >.

36   "Dangerous Liaisons, Mergers and Acquisitions: The Integration Game."
Haygroup.com. Hay Group, 2007. Web. 3 Sep. 2009.

<http://www.haygroup.com/au/downloads/details.aspx?ID=15965>.

37   "The Morning After – Driving for Post Deal Success." *Kpmg.com*. KPMG
International, 2006. Web. 6 Feb. 2011.

<http://www.kpmg.com/CN/en/IssuesAndInsights/ArticlesPublications/Pages/
Driving-for-post-deal-success-200602.aspx>.

38   Accenture. "Accenture/Economist Intelligence Unit 2006 Global M&A Survey." *Accenture.com*. Accenture, 2006. Web. 2006.

39   "One Size Doesn't Fit All: The Distinct Leadership Capabilities for Organic, Alliance, and M&A Growth." *Forum.com*. IIR Holdings, Ltd., 2007. Web. 1 Dec. 2011.

< http://www.forum.com/_assets/download/acf2f454-dd96-48cc-95ce-8cbd74b-6d7cf.pdf>.

40   Davison, Dean. "Top 10 Risks of Offshore Outsourcing." *Zdnet.com*. CBS Interactive, 9 Dec. 2003. Web. 6 Feb. 2011.

<http://www.zdnet.com/news/top-10-risks-of-offshore-outsourcing/299274>.

41   neoIT. "Healthcheck on Global Operations." *Neoadvisory.com*. neoIT, Jan. 2005. Web. 6 Feb. 2011.

<http://www.neoadvisory.com/pdfs/whitepapers/OIv3i01_0105_Healthcheck-on-Global-Operations.pdf>.

42   neoIT. "Challenges with Offshore Business Process Outsourcing." *Neoadvisory.com*. neoIT, Nov. 2003. Web. 6 Feb. 2011.

<http://www.neoadvisory.com/pdfs/whitepapers/Challenges_in_BPO.pdf>.

43   Keizer, Gregg. "Gartner Says Half of Outsourcing Projects Doomed To Failure" *Crn.com*. Everything Channel, 26 Mar. 2003. Web. 3 Feb. 2004.

<http://www.crn.com/news/channel-programs/18822227/gartner-says-half-of-outsourcing-projects-doomed-to-failure.htm;jsessionid=ulqzM3WixbhNMAvoB0WcqQ**.ecappj01>.

44   Goolsby, Kathleen, "What Causes Outsourcing Failures?" *Outsourcing-center.com*. Alsbrige Inc., 1 Aug. 2004. Web. 6 Feb. 2011.

<http://www.outsourcing-center.com/2004-08-what-causes-outsourcing-failures-article-37826.html>.

45   Covey, Stephen R. *The 7 Habits of Highly Effective People*. New York: Simon & Schuster Inc., 1989. Print.

46   Jehn, Karen A., Margaret A. Neale, and Gregory B. Northcraft. "Why Differences Make a Difference: A Field Study of Diversity, Conflict, and Performance in Workgroups." *Jstor.org*. Administrative Science Quarterly, Dec. 1999. Web. 5 Apr. 2011.

<http://web.mit.edu/cortiz/www/Diversity/Jehn%20et%20al%201999.pdf>.

47   Keen, Cathy. "UF Study: Rudeness Hurts Performance and Willingness to Help on Job." *UFl.edu*. University of Florida, 24 Jan. 2008. Web. 20 Mar. 2011.

<http://news.ufl.edu/2008/01/24/rude-workplace-2/>.

48   Institute of Industrial Engineers. "Missed Manners: Injurious Behaviors on the Job Harm Workplace Productivity (Punchline)." *highbeam.com*. Institute of Industrial Engineers, Inc., 1 May 2003. Web. 1 Dec. 2011.

<http://www.highbeam.com/doc/1G1-112818171.html>.

49   Crum, Thomas F. *The Magic of Conflict: Turning a Life of Work into a Work of Art*. New York: Simon & Schuster Inc., 1987. Print.

50   Capek, Frank. "How Employee Experiences Drive Organizational Behavior." *CustomerInnovations.com*. Customers Innovations, Inc, 5 Dec. 2007. Web. 9 May 2008.

<http://customerinnovations.wordpress.com/2007/12/05/how-employee-experiences-drive-organizational-behavior/>.

51   Selden, Bob. "Are Happy Employees Motivated Employees?" *Employer-Employee.com*. Employer-Employee.com, 2006. Web. 18 July 2008.
<http://www.employer-employee.com/happymotivated.html>.

52   Crainer Dearlove. "The Global Ranking of Business Thinkers." *Thinkers50.com*. Crainer Dearlove, 2010. Web. 14 July 2008.
<http://www.thinkers50.com/results-2007>.

53   Goolsby, Kathleen. "C. K. Prahalad on the New Age of Innovation." *Sand-Hill.com*. Sandhill Group, 18 Aug. 2008. Web. 18 Aug. 2008.
<http://www.sandhill.com/opinion/editorial.php?id=202>.

54   Wolfe, Ira S. "Competent Chaos: Creating High Performance Teams." *Super-Solutions.com*. Business 2 Business, June 2006. Web. 5 June 2008.
<http://www.super-solutions.com/CompetentChaos_Interdependence.asp>.

55   Phillips, Donald T. *The Founding Fathers on Leadership: Classic Teamwork in Changing Times*. New York: Warner Books, Inc., 1997. Print.

56   "Frederick Winslow Taylor." *Wikipedia: The Free Encyclopedia*. Wikimedia Foundation, Inc., 23 Nov. 2011. Web. 2 Dec. 2011.
<http://en.wikipedia.org/wiki/Frederick_Winslow_Taylor>.

57   Kantor, Donald L., and Philip H. Mirvis. *The Cynical Americans: Living and Working in an Age of Discontent and Disillusion*. Hoboken: Jossey-Bass, 1989. Print.

58   Tischler, Linda. "The CEO's New Clothes." *Fast Company*. Mansueto Ventures LLC, 1 Sep. 2005. Web. 5 May 2011.
<http://www.fastcompany.com/magazine/98/open_essay.html>.

59   Lipman-Blumen, Jean. "Connective Leadership – A New Paradigm." *Connective Leadership Institute*. Drucker Magazine, Vol. 1, No. 1, 1997. Web. 29 Dec. 2005.
<http://www.achievingstyles.com/articles/a_new_paradigm.asp>.

60   Senge, Peter M. *The Fifth Discipline: The Art & Practice of the Learning Organization*. New York: Doubleday, 1990. Print.

61   Smith, Michael L. and James Erwin. "Role & Responsibility Charting (RACI)." *PMForum*. Pmforum.org, Inc., Web. 5 Nov. 2011.
<http://www.pmforum.org/library/tips/pdf_files/RACI_R_Web3_1.pdf>.

62   Hutchins, David. *Hoshin Kanri*. Burlington: Gower Publishing Company, 2008. Print.

63   Saxena, Sanjaya Kumar. "SIPOC." *Discover 6Sigma The Science Behind Breakthrough Improvements*. June 2007. Web. 22 July 2011.
<http://www.discover6sigma.org/post/2007/06/sipoc/>.

64   Prahalad, C.K., and M.S. Krishnan. *The New Age of Innovation*. McGraw-Hill, 2008. Print.

65   Herrmann, Ned. *The Whole Brain Business Book*. New York: McGraw-Hill, 1996. Print.

66   Crum, Thomas F. *The Magic of Conflict*. New York: Touchstone, 1988. Print.

67   Carnegie, Dale. *How to Win Friends and Influence People*. New York: Simon & Schuster, 1936. Print.

68   Wolcott, William Linz, Trish Fahey. *The Metabolic Typing Diet: Customize Your Diet to Your Own Unique Body Chemistry*. New York: Broadway Books, 2000. Print.

69   Mercola, Joseph M, DO. "Achieve Independent Health With Your Optimized Nutrition Plan: Getting Started." *Mercola.com*. Dr. Joseph Mercola, 2011. Web. 21 Nov. 2011.
   <http://www.mercola.com/nutritionplan/index.htm>.

70   Mercola, Joseph M. DO. *Mercola.com*. Dr. Joseph Mercola, 2011. Web. 21 Nov. 2011.
   <http://search.mercola.com/search/Pages/results.aspx?k=stress%20management>.

71   Dworkin, Andy. "Pain from the brain; Migraine activism calls attention to debilitating headaches." *Highbeam Research*. The Post-Standard, 12 Aug. 2008. Web. 15 Aug. 2011.
   <http://www.highbeam.com/doc/1G1-182780419.html?key=01-42160D517E1
91C6B1402021B07674B2E224E324D3417295C30420B61651B617F137019731
B7B1D6B39>.

72   "Britain's Workers Are Hiding Depression From Their Bosses." *The Free Library by Farlex*. Scottish Daily Record & Sunday, 21 Apr. 2008. Web. 15 Aug. 2011.
   <http://www.thefreelibrary.com/vital%3A+BRITAIN'S+WORKERS+ARE+HID
ING+DEPRESSION+FROM+THEIR+BOSSES.-a0178070312>.

73   Covey, Stephen. *The 7 Habits of Highly Effective People*. New York: Fireside, 1989. Print.

74   "Butterfly effect." *Wikipedia, The Free Encyclopedia,* Wikimedia Foundation, Inc., 3 Aug. 2011, Web. 15 Aug. 2011.
   <http://en.wikipedia.org/wiki/Butterfly_effect>.

Index

Page numbers followed by suffix "t" indicate tables.

For More Information

This book is only the beginning of how appropriate application of employee behaviors, leadership behaviors, and business system characteristics can be applied to the business environment. Additional resources to help you apply these concepts to various situations are provided on my Web site Metargymedia.com.

I also welcome your comments, stories, and case studies on how you've applied these concepts on my Web site. You may also contact me at the following address:

Mary Vaughn
Metargy Media
PO Box 4010
Parker, CO 80134